M. L. Wilson and the Campaign
for the Domestic Allotment

M. L. Wilson
and the Campaign
for the Domestic Allotment

by

WILLIAM D. ROWLEY

HD
1761
R66

UNIVERSITY OF NEBRASKA PRESS · LINCOLN

Publishers on the Plains
UNP

Copyright © 1970 by the University of Nebraska Press
All Rights Reserved
Standard Book Number 8032–0726–3
Library of Congress Catalog Card Number 69–19106

Manufactured in the United States of America

For my parents

Contents

Preface

An Iowa farm, the agricultural college at Ames, tenant farming in Nebraska, the Montana wheat country, and graduate study at Wisconsin and Cornell all served to mold the life of one of the foremost New Deal agricultural planners—M. L. Wilson, known to many as the apostle of the domestic allotment. From 1930 to 1932, operating from his remote base at Montana State College in Bozeman, Professor Wilson informed a broad cross section of farm and business leadership about the merits of the domestic allotment plan for raising the price of wheat. In 1932, Wilson brought the plan to the attention of Democratic presidential candidate Franklin D. Roosevelt. After the passage of the Agricultural Adjustment Act, the administration invited Wilson to head the Wheat Section of the AAA and administer the program he had advocated. Wilson's approach was a curious blend of theoretical economics, loyalty to the free market system, and political realism. The following pages will, I hope, illustrate this combination. The general problem of agriculture in the first three decades of the century is beyond the scope of this study. Rather the attempt here is to concentrate on the role one individual played in bringing about a significant experiment of government in agriculture.

In this study I have been assisted by several people, whom I wish to thank. James C. Olson, my mentor at the University of Nebraska, encouraged me to undertake the work and carry it through to its conclusion. David F. Trask of New York State University at Stony Brook offered helpful comments on the manuscript, and my colleagues afield W. Gerald Berberet and Edward A. Cole did likewise. For financial aid in this project I wish to acknowledge the A. E. Sheldon Fund for Research in Nebraska History and the Desert Research Institute at the University of Nevada. I wish to recognize also the state historical societies of Nebraska, South Dakota, North Dakota, and Montana for their cooperation. Special assistance has been given by Gladys L. Baker, Wayne D. Rasmussen,

x   *Preface*

and Elmer A. Starch of the United States Department of Agriculture, by the staff librarians at Montana State University and by Professor Richard S. Kirkendall of the University of Missouri. M. L. Wilson extended the hospitality of his home for several sessions of interviewing, and for all of that I wish to record my gratitude. Of course, shortcomings in the book must rest entirely at my doorstep.

WILLIAM D. ROWLEY

M. L. Wilson and the Campaign
for the Domestic Allotment

Wheat—Symbol of Agricultural Despair

My symbols involved my talking about wheat all the time,
partially and I suppose principally, because I came from the
wheat country.—M. L. Wilson

On the fringes of America's interior agricultural empire northwest
from the Mississippi Valley are the vast wheatlands of the northern
plains. These lands tempted settlers when, in the latter part of the
nineteenth century, railroads unlocked the area's agricultural potential. People came, lured on by extravagant claims of mild climate
and fertile soil, and by faith in the ever expanding demand for the
staff of life—wheat. But the dream of a great wheat empire on the
northern plains was a dream filled with nightmares and catastrophes.
Drought, grasshoppers, harsh winters, wheat rust, and declining
wheat prices all plagued the growth of a wheat empire. Bright
spots did appear in certain years, especially in World War I, when
wheat prices soared, but after the war years, declining prices depressed the wheatlands. The problem of wheat persisted even when
nature was bountiful. The cause of the downward movement of
prices was not easily identified; still more difficult was a solution.
Both were illusive ghosts that haunted the agricultural depression
of the 1920's and the deeper economic crisis which followed. The
people of this region became the victims of wheat and its special
problems on the periphery of an expanding, prosperous society.

The wheat problem was the most critical agricultural question
in the postwar period. Hard times in the wheat areas were sympto-
matic of a general and spreading agrarian depression in the midst of
apparent urban and industrial prosperity. The futility of increased

and efficient production in the face of declining income was most marked in the wheat region. Increased farm mortgages, farm tenancy, prices below cost of production, and bank failures were grim realities. The pioneer dream of an agricultural Eden in the West was thwarted in this decade of prosperity. In response, spokesmen from the northern wheat region mounted successive campaigns for agricultural relief legislation in the 1920's, but only through the New Deal and the domestic allotment plan in the following decade was the national government placed directly behind the northern wheat farmers' drive for higher domestic prices.

M. L. Wilson, professor of agricultural economics at Montana State College in Bozeman, Montana, emerges as one of the most outstanding and effective portrayers of the problems besetting his region. His concern was with the plight of agriculture and in particular with the complicated problem of wheat. By the mid-twenties, Wilson actively supported national relief legislation for the wheat crop and endorsed programs both to aid in the disposal of surplus wheat and to increase the efficiency of the American wheat farmer. Active participation in campaigns for agricultural relief legislation added a new dimension to the role of a western college professor whose traditional function confined him to the state college's search for improvements in applied agricultural science. Eventually Wilson came to believe that the solution to the wheat problem did not lie in further research into the biological and mechanical problems of wheat farming, but rather in the economics of marketing and in a nationally directed program of restricted wheat production.

Wilson's work for wheat-relief legislation began during the McNary-Haugen struggles in the twenties. After the failure of the battle for "agricultural equality," Wilson found little encouragement in his attempt to meet the wheat problem through application of efficient farm techniques. With the onslaught of the Great Depression, he turned to the domestic allotment. His campaign for the plan won him an interview with Democratic candidate Franklin D. Roosevelt, who sought many councils on the perplexing agricultural question. Wilson's successful meeting with the future President prompted Roosevelt to move cautiously in the direction of a domestic allotment approach to farm relief. After Roosevelt's triumph, Wilson's leadership in the campaign for the domestic allotment and his familiarity with the problems of wheat made him the logical choice of the New Deal administration to head the Wheat Section of the AAA in administering the 1933 domestic allotment plan for wheat.

Milburn Lincoln Wilson, born in Atlantic, Iowa, in 1885, grew up on an Iowa farm and, like so many other Iowans of his generation, was destined to contribute to the national life. Looking back, he painted no idyllic picture of agrarian life in late nineteenth-century Iowa. Farm life involved drudgery, hard work, and long hours. In part to escape those aspects of rural life, he went to Iowa State College in Ames and took a degree in agriculture. From there he tried tenant farming in northeastern Nebraska, and when the Enlarged Homestead Act in 1909 lured farmers farther west, Wilson took up a homestead in Montana and concerned himself with the technological conquest of the land. He experimented with the application of steam power to farm machinery, and when a series of dry years struck, the state college at Bozeman called Wilson in to study dry-land farming—"to find out how we could work an adjustment here, and farm so as to stay." Upon passage of the Smith-Lever Act in 1914, Wilson became Montana's first state county agent leader. His interests eventually led him to graduate studies at the universities of Wisconsin and Chicago and Cornell University, where he worked with economists Richard T. Ely, John R. Commons, E. A. Ross, and George F. Warren. Wilson obtained a Master of Science degree from the University of Wisconsin in 1920. His subsequent career illustrated that agricultural economics need not be a narrow, technical subject confined to the problems of production.[1]

On the national level, the establishment of the Bureau of Agricultural Economics as the principal research arm of the Department of Agriculture in 1922 injected new imagination into approaches to farm problems. The bureau emphasized statistical knowledge of farm production in an effort to estimate future market requirements for production, thereby providing a center of creative thinking oriented toward a national program for the alleviation of the farmer's

[1] M. L. Wilson, Columbia Oral History Collection (hereafter cited as COHC), Columbia University, New York, N.Y.; Wilson Papers, Montana State University Library, Bozeman, Montana (hereafter cited as Wilson MSS); Russell Lord, *The Agrarian Revival: A Study of Agricultural Extension* (New York: American Association of Adult Education, George Grady Press, 1939), pp. 132–133; Louis Finklestein, ed., *American Spiritual Autobiographies* (New York: Harper & Brothers, 1948), p. 15.

cost-price squeeze; it showed special interest in the plight of the wheat farmer in an extensive report to the President in November, 1923, entitled "The Wheat Situation." [2] Henry C. Taylor, head of the new bureau, looked to the northern wheat region for support of a national agricultural program in late 1923. His trip to the Northwest in the fall of that year brought news of a proposal to establish an export corporation for the disposal of wheat abroad. Shortly thereafter, Montana's Commissioner of Agriculture, Chester C. Davis, came to Washington as a permanent lobbyist and associate of George N. Peek in the "equality for agriculture" fight. Wilson from the state college and W. L. Stockton, president of the Montana State Farm Bureau, responded to Taylor's gesture by forming the Montana Equalization Fee Committee, devoted to promoting export legislation within Montana.

Numerous farm relief plans took shape in the twenties, but few were chosen. Most economists had serious doubts about the export commission and McNary-Haugen proposals. These plans all looked to surplus wheat disposal on foreign markets and were internationally irresponsible. They refused to recognize that the limitations of the domestic market demanded that production be cut back as the first step toward attacking the heart of the wheat problem. President Hoover's Farm Board tried to regulate and adjust the flow of commodities on the market to ensure adequate prices, but here again the plan attacked symptoms and not root problems. The Farm Board's failure to stabilize prices made it a political liability. This danger threatened every attempt by the national government to implement a farm plan. A new breadth of vision was needed to look realistically at the markets open to American producers and to recognize the ability of the American farmer to overproduce for these limited markets.

Neither the political name-calling in Washington nor the discontent at the grass-roots level of American agriculture produced a plan involving production control. Rather, it was in the Bureau of Agricultural Economics that bold new thinking about the problem of limited markets and increasing production occurred. And Wilson, who spent a year and a half with the bureau (from 1924 to 1926), moved with the new intellectual currents in the department.

[2] *United States Department of Agriculture Year Book of Agriculture, 1923* (Washington, D.C.: Government Printing Office, 1924), pp. 95–150.

In 1926 he returned to Montana to resume his academic duties and to participate in the Fairway Farms experiments in efficient wheat farming in several of the most distressed wheat areas of Montana. Although farming suitable units with machinery meant efficiency and lower production cost per bushel of wheat, reduced costs could not keep pace with declining wheat prices, and Wilson eventually had to concede defeat for farm efficiency as the way out for the farmer. In 1929, Wilson accepted an offer from the Soviet Union to spend several months in Russia as an adviser in the development of newly mechanized wheat farms there. Although he observed a primitive agriculture in the Russian countryside, he was not blind to the Russian potential for wheat exportation and the progress already under way in mechanizing the industry. In the fall of 1929, he returned, completely shaken in his belief that efficiency in American wheat raising could keep foreign markets open to the American farmer.

A man close to the problems of his region, Wilson clearly saw the consequences of the loss of foreign markets. Wheat, the main agricultural export crop of the northern plains, suffered throughout the twenties from dwindling foreign markets and lower per capita consumption at home. Faced with a depressed world economy and increasing competition from other wheat-producing regions, American wheat appeared to have traveled the road to ruin despite heroic efforts at efficiency. Now Wilson saw that foreign markets must soon be written off entirely; the only remaining market was the domestic one with its relatively declining demand for wheat. These facts, plus Wilson's familiarity with production-control schemes conceived in the Bureau of Agricultural Economics, gradually led him to the principles of a restricted production plan for wheat. In a 1929 book, *Agricultural Reform*, John D. Black, dean of American agricultural economists, included a chapter on "the Domestic Allotment Plan." Black suggested that production should be restricted to meet the domestic market needs of the country by paying farmers to plant less wheat; the result would be a higher wheat price in a market freed from the glut of overproduction.[3]

Thus a fresh and practical approach to the problem had appeared. Admittedly it sprang from the minds of academicians and did not fully consider the problems of administration, but the freshness of the

[3] John D. Black, *Agricultural Reform in the United States* (New York: McGraw-Hill Book Co., 1929), pp. 271–308.

attack and the pinpointing of the overproduction problem, or the need to produce only for market demand, seemed within the mainstream of American economic thought and practice. Yet such a scheme required a small revolution in the thinking of many agricultural economists, including M. L. Wilson. Now the traditional American effort toward agricultural expansion was to be curbed, and apparently the strides of the agricultural schools for greater yields was to be countered by a production-control program. Although this plan made sense to a few in agriculture's academic community, its chances of winning approval of the political powers in Washington were doubtful.

To acute observers of the world wheat situation, it appeared that time was running out for the basic crop on the northern plains in late 1930. While Hoover's Farm Board worked to reduce marketing expenses, it also began to suggest that wheat farmers curtail production, but it could do no more than suggest, and the wheat problem finally broke the back of the Farm Board and its cooperative marketing solutions. When Wilson began the campaign for the domestic allotment plan, he converted the symbols of farm distress into concrete action; his proposals went beyond soapbox pronouncements concerning the justness of agriculture's cause. In 1930 the professor from Montana entered the battlefield of farm politics in a broad effort to bring to the attention of many influential leaders in the country the merits of the domestic allotment program, which included a land reform program designed to remove submarginal lands from production. Wilson was determined that ground swells for various farm relief measures from the northern plains should be channeled into an effective program and be accepted by important segments of business leadership, by farm organizations, and by a popular and inspiring leader of a national party. His success in this task earned him a foremost place in the ranks of what one historian has called the "service intellectuals" of the New Deal.[4]

[4] Richard S. Kirkendall, "Four Economists in the Political Process," *Journal of Farm Economics*, XLI (May, 1959), 202–203; Kirkendall, "The New Deal Professors and the Politics of Agriculture" (Ph.D. dissertation, University of Wisconsin, 1958), p. 129; Kirkendall, "A Professor in Farm Politics," *Mid-America*, XLI (October, 1959), 210–217; Kirkendall, "Franklin D. Roosevelt and the Service Intellectual," *Mississippi Valley Historical Review*, XLIX (December, 1962), 456; Kirkendall, *Social Scientists and Farm Politics in the Age of Roosevelt* (Columbia, Missouri: University of Missouri Press, 1966), p. 6.

The evolution of Wilson's thought marks him as a man whose thinking had been shaped by the needs of the crop upon which his region depended. Despite this, his thinking ranged beyond regional parochialism. Wilson's observations in Washington during the farm battles of the twenties taught him that the success of any plan depended upon both the universality of its appeal and the political sagacity of the national administration. Years later, Wilson vividly described his central interest in obtaining relief for the wheat-raising area and his utilization of wheat as a symbol for general agricultural distress. He commented:

> But you will notice that in my activities in this whole story up to date, I kept over on wheat. My symbols involved my talking about wheat all the time, partially and I suppose principally, because I came from the wheat country and the economic interest with which I was identified was wheat. Secondly, I did not know enough about cotton, but if you go back over the McNary-Haugen history, you find that they were talking about wheat all the time. Wheat was the symbol that was used for farm relief. [5]

Wheat was the crop which had suffered the longest and borne the brunt of the agricultural depression. Yet the cause of wheat had to be activated by alert and competent leadership capable of turning voices crying in the wilderness into voices that talked sound economic and political sense to the receptive ears of a concerned national administration. The challenge, as Wilson stressed, was to transform the tragic situation in the wheat region into a clarion call for farm relief, a "symbol" for urgent action on the part of the national government. M. L. Wilson, concerned primarily with the wheat problem, made this symbol a concrete touchstone for immediate and long-range agricultural reform on a national level.

[5] Wilson, COHC.

CHAPTER TWO

Postwar Wheat Politics:
Prelude to Reform

The wheat situation is a symptom of a pathological condition
in Agriculture which extends to nearly every branch of the
industry.—H. C. Taylor

Armistice Day, November, 1918, pointed to the end of a boom
period in the wheat areas of the northern plains. The wartime slogan
"Food will win the war" and skyrocketing prices, which prompted
government controls, spurred production of the staples wheat, hogs,
and cotton. Despite loud demands for increased wheat production,
some termed the expansion reckless and said it was based on "loose
thinking" about the permanency of the demand.[1]

Wheat prices immediately felt the impact of the war's end. The
threat of price recession prompted Congress to expand the War
Finance Corporation in March, 1919, to aid agriculture by supplying
credits for exports. Also, the Food Administration called upon
Congress to appropriate funds to extend the minimum wheat price
of $2.26 to the middle of 1920. The result was the Wheat Stabiliza-
tion Act of March 4, 1919, which appropriated one billion dollars
to meet previous commitments until June 1, 1920. Through extensive
operations, the grain corporation kept the government price during
1919. Continuation of the price guarantee represented a victory for
the wheat interests and agriculture in general. Suspicion in farm
circles, however, that prices were repressed in relation to manufactured goods qualified the success. But most important it postponed
the moment of painful readjustment to a peacetime market.[2]

[1] *United States Department of Agriculture Year Book of Agriculture, 1920*
(Washington, D.C.: Government Printing Office, 1921), p. 34.
[2] James H. Shideler, *Farm Crisis, 1919–1923* (Berkeley: University of
California Press, 1957), pp. 22–23; A. B. Genung, *The Agricultural Depression*

Government efforts to support wheat prices did not go unaided by the perverse forces of nature in the northern wheat areas in 1919. Winter and spring wheat plantings combined amounted to 71,854,000 acres, or 7,200,000 acres more than the previous record set in 1918. But the yield of 918,471,000 bushels exceeded that of 1918 by only 1,000,000 bushels and did not equal the 1915 record yield of 1,025,801,000 bushels.[3]

The year 1919 brought widespread drought in the northern hard spring wheat areas. Spring wheat in Montana yielded only an average of 4.7 bushels per acre. The story was similar in North Dakota where the average yield was 6.9 as compared to 10.5 average for the ten-year period from 1910 to 1919. Taken together, South Dakota and Nebraska had about equal amounts of spring and winter wheat planted, and suffered more moderate yield reductions. The value of the North Dakota crop suffered an almost 50 per cent reduction in 1919 from the 1918 crop. Statistics for the state show that it sustained huge losses in comparison with acreage planted. National statistics indicate that the drought predominated only in this northern region. Unfortunately for the region, government activities in the market could do little for a condition produced by adverse climate.[4] The table shows comparatively poor wheat yield in 1919:

Average Bushels Per Acre   1910–1919*

	10 yr. Average 1910–1919	1910	1911	1912	1913	1914	1915	1916	1917	1918	1919
Nebraska	16	16.2	13.4	17.6	17.9	18.6	18.3	19.4	13.8	11.2	13.8
North Dakota	10.15	5	8	18	10.5	11.2	18.2	5.5	8	13.6	6.9
Montana	19.2	22	28.7	24.1	23.8	20.2	26.5	19.3	10.4	12.6	4.8
South Dakota	11.4	12.8	4.0	14.2	9.0	9.1	17.1	6.8	14	19	8.1

* *Year Book of Agriculture 1919*, p. 526.

Following World War I and Its Political Consequences (Ithaca, N.Y.: Northeast Farm Foundation, 1954), p. 6; John D. Hicks, *Rehearsal for Disaster: The Boom and Collapse of 1919–1920* (Gainesville: University of Florida Press, 1961).

[3] *Year Book of Agriculture, 1919*, pp. 10–13.

[4] *Ibid.*, pp. 522–526.

The wheat situation in 1919 showed three distinctive traits present in the politics of wheat until the advent of the New Deal—overproduction, limited government intervention, and drought. Although the 1920 *Year Book of Agriculture* spoke optimistically about the contraction of wheat acreage and about the need to understand the temporary nature of the war market, wheat production continued to overreach the market potential in the coming years.[5] Expansion beyond market needs and the disadvantageous price-ratio between farm products and general commodity prices plagued the wheat farmer's bid for a rewarding slice of American prosperity. The question of how and the extent to which government should intervene to improve the wheat situation loomed behind the outstanding agricultural political battles in the twenties. Finally, the long shadow of drought lingering over the northern plains added to the miseries of harsh climate and inadequate institutional devices to bring wheat production in line with prospective markets. These issues persisted, provoking protests, responses, and despair.

From the beginning, life had been hard on the northern plains. O. E. Rölvaag's *Giants in the Earth*, published in the mid-twenties, described the early settlement of the northern plains in terms of broken men, demented women, and generally painful adjustment to a hostile environment.[6] When M. L. Wilson returned to Montana from the University of Chicago in 1920, he recalled:

> I didn't realize it then, but as I see it in perspective, this was a culmination of hard luck, dry years, and prices that were out of line with costs. It was the beginning of a long period of hard times with relatively low agricultural prices especially in wheat.[7]

Reacting to these "hard times," one Depression farmer later called Dakota "one Hellova place" in a poem submitted to the *Dakota Farmer:*

> So, Dakota, you've just about wrecked us
> And at wrecken' you're not such a slouch
> But listen to this, Old Dakota:
> You're in for one Hellova grouch!

[5] *Year Book of Agriculture, 1920*, p. 34.

[6] O. E. Rölvaag, *Giants in the Earth* (New York: Harper and Brothers, 1927); Elwyn B. Robinson, *History of North Dakota* (Lincoln: University of Nebraska Press, 1966), p. 10.

[7] M. L. Wilson, Columbia Oral History Collection, Columbia University, New York, N.Y.

When the jackrabbits, and thistles, an' coyotes
Are a-trampin' an marrin' your face,
I'm a-gon'a laugh—don't forget it—
For Dakota'll be one Hellova place! [8]

Despite the deprivations of climate, isolation, and grasshopper scourges, the commercialized American farmer pushed continuously into the plains, adapting farming methods and fighting each successive obstacle that nature placed in his way. Wheat's drought tolerance and the availability of railroad shipping facilities made it the most profitable cash crop in the area. From one standpoint the prairie grasslands and the means to bring them under cultivation were a "bonanza" discovery of the generation at the turn of the century, just as the gold in the Far West and the fertile lands of the Middle West were a bonanza to an earlier generation. The inflated war market was by no means the only cause of increased wheat acreage and expansion into the marginal areas. Expansion of wheat production was well under way before the beginning of the war. [9]

The stubborn refusal of wheat production to decline measurably turned wheat into the most critical agricultural problem in the postwar period. Solutions for the problem in the early part of the decade involved several approaches. The policy asking for the least extension of government aid simply called for supplying the farmer with better information about production and markets. With market information readily available, it was argued that production could be adjusted to the prospective conditions of the market. Government feed and seed loans were based on the assumption that the crisis was temporary and would soon pass. The youthful head of the Montana State College Department of Agricultural Economics, M. L. Wilson, observed that such policies followed the "farm fallacy

[8] *Dakota Farmer,* May 12, 1934 (Aberdeen, South Dakota), from A. J. White, Brookings County, South Dakota.

[9] Mary Wilma M. Hargreaves, *Dry Farming in the Northern Great Plains, 1900–1925* (Cambridge: Harvard University Press, 1957), pp. 23, 536; Helen M. Strong, "Export Wheat Producing Regions," *Economic Geography,* VIII (April, 1932), 161; also Wilfred Malenbaum, *The World Wheat Economy, 1885–1939* (Cambridge: Harvard University Press, 1953), pp. 127–153, points to the development of wheat raising in many areas of the world; Hiram M. Drache, *The Day of the Bonanza: A History of Bonanza Farming in the Red River Valley of the North* (Fargo: North Dakota Institute for Regional Studies, 1964); Lloyd P. Jorgenson, "Agricultural Expansion into the Semiarid Lands of the West North Central States During the First World War," *Agricultural History,* XXIII (January, 1949), 32.

theory," which held that holding actions would be adequate until normal prosperity returned.[10]

A step beyond providing information services about prices was the policy of offering the services of government officials in inspecting and grading commodities. In addition, government assistance went to organizing producers' cooperatives and in supplying them with technical and even financial aid. On the recommendations of both the Joint Commission and the National Agricultural Conference, Congress in 1922 enacted the Capper-Volstead bill which exempted cooperatives from prosecution under the Sherman Anti-Trust laws and was generally referred to as the "Magna Carta of Cooperative Marketing." The Grain Futures Act of the same year required the private grain trade to admit cooperatives without discrimination to the normal channels of trade. Financial help for the cooperatives came from the continued activities of the War Finance Corporation and the Intermediate Credits Act of 1923. One of the reasons for the acceptance of the cooperative idea grew out of the nationwide promotional campaign of Aaron Sapiro, who preached that the cooperative would solve the farm problem.[11]

Two other proposals that called for increased government intervention centered upon the surplus problem. The first wanted government to move into the market, purchase surpluses, and perform a holding action until the market might profitably absorb them. In a revolving fund, public support would be placed at the disposal of producers. Essentially this was Senator George Norris' export corporation plan, which he suggested in June, 1921, for the purpose of buying farm surpluses and selling them abroad. The second proposal, or the Peek-Johnson plan, which later developed under the banner of McNary-Haugenism, also called for a government export corporation designed to buy up domestic surpluses and dispose of them in the world market until the domestic price reached

[10] Theodore Saloutos, "Spring Wheat Farmer in a Maturing Economy," *Journal of Economic History*, VI (November, 1946), 176: "In 1921 more than half, and in large areas over 80 per cent, of the farmers in many northern states raised wheat, which meant that prices affected the entire communities that depended on the crop"; M. L. Wilson interview, November, 1965.

[11] Theodore Saloutos and John D. Hicks, *Agricultural Discontent in the Middle West, 1900–1939* (Madison: University of Wisconsin Press, 1951), p. 288; Grace H. Larsen and Henry E. Erdman, "Aaron Sapiro: Genius of Farm Co-operative Promotion," *Mississippi Valley Historical Review*, XLIX (September, 1962), 242–268.

a defined parity that would create "agricultural equality." Only a few recognized that such plans must be coupled with production restrictions. This question was to remain unexplored until the holding activities of President Hoover's Farm Board proved ineffective in the face of mounting production.[12]

The newly appointed Secretary of Agriculture, Henry C. Wallace, came to Washington at the beginning of the Harding administration under the heavy obligation to find ways of improving the agricultural situation. Wallace was the son of a famous farm editor and had a scientific and practical approach to agriculture. Wallace's efforts gradually remodeled the department into a policy-making agency instead of a purely administrative arm of the national government. He supported research in overproduction problems and lower farm costs. By July, 1922, he succeeded in establishing the Bureau of Agricultural Economics which coordinated the work of the Bureau of Markets and Crop Estimates and the Office of Farm Management and Farm Economics. This was to be one of the strongest bureaus in the government.[13]

[12] Various works have dealt extensively with these movements. Parity was the most enduring concept to grow out of the early struggles in the twenties. James H. Shideler, "The Development of the Parity Price Formula for Agriculture, 1919–1923," *Agricultural History*, XXVII (July, 1953), 77–84, suggests that the unique contribution of George N. Peek and Hugh Johnson was not their ability to invent a plan for farm relief, but their determination to attract popular support and diminish opposition to political price management. Robert L. Tontz, "Origins of the Base Period Concept of Parity," *Agricultural History*, XXXII (January, 1958), 3–13, agrees with Shideler. Tontz asserts that the parity, or "ratio idea," which goes back to the Grange in the post-Civil War in its origins, was so well championed by Peek and Johnson that it developed an appeal all its own. Gilbert C. Fite, *George N. Peek and the Fight for Farm Parity* (Norman: University of Oklahoma Press, 1954), outlines clearly the struggles of the decade in this biography of the leading farm spokesman in the period; see also Norman L. Zucker, *George W. Norris: Gentle Knight of American Democracy* (Urbana: University of Illinois Press, 1966), p. 88; George W. Norris to W. T. Farnsworth of Minatare, Nebraska (December 31, 1922), Norris Papers, Library of Congress, Tray 80, Box 2; Norris, "Farmers' Export Finance Corporation Act," Senate Report No. 192, 67th Cong., 1st sess. (Washington, D.C.: Government Printing Office, June 30, 1921).

[13] John D. Black, "The Progress of Farm Relief," *American Economic Review*, XVIII (June, 1928), 268: "Secretary Wallace came to Washington with a splendid vision of converting the Department of Agriculture into an agency that would take heed of economic as well as cultural factors, so that in the future farm leaders would not be able to point the finger of derision at it and accuse it of only helping the farmers to overproduce"; Donald L. Winters,

Work in the bureau attracted young economists trained by Professors Richard T. Ely and John R. Commons, who were noted for their social theories of property. Henry C. Taylor came from the progressive University of Wisconsin to head the bureau. Mordecai Ezekiel, L. H. Bean, and M. L. Wilson, who were later to play prominent roles in agricultural programs, worked in various capacities in the bureau. Economists who shared some of Wallace's views and worked with him were O. C. Stine, John D. Black, George R. Warren, Howard R. Tolley, and O. E. Baker. Attacks on the bureau by Secretary of Commerce Herbert Hoover, who thought that only his department should assist farmers with marketing problems, served to promote a spirited determination among this group to prove the value of the bureau to farmers.[14]

The bureau's research focused on the relation of agriculture to the distribution of national wealth. In relation to other segments of the economy, did agriculture reap its fair share on the open market? Agricultural economists invariably gave a negative answer. They began to stress a balance of what they called economic and social forces. Under the law of supply and demand in the "free" economy, agriculture's share of the national product each year diminished. Since the mid-nineteenth century, the official doctrine had been that if both seller and buyer were informed, the supply and demand price would be fair. The heresy of the new economic thinking asserted that the supply and demand price might not be the fair price. It dared to ask questions about the stabilization of farm purchasing power by government intervention into the free play of economic forces.[15]

When Wilson was a student of Professor Commons, he asked the professor what determined the division of national wealth among the various producers in an economy. Commons replied that classical

---

"The Persistence of Progressivism: Henry Cantwell Wallace and the Movement for Agricultural Economics," *Agricultural History*, XLI (April, 1967), 112.

[14] Taylor emphasizes that Ely's influence was especially profound on him because he came from a line of Iowa farmers who had a stewardship view of property. H. C. Taylor Papers, Collection Various, Columbia University, vol. 8 (1926), 26; John M. Gaus and Leon O. Wolcott, *Public Administration and the United States Department of Agriculture* (Chicago: Public Administration Service, 1940), p. 54.

[15] Henry C. and Anne Dewess Taylor, *The Story of Agricultural Economics in the United States, 1840–1932* (Ames, Iowa: Iowa State College Press, 1952), pp. 597–598.

economies was logical in theory, but in actuality the pressure brought
to bear by various producing classes through institutions in the
society on the social product more often determined their share of
the national product.[16] From this Wilson eventually concluded that
agriculture did not possess effective institutions to compete for a
fair share of the total national product. If a degree of social justice
were to be achieved for agriculture, reform was needed.

The new breed of agricultural economists in the Bureau of
Agricultural Economics maintained close contact with the rural
distress in the areas of the northern wheat region. The statistical
tables became more than figures and reflected the profound hardships
under which the countryside suffered. New recruits from the schools
of agricultural economics began to think in terms of "things" and
"people" instead of words and statistics only. From the beginning,
Wallace pushed Harding to call a National Agricultural Conference.
In January, 1922, the conference was held with a cross section of the
American economic community represented. Taylor came to the
conference armed with ideas from the unorthodox economists Ely
and Commons. He tried to impress upon the delegates the necessity
for social justice in agriculture. But Taylor was disappointed in the
conference. It only stated that further study should be made of
measures to re-establish farm purchasing power and made no positive recommendations.[17]

Recoiling from the failure of national conferences to produce
results and from the attack by Hoover's department on the enlarged
functions of the Department of Agriculture, Wallace began to beat
the drums openly for a sweeping reform in agricultural policy. In a
letter to his son Henry A. Wallace on September 18, 1922, he said:

> I agree with you that we should cut down production to our
> own needs, or a little more. I am going to make a speech some
> time soon, in which I shall say this in effect, if not directly.[18]

[16] Wilson interview, November, 1965; Joseph Dorfman, *The Economic Mind
in American Civilization, 1865–1918* (New York: The Viking Press, 1949), III,
278–292; John R. Commons, *The Distribution of Wealth* (New York: Macmillan
and Company, 1893).

[17] Gaus and Wolcott, *Public Administration and the USDA*, p. 53; Russell
Lord, *The Wallaces of Iowa* (Boston: Houghton Mifflin Company, 1947), p.
236; Taylor Papers, vol. 8, 249.

[18] Files of the Economic and Statistical Analysis Division of the Economic
Research Service, "Production Control Proposals," United States Department
of Agriculture.

The department aimed at voluntary production control by individual farmers when it inaugurated a forecasting or Outlook program in 1921 to give farmers some indication of the market demand and future price on various crops in the coming year.

Volunteerism was an unrealistic approach to the problem. The Outlook programs, which developed from the crop-forecasting services, were a part of the general theoretical work that went on in Washington in relation to agriculture's declining place in the economy. Soon, Wallace began to move beyond the realm of the theoretical in his support of concrete legislative measures for agricultural aid. In late 1922 and early 1923 he caused concern in the administration over his flirtation with the export corporation plan for wheat that was sponsored by the "industrial agrarian," George Peek.[19]

The flurry of activity in Washington and the coming battles over farm policy reflected the continuing unsatisfactory conditions in the various agricultural sections of the country, and in particular the overriding distress in the northern wheat regions. A department memorandum in December, 1922, dealt with the situation in the spring wheat states. For a solution it suggested diversification of agriculture to escape the one-crop complex of the region. On the other hand, the report made a good case for wheat as the only suitable money crop for the area. It pointed out that the relatively high price per pound of wheat made it possible for the crop to stand the high cost of transportation. For this reason it predicted that since the territory was some distance from the market, wheat would by necessity remain the major source of the cash income for farmers in the region. In many respects it was a contradictory report, first describing what would be an ideal solution and then looking at the realities of economic life on the northern plains that might preclude diversification.[20]

Although diversification took place after the war, it occurred primarily in the eastern parts of North and South Dakota and in

[19] Fite, *Fight for Farm Parity*, p. 55; Russell Lord, *Agrarian Revival: A Study of Agricultural Extension* (New York: American Association for Adult Education, George Grady Press, 1939), p. 155, refers to Peek as an "industrial agrarian."

[20] W. S. Spillman, "Memorandum for the Assistant Secretary Relating to Agricultural Problems in the Spring Wheat States" (December 7, 1922), Miscellaneous Manuscripts, 1915–1929, RG83, National Archives and Records Service [hereafter referred to as NARS], Washington, D.C.

states such as Nebraska where weather, soil, and transportation costs could permit diverse crops. An extensive report in the 1923 *Year Book of Agriculture* on "The Wheat Situation" revealed that most of the 6,500,000 acres added to spring wheat acreage during the war were no longer sown in wheat. It also showed that the region reduced its 1923 wheat area to 700,000 acres less than the average before the war (1909–1914). But the reduction was in the eastern part of the Dakotas and Minnesota. In the semiarid sections of North Dakota, South Dakota, and Montana, wheat acreage in 1923 was 176 per cent greater than in 1909. Generally, the area of cultivated crops in the region continued to expand after the war.[21]

Because of crop failures in the semiarid regions in 1921 and 1922, Montana, North Dakota, and South Dakota were heavy recipients of federal seed and grain loans. This complicated the farm indebtedness problem in the area where wheat farming was a specialized industry operating under conditions of high risk. Continued expansion in the face of declining markets and persistent crop failure, although a tribute to the wheat farmer's great faith in the future, also marked him as an unimaginative businessman who refused to adjust and who flouted the warnings of the market indicators. One writer has said that Montana would always be "next year country," implying that hope in the future was the only reason for staying on the plains. Another has suggested that the wheat growers in these areas were not the traditional agriculturalists, but were soil miners, land gamblers, and reckless borrowers of credit who bought their food in the city and charged their losses to the government.[22]

The northern plains states, especially the predominantly wheat areas, were not without their distinctive political reactions to the prevailing distress in agriculture. In North Dakota the ruling Nonpartisan League, originally a protest against Twin Cities' exploitation of the wheat area, came under heavy attack and eventual defeat. It took all of the political genius of progressive Republican Peter Norbeck to defeat the Nonpartisan League in South Dakota after embracing some of its program of state industries. In Montana progressive reform flourished under Republican Governor

---

[21] *Year Book of Agriculture, 1923*, pp. 135–136.

[22] *Ibid.*, p. 120; Joseph Kinsey Howard, *Montana: High, Wide, and Handsome* (New Haven: Yale University Press, 1959), p. 305; Garet Garrett, "That Pain in Our Northwest," *Saturday Evening Post*, CXCVI (April 12, 1924), 47.

Joe Dixon from 1920 to 1924, but tax reform aimed at the Anaconda Mining Company sealed his defeat when an alliance of the mining company, bankers, ranchers, and mercantile interests defeated him and progressivism in 1924. To the south, in Nebraska, there was no violent political reaction. Nebraskans did show their chagrin at Republican farm policies by consistently returning to office Democratic representatives from rural areas and in their loyalty to George W. Norris in his fight against the Republican position on the farm issue. Perhaps the "enemy" was never as identifiable in Nebraska as it was in the Dakotas and Montana in the form of the Twin Cities' grain trade or the "company." Also, one investigator contends that the Populist heritage in Nebraska never presented a united front in the twenties because of its ambivalence toward the use of government in meeting economic problems.[23]

In the long run, the problem was beyond the meager resources of a region that in many respects stood in economic dependence on the national and international markets. Powerful conservative forces in these states were convinced that the current period of deflation was a passing phenomenon. Since it was not, thwarting state enterprises fortunately saved them from more extensive catastrophe. Unfortunately, the deteriorating situation seemed to produce a general disillusionment with reform in state government. It did, however, carry the lasting message that possibly reform had to

[23] Robert L. Morlan, *Political Prairie Fire: The Nonpartisan League, 1915–1922* (Minneapolis: University of Minnesota Press, 1955), p. 327; Theodore Saloutos, "The Expansion and Decline of the Nonpartisan League in the Western Middle West, 1917–1921," *Agricultural History*, XX (October, 1946), 235–252; Gilbert C. Fite, *Peter Norbeck: Prairie Statesman*, University of Missouri Studies, XXII (Columbia: University of Missouri Press, 1948), 68–69; Fite, "Peter Norbeck and the Defeat of the Non Partisan League in South Dakota," *Mississippi Valley Historical Review*, XXXIII (September, 1946), 234; Herbert S. Schell, *History of South Dakota* (Lincoln: University of Nebraska Press, 1961), p. 276; K. Ross Toole, *Montana: An Uncommon Land* (Norman: University of Oklahoma Press, 1959), p. 266; Howard, *Montana, High, Wide, and Handsome*, pp. 246–249; Jules Alexander Karlin, "Progressive Politics in Montana," in *History of Montana*, eds. Merrill G. Burlingame and K. Ross Toole (New York: Lewis Publishing Company, 1957), I, 271; James C. Olson, *History of Nebraska* (Lincoln: University of Nebraska Press, 1955), pp. 302–304; James A. Stone, "Agrarian Ideology and the Farm Problem in Nebraska State Politics with Special Reference to Northeast Nebraska, 1920–1933" (Ph.D. dissertation, University of Nebraska, 1960), pp. 2, 285–287.

come from a different level. That level was the national government —the only source of power strong enough to deal with the problems of the national market.

In Washington the untiring efforts for agricultural reform by Secretary Wallace put him on a collision course with powerful elements in the Republican administration. The rift with Secretary Hoover was widening. Hoover's conviction that private associations of cooperatives could solve the farm problem drew little enthusiasm as the light of cooperative marketing dimmed in 1923. Although special national legislation favored cooperatives, the movement failed to attract a national following in large numbers to bring the markets under control of the producers.[24]

Clearly, Wallace took little stock in the cooperative marketing panacea. The 1923 departmental statement on the wheat situation said cooperatives had not shown themselves capable of organizing the producers of the great staples to give them that control over supply which is necessary to influence prices. After a discussion of the world wheat surplus problem, the report went so far as to conclude, "The suggestion that the Government set up an export corporation to aid in the disposition of this surplus is worthy of the most careful consideration."[25] In advocating an export corporation through departmental publications, Wallace moved the department into a policy-forming position it had not held before. He permitted the first steps in this direction when economists in the Bureau of Agricultural Economics were encouraged to define the problem. Once the problem was identified, it was only a short step to suggest solutions.

[24] Shideler, "Herbert Hoover and the Federal Farm Board Project, 1921– 1925," *Mississippi Valley Historical Review*, XLII (March, 1956), 713. In defense of the cooperative movement, Hoover wrote, "I believe it to be one of the most hopeful undertakings, for according to my social theories any organization by citizens for their own welfare is preferable to the same action by the Government," Herbert Hoover, *The Memoirs of Herbert Hoover, The Cabinet, and the Presidency, 1920–1933* (New York: The Macmillan Company, 1952), II, 110.

[25] *Year Book of Agriculture, 1923*, "The Wheat Situation," p. 150: "The prime duty of such an export corporation would be to restore, so far as possible, the pre-war ratio between wheat, and other farm products of which we export a surplus, and other commodities. Its activities would therefore expand or contract accordingly as the relative prices for farm products varied with other commodities, and it would cease to function as pre-war ratios become fairly well restored."

While Harding lived, Wallace believed there was some chance to educate the administration toward a positive farm program. Harding's trip to the Northwest in the summer of 1923 raised hopes that he would recognize the possibility of political revolt in the deflated wheatlands as he traveled from Kansas northward. Early rains, however, had turned the country green and it looked prosperous. Throngs of northwesterners greeted the President, and "all he heard was talk about this 'God's country' and a boundless, buoyant future." Montana's Commissioner of Agriculture, Chester Davis, remembered that cheering crowds in Helena gave the Harding party an especially warm welcome: "Yet nearly half of Montana's wheat farmers had lost their lands and homes in the postwar land crash." [26]

With the death of Harding on his return from Alaska in August, 1923, Wallace's plans for converting the administration to the export corporation plan evaporated. Vice-President Coolidge had little interest in problems west of the Alleghenies, and, what was more critical, Hoover now moved to a position of more power as he gained Coolidge's ear on agricultural matters. [27]

After Harding's death, Wallace openly supported the movement for an export corporation plan in the fall of 1923. To counter the move, the administration made a strong bid to rekindle enthusiasm and faith in the cooperative movement. Prices of corn and cotton improved in the summer of 1923, but the wheat situation remained gloomy and was headed for another crisis. Wheat presented the most difficult problem for the cooperative movement. [28] In the wheat regions prices fell to below a dollar a bushel for almost the first time since 1914. The crisis in wheat showed the inadequacy of the explanation that the farm crisis was short-lived and that voluntary cooperative efforts by wheat farmers would solve their problems.

[26] Lord, *The Wallaces of Iowa*, pp. 244–245.

[27] Black, "Progress of Farm Relief," p. 268; H. C. Taylor is especially harsh on Coolidge's limited view of American life that excluded agriculture, Taylor Papers, vol. 8, 252; O. C. Stine asserts, "With the death of Harding and the coming in of Calvin Coolidge, H. C. Wallace was in a somewhat more difficult position. In my view this was because Coolidge was a little more susceptible to the Hoover influence than was Harding," Stine, Columbia Oral History Collection, Columbia University, New York, N.Y.

[28] Shideler, *Farm Crisis, 1919–1923*, p. 251.

The Coolidge administration could not ignore requests pouring in from groups in the Northwest for the creation of an export corporation. The heightened crisis in wheat pushed the administration to send Eugene Meyer and Frank Mondell, directors of the War Finance Corporation, to the Northwest in an effort to win sentiment for a national wheat marketing cooperative. On the advice of Hoover, Coolidge initiated the trip without consulting Secretary Wallace. In the Northwest, the trip met with much skepticism from farmers who had heard too much about self-help schemes and from the private grain trade that had always been suspicious of government-sponsored cooperatives. The Meyer-Mondell mission went first to Chicago where they conferred with Sapiro men and envisioned a new grain-marketing corporation to be known as the "Coolidge Pool."

The *Montana Record-Herald* in Helena began covering the trip when it reached St. Paul. The October 12 issue of the paper reported that the special committee sent to the wheat belt by President Coolidge told a meeting of seventy local businessmen, bankers, farmers, and others interested in the Minnesota Club that cooperative marketing was the best solution to the northwest wheat situation. Meyer said that he did not believe statistics gave a true picture of the wheat surplus and that he did not consider the wheat surplus in the United States dangerous "if deficiency of stocks in Europe, and the world demand, were taken into consideration."

A week later in Helena, after stops in North Dakota, the Meyer-Mondell team made a special appeal to bankers for support of cooperatives and the orderly marketing of the wheat crop. In a call for continued credit to the wheat farmer, Meyer said bankers should not adopt shortsighted policies toward farmers and especially toward those participating in pools. Meyer swiped at the private grain trade when he called for an elimination of speculative marketing by the formation of wheat pools.[29] Throughout its support of cooperatives, the administration constantly placed itself in a difficult position in relation to the private grain trade. Eventually the Republicans were caught with a program for action that on the one hand did not answer the needs of the wheat problem for the farmer and on the other hand offended the interests of the private grain trade. Its cooperative approach left the administration with few allies in a sea of trouble.

[29] *Montana Record-Herald,* October 16, 1923.

Not to be outdone, Wallace gave the green light to his own emissary, H. C. Taylor, to travel through the Northwest in October. Taylor was to assess farmer opinion and privately sound out sentiment toward the export corporation plan. The expeditions crisscrossed paths on the plains and took on an air of competition as they met with local groups. Before the trip, on September 22, 1923, Taylor had presented a report to Wallace entitled "The Agricultural Situation and the Means of Setting It Right." Taylor's central thesis in the report was that the "wheat situation is a symptom of a pathological condition in Agriculture which extends to nearly every branch of the industry." [30] This report and its theme—that the agricultural problem must be attacked first in the wheat areas to restore an equilibrium between farm prices and manufactured goods—played a large role in Wallace's decision to approve the Taylor mission in what he knew would be an open break with administration policy.

Taylor's reports on the trip reveal a widening picture of distress as he moved into the wheat areas of the Northwest. In the Wisconsin dairy- and diversified-farming area, Taylor found some complaints among farmers, but as a whole they felt they were doing rather well. But he writes, "This was in marked contrast to the conditions I was to find a few days later in the wheat region." [31]

Taylor arrived in Montana before the Meyer-Mondell mission. Alerted to the coming visit of Meyer and Mondell, Lester Cole, editor of the *Montana Farmer*, asked Taylor whether their visit was sincere or political. This incident and open newspaper denials about the political intent of their mission shows the presence of a widely held skepticism toward their effort. [32] In Helena, Taylor held an extended conference with Governor Dixon. This was followed by a dinner party with the Governor; Chester Davis; M. L. Wilson; W. S. McCormick, director of the Farm Loan Bank of Spokane and farmer; W. J. Hopper of Joliet, Montana, president of State Farmers Union; A. H. Stafford, state Farm Bureau president; Dwight R. Cresap of Lewistown, president of the Montana Wheat Growers Association; and George A. Scott, state agricultural statistician.

[30] Taylor Papers, vol. 8, 255.
[31] *Ibid.*, p. 262.
[32] *Montana Record-Herald*, October 12, 1923.

In his memoir, Taylor does not say that his mission was to sell the idea of an export corporation plan. He maintains that he was only testing sentiment in its favor. Certainly there must have been a fine line between Taylor's task of testing sentiment in favor of the plan and of actively favoring it among these people as a feasible outlet for the wheat surpluses. The next day, Taylor telegraphed Wallace, "Ideas of everyone present in line with previous telegram. Governor Dixon will be in Washington twentieth and wants to see you." What he meant by this message is not exactly known, but M. L. Wilson explains that Taylor wanted Dixon to press Coolidge on the Peek plan when he was in Washington. According to Wilson, Taylor talked at great length of the plan and asked if it did not merit national action.[33]

That evening Wilson and Davis discussed the plan privately. Davis had previously been editor of the *Montana Farmer* and had been appointed by newly elected Governor Dixon as Montana's Commissioner of Agriculture in 1921 as part of a drive by the new administration to revitalize that department of state government. Montana's new Commissioner of Agriculture and future director of the AAA in the early New Deal was born in Linden, Iowa. He received his B.A. from Grinnell College in 1911 and later did graduate work at Cornell University. Davis suggested that they not go into the plan's details, but simply ask the most important question, Could it bring quick results to the stricken area? Wilson admits that he had never thought much about a comprehensive plan to aid the wheat region, but he also remembered that he never took much stock in the "monopolistic marketing of the Co-ops."[34]

When informed of the Taylor trip, President Coolidge immediately saw that it undermined the Meyer-Mondell mission. Wallace was instructed to recall his man. Before Taylor could swing back

[33] Taylor Papers, vol. 8, 289; Wilson, COHC.

[34] Wilson interview, November, 1965; Wilson, COHC; Chester C. Davis Papers, Western Historical Manuscript Collection, University of Missouri, Columbia, Missouri. Professor Jules Alexander Karlin of the University of Montana, who is currently writing a biography of Governor Dixon, finds no evidence in the Dixon papers of any effort by the governor to promote the export corporation plan with the Coolidge administration. Professor Karlin writes, "Although I would like to portray Dixon as an exponent of a new form of farm aid, the evidence I have will not substantiate this thesis." Karlin to author (October 2, 1967).

through the winter wheat regions, he received a telegram from Wallace to return to Washington and report his findings to the President. But Taylor never was called to the White House to deliver the report. He admits that many persons he met on the trip later came to Washington and urged Secretary Wallace to back plans for re-establishing a just price-ratio for agriculture, but Taylor denied that the real purpose of his trip was to arouse support in the Northwest for a specific farm relief plan. [35]

Despite controversy that may exist over the purpose of the trip, it is clear that Taylor represented an opposing viewpoint within the administration. Taylor explained that although his interest centered in the farm sections of the economy, he always approached economic questions from a national standpoint. He believed that each group in the economy should compete on an equal basis with other groups without special favors. As a farm economist he never favored farmer movements that produced a psychology of class struggle. Now, however, Taylor moved to a position of government intervention in the interests of the farm population. He related:

> But my association with Wallace and my contacts with the realities of life, particularly on my western trip in 1923, had brought me to a vivid realization that the interests of the farmers must be protected in this period of great disaster. [36]

Although Taylor voiced his belief in the need for some type of relief legislation from Congress, he asserted that he had no part in promoting such legislation in or out of Congress. In his memoirs he tried to extricate himself from the charge that he was playing politics under the table in sounding out grass-roots support for what was later to develop into the McNary-Haugen bill. In concluding the matter, he wrote that both he and Wallace recognized that political activity was not his function. Taylor attempts to show that the function of the Bureau of Agricultural Economics was an information-gathering agency and without the ability to prescribe

[35] Taylor, *Story of Agricultural Economics*, pp. 595–596. This is, of course, somewhat at variance with Wilson's recollection of Taylor's visit to Montana. O. C. Stine comments that Taylor's account of his western trip in the material at Columbia is not a detailed report and that many experiences are not included. Stine, COHC.

[36] Taylor Papers, vol. 8, 310.

policy. Yet in defining the wheat problem in "The Wheat Situation" report of 1923, he strongly suggested that the export corporation plan be tried.

The wheat disaster on the plains, standing as a "symptom of a pathological condition" in all agriculture, had finally caused deep consternation in Washington. Overproduction and what the bureau preferred to call low price-ratios persisted in the country's wheat situation through the succeeding Republican administrations. Still, people stayed on the plains, and the "Honyockers" in Montana clung to their "next year" philosophy. On the state level these years pointed to the necessity for a solution beyond the actions of state political experiments. In academic circles a rethinking of agriculture's position in the mature industrial economy occurred. BAE chief Taylor is an outstanding example of a leading agricultural economist re-examining his traditional thinking about the role of government in relation to agriculture. Wilson admits that he had never given much thought to a national plan when he heard of the export corporation proposal. Moreover, he never seriously entertained the cooperative approach as an answer.

In the following years, attention fixed on a national solution. The regional and minority status of agriculture became increasingly apparent as proposed solutions failed to win sympathy on a broad national level. The administration, while recognizing the existence of a problem, refused to involve government in the economy of agriculture and wheat on the scale that many farm leaders demanded. The refusal sowed the seeds of frustration and split the personality of Republicanism in the Northwest as loyalty to the party conflicted with the recognition that the region needed a nationally backed program for salvation.

CHAPTER THREE

Disappointment in Washington
1924-1929

> The trouble is most people are interested in maintaining the status quo, particularly those parts of our population that are articulate in civic organizations and through the press.—Chester C. Davis.

Growing agitation in the Northwest for a national solution to the wheat problem eventually reached Washington. The Peek-Johnson plan stirred imaginations, and through the cooperation of the Agricultural Department the first McNary-Haugen bill was introduced in congress on January 16, 1924. After a bitter fight, Congress rejected it the following June. Clearly, the farm bloc and lobbyists had gathered surprising support for their proposal. Some had called for price-fixing in 1921 and 1922, but their pleas were dismissed as untenable. When the first McNary-Haugen bill came within forty votes of winning a majority of the votes cast in the House in June, 1924, the untenable came close to reality, and Washington began to reap the harvests of discontent in the hinterland. Secretary Wallace had made extensive preparations for the legislative battle. The general public took notice, and the administration became increasingly alert to the danger within its ranks.

The Coolidge administration took steps to head off radical measures. Wallace's death on October 25, 1924, gave the President control of an upcoming conference of agricultural leaders that had been promised in his campaign. Hoover played a major role in the selection of delegates and told the president they should be men who had not been "infected by McNary Hougen [sic] stuff." The

President chose the names on the invitation list carefully and the conference performed accordingly:

> What little it did say strongly suggested the Republican doctrine of protective tariffs for agriculture, self-sufficiency, and reduced exports of farm products. It was a Republican Conference.[1]

The conference's recommendations gave major impetus to the Farm Board idea which envisioned stabilization through cooperative marketing associations on the producer level. The farm bloc's defeat of the Capper-Haugen bill in February, 1925, which embodied the Farm Board proposal in preference to an export plan, drew battle lines on the two issues that were to provide the sparks for the agricultural tinderbox until the appearance of the domestic allotment program. The McNary-Haugen export solution versus the Farm Board cooperative-marketing solution represented four years of harried search for an adequate farm program. Some believe that neither solution offered a constructive program.[2] The establishment of the Farm Board and its failure proved to many influential groups, congressmen, and government officials the inadequacies of cooperative marketing even when accompanied by withholding actions. Moreover, the Farm Board's trial and error delayed the implementation of effective production-control programs.

Wallace's independent course during his years as Secretary of Agriculture and his ability to gain a following in Congress prompted Coolidge to fill the now-vacant post with a man whose views were acceptable and loyal to the administration. His task would be to rid the department of everyone connected with the McNary-Haugen movement and those who did not support the administration's program of cooperative marketing. W. M. Jardine, president of Kansas State College in Manhattan, filled these requirements. After Jardine's appointment, H. C. Taylor soon found himself without a job.[3] Hoover was especially bitter toward the Bureau of Agricultural Economics. He said it had originated the McNary-Haugen Bill and

[1] James H. Shideler, "Herbert Hoover and the Federal Farm Board Project, 1921–1925," *Mississippi Valley Historical Review*, XLII (March, 1956), 727; John D. Black, "The Progress of Farm Relief," *American Economic Review*, XVIII (June, 1928), 270.

[2] Shideler, "Herbert Hoover and the Federal Farm Board Project," p. 729.

[3] Wilson, Columbia Oral History Collection, Columbia University, New York, N. Y.

would not support legislation favorable to cooperatives. Convinced that extensive government intervention on behalf of agriculture was tantamount to socialism, the future President wrote to a friend, "That Bureau has never, so far as I am aware offered a constructive idea for the assistance of co-operatives. . . . Being naturally Socialistic in my mind they turn to Socialism as a solution." [4] Secretary Wallace had been a persistent critic of Hoover's Farm Board idea and schemes for large government-backed cooperatives. Wallace wrote President Coolidge in April, 1924, that it would be a mistake for the administration to support a bill for a federal marketing board under the illusion that it would relieve the agricultural situation. "It would not be accepted by farmers generally as offering any substantial measure of relief from their present troubles," he wrote. [5]

In Washington the agricultural battle lines formed on two defensive fronts. The first wished to protect the farmer from the city by establishing a system to equalize economic conditions in the city and country. The other threw up bulwarks around the Department of Agriculture in an effort to protect it from administration domination. To some extent the effort collapsed when Jardine became secretary in 1925. But these two aspects of the agricultural battle in Washington were part of the growing movement to keep agriculture free from domination by the business interests of the country represented by the administration and Hoover's Department of Commerce. Nationally, however, the McNary-Haugen campaigns of the twenties helped to prepare business for the agricultural reform legislation of the 1930's. [6]

In the Northwest, Senator Norbeck was determined to inform the administration and the Republican party that his state and region were not going to fall in line behind its policies. Agricultural work in Washington called M. L. Wilson and Chester C. Davis from Montana. Davis went immediately into the fray of agricultural politics by joining George Peek on the congressional lobbying front

---

[4] Hoover to Charles C. Teague (December 1, 1924), in Shideler, "Herbert Hoover and the Federal Farm Board Project," p. 721.

[5] Wallace to Coolidge (April 8, 1924), Herbert Hoover Library, West Branch, Iowa, Container No. 1-I/2.

[6] Black, "Progress of Farm Relief," p. 269; J. P. Gleason, "The Attitude of the Business Community Toward Agriculture During the McNary-Haugen Period," *Agricultural History*, XXXII (April, 1958), 128.

as the "equality for agriculture" struggle moved into the McNary-Haugen phase. Staying outside the political infighting, Wilson joined the mistrusted Bureau of Agricultural Economics in May, 1924.[7]

The Montanans felt they had been called to Washington at the express invitation of Secretary Wallace. When Governor Dixon met with Wallace in October, 1923, the secretary candidly told him that he would like to have any qualified people from Montana who were interested in farm relief legislation to come to Washington and meet with George Peek.[8] By December, 1924, Davis was in Washington at work on a farm relief bill with Peek. For the next four years Davis provided much of the brains behind the political battles for a McNary-Haugen bill and became one of the most valuable recruits to the agricultural crusade. In January, 1924, when the new bill was presented, Davis, Wilson, and W. L. Stockton, president of the Montana State Farm Bureau were on hand to cheer it on in Washington.[9]

Back in Montana, Governor Dixon recognized the loss of leadership from the state to the national level. In April, 1924, he answered Davis's announced intention to stay in Washington permanently with the lament:

> While I feel heart broken to think of your leaving the work here in Montana I could not stand in the way of what I feel may be your personal advancement. My great problem is where is there another man to take your place. We will feel lost without you.[10]

In Washington, Davis had no illusions about simplistic solutions to the farm problem. He frankly admitted to Wilson in the summer of 1925 that from an economic standpoint, the position taken by Mr. Peek and "our associates" on the export-surplus problem was indefensible. He seemed to ridicule the argument that if the wheat surplus could be disposed of overseas, wheat would obtain a fair price-level behind the protective tariff. There was no evidence that

[7] Peter Norbeck to W. R. Ronald (November 27, 1923), Norbeck MSS, University of South Dakota, Vermillion, South Dakota; Wilson, COHC.

[8] Wilson, COHC.

[9] Gilbert C. Fite, *George N. Peek and the Fight for Farm Parity* (Norman: University of Oklahoma Press, 1954), p. 85; *Washington Post*, January 29, 1924 (Washington, D.C.).

[10] Dixon to Davis (April 19, 1924), Davis MSS.

low agricultural prices were caused by the American high protective tariffs since the difference in price levels between agriculture and industry seemed to be a world-wide phenomenon.[11]

Somehow relief measures must be extended beyond the law of supply and demand that was supposed to set the fair exchange rates between industry and agriculture. Actually Davis was complaining that the price-ratio feature had to be dropped from the export bill for political reasons to avoid the charge of price-fixing. On this issue Peek said, "We switched from a ratio price basis to world price plus the tariff for political reasons. . . . Chester and I will have to assume the responsibility for that."[12]

By 1926, Davis began to sense the futility of his work in Washington and sympathized with Wilson's desire to return to Montana. He wrote to Wilson in February, 1926, "I do not see how they can afford to let you get away. At the same time I cannot help but wish that I were going back with you." Regardless of how much its backers streamlined the export bill for "political reasons," the administration and its supporters would not buy it. On the local level in Montana, Davis saw a continued drift away from the progressivism that the state had experienced under the leadership of Governor Dixon. All he saw in the political news coming out of Montana was "popular ignorance or indifference." In his opinion the state legislative ticket did not offer a single progressive leader with courage and ability.[13]

In Washington and throughout the country, public opinion generally favored Coolidge and the course of administration policy. "The trouble is most people are interested in maintaining the status quo," wrote Davis in the summer of 1926, "particularly those parts of our population that are articulate in civic organizations and through the press." Before broad national agricultural reform could be achieved, these people would have to be jarred from their present indifference. Davis recognized that discontent in one region or among wheat farmers was not enough to promote sweeping changes in the national government's policy toward agriculture. One sign of hope did appear on the horizon. The downward trend of cotton

[11]   Davis to Wilson (July 28, 1925), Wilson MSS.

[12]   As quoted in Fite, *Fight for Farm Parity*, p. 108.

[13]   Davis to Wilson (February 16, 1926); Davis to Wilson (August 18, 1926), Wilson MSS.

prices brought into focus the much-hoped-for wheat-cotton alliance on the McNary-Haugen issue. According to Davis, this would result "in opening the eyes of the South" and was now causing eastern politicians sleepless nights. But even senators from the Northwest could not unite on a single agricultural program. Senator Norbeck believed this was the reason northwestern farmers did not obtain helpful legislation from Congress.[14]

Amidst the despondency in Washington, Wilson retreated from the national scene in July, 1926, to continue his work at the college and his experiments in large-scale mechanical wheat farming. Wilson was secretary and managing director of the Fairway Farms Corporation in Montana, which controlled seven wheat farms in the state. The large-scale wheat farm in Montana during the twenties ranged from eight hundred to two thousand acres. Taylor, on his trip to Montana in the fall of 1923, had suggested the formation of this corporation with the aid of the Rockefeller Foundation. Before leaving Montana he wrote to Beardsley Ruml, director of the Rockefeller Memorial Spielman Foundation, in behalf of the project, outlining a plan for the acquisition of abandoned farms and bringing tenants with machinery onto the land, which they would then be permitted to buy from the corporation over a period of time. The project aimed to help tenants climb the "agricultural ladder" to landownership and, in conjunction with the college, provided the most advanced knowledge in organizing farms adapted to the climatic environment. The forthcoming Rockefeller appropriation subsidized local efforts to reconstruct the wrecked agriculture of Montana on a solid social and economic base.[15]

Like many Montanans and northwesterners, Wilson had taken a positive stand on the McNary-Haugen issue before he came to Washington. Wilson maintained, however, that his two years of service with the Bureau of Agricultural Economics saw strict neutrality on his part. Despite this, Wilson narrowly missed an earlier trip home when Jardine purged the department of the McNary-Haugenites. Like Taylor, Wilson had been placed on the

[14] Davis to Wilson (August 18, 1926), Wilson MSS; Fite, *Peter Norbeck: Prairie Statesman*, University of Missouri Studies, XXII (Columbia: University of Missouri Press, 1948), 105.

[15] M. L. Wilson, "The Fairway Farms Project," *Journal of Land and Public Utility Economics*, II (April, 1926), 156–171; Elmer Starch to author (May, 1966).

firing list, but Taylor's successor, Nils Olsen, persuaded the secretary that Wilson was free of any serious involvement in the McNary-Haugen plot.[16]

As a result of his Washington experience, Wilson gained many contacts throughout the country in his dealings with officials in the various land-grant institutions and his association with such leading agricultural economists as John D. Black, Howard R. Tolley, and Mordecai Ezekiel. Tolley, then head of the Farm Management Division of the Bureau of Agricultural Economics, described the Wilson he knew in Washington as a man intensely interested not only in improving farm income, but also in the needs of farm families and communities that were "more than material in nature." His broad-gauged view of life enabled him to look at farm life in general terms, its variations in different parts of the United States, and its particular regional problems. More than any other person, Tolley said, Wilson emphasized a type of thinking that went beyond statistics and asked questions about the quality of American rural life, aside from the pressing question of farmer income in comparison with the rest of the nation.[17] No doubt Wilson's interests brought him into a wide range of acquaintances in Washington. They were later to serve him well when he embarked on the task of selling the production-control philosophy as the first step in solving the farm dilemma.

The origins of the production-control philosophy are vague. In 1921, *Wallace's Farmer* called for regulation of acreage in the corn belt:

> Careful estimates of future demand, together with regulation of acreage to fit that demand, make up two parts of the big job that farm organizations must some day have nerve to tackle.

Justifying the step as traditional and orthodox, the editorial asserted that industry had always estimated future demand and regulated its production accordingly. The export-surplus plans never met the question of overproduction squarely. In 1924, Senator Norbeck advocated acreage restriction in answer to critics who charged that the McNary-Haugen bill would increase production through

[16] Wilson interview, November, 1965.
[17] Howard R. Tolley, COHC.

stimulated acreage expansion. His advocacy, however, was short-lived:

> . . . he did not dwell on this point when speaking on the measure two years later. He seemed unable to decide on this problem which obviously bothered him. Publicly he would not admit this weakness in the bill, but privately he did. Thereby he tacitly agreed with the opposition's argument that the bill would tend to increase production through greater acreage.

If those in the front ranks of the battle for "agricultural equality" did not admit the necessity for production controls, neither did any of the farm organizations think in these terms in the 1920's.[18]

The Outlook programs in the newly established Bureau of Agricultural Economics took some of the first steps toward promoting a crop-regulation philosophy by estimating future needs so that farmers could plant accordingly. The appearance of a comprehensive production-control proposal along the lines of the later domestic allotment program in one of the Northwest's leading farm magazines in 1926 marks the entrance of the domestic allotment plan onto the public stage.[19]

Harry N. Owen, editor of *Farm, Stock and Home,* in an article entitled "Getting the Tariff to the Farmer," presented the basic outline of the domestic allotment plan on February 1, 1926. The plan, based on the thinking of Dr. W. S. Spillman in the Bureau of Agricultural Economics, later appeared in a more detailed form in Spillman's book, *Balancing the Farm Output,* the following year. The first question the Owen article asked was the one McNary-Haugenites wished to avoid: How can farmers get the full benefit of the tariff on agricultural products without at the same time increasing production and making their future situation worse than the present? The article asserted that editor Owen was the first to suggest the formation of an export corporation in the fall of 1920. It sought to segregate the exportable surplus of wheat by purchase

[18] *Wallace's Farmer,* July 1, 1921; Fite, *Peter Norbeck,* pp. 124–125; Clifford V. Gregory, "The American Farm Bureau Federation and the AAA," *Annals of the American Academy of Political and Social Science,* CLXXIX (May, 1935), 153.

[19] Black, *Agricultural Reform in the United States* (New York: McGraw-Hill Book Co., 1929), p. 271; *Readings in the History of American Agriculture,* ed. Wayne D. Rasmussen (Urbana: University of Illinois Press, 1960), p. 248.

at market prices during the months of heavy marketing and merchandize it abroad at the best advantage and charge the loss, if any, to the producers.

While lauding the effort and thought behind it, Owen admitted that attempts to achieve the desired end had failed. "The McNary-Haugen bill was a blundering, uneconomic, cumbersome attempt to do this." Upon reflection, the whole export corporation idea was open to many objections. First, it put the government into the grain business, presenting numerous difficulties in assessing losses back to the producer, and it could not be made effective in the case of meats and meat products. Finally, it would destroy the business of grain exporters. Having acknowledged the shortcomings of the export corporation idea, Owen attacked the unsound economic principle in the tariff, but conceded that the principle was so deeply imbedded in the economic structure of the nation that to disrupt it would be extremely dangerous. Operating on this premise, Owen asserted that the only thing to do in the attempt to achieve "agricultural equality" was to try for it through extension of tariff benefits to the agricultural population.[20]

While Owen believed this new plan could apply to all agricultural products, for the sake of simplicity he chose wheat as the most lucid illustration. Starting with the base figure of one hundred bushels of wheat, he assumed that it was estimated that the probable exportable surplus of wheat was 15 per cent of the crop. The local elevator terminal would be required to pay 42 cents a bushel (current level of the tariff on imported wheat) over the domestic price for the hundred bushels, but the producer would get the 42 cents on only 85 bushels and the going market price for the other 15. In the end, the consumer would pay the bill because when the wheat was sold the elevator man added this 42 cents to his price.

> The price then automatically becomes the market price at terminals. The station, or local market, price will be figured at 42 cents, plus freight, lower than the terminal price, but that is a mere matter of establishing the basis. When the farmer sells, he gets the 42 cents added to the local price.[21]

[20] *Farm, Stock and Home*, February 1, 1926.
[21] *Ibid.*

What would the elevator man do with the 42 cents profit that he received on the fifteen bushels ? He would, according to this plan, be required by law and under bond to send the money to a finance board, which in turn would pay the wheat exporter 42 cents a bushel over the price for which he must sell the wheat in competition with the world. The miller exporting flour would be paid on the same scale, or about a cent a pound for exported flour. This would be necessary or otherwise it would be impossible to export any wheat or flour, because no exporter could sell wheat for which he had been compelled to pay 42 cents a bushel more than the world market price.

The chief benefit of the plan would be to encourage the farmer to produce up to the level of domestic requirements and penalize him 42 cents below the domestic price on those bushels he produced over these requirements. The advantage of the plan, according to Owen, was that it eliminated the complicated equalization fee, and the transaction was completed for the farmer when he delivered his wheat. To administer the plan it would be necessary to establish a finance board to receive and administer the funds sent in by the wheat buyers. The salaries and expense of carrying on the work of this five-member board would be paid out of the funds collected. The only connection the government would have with the board would be to appoint the members and supervise it for any misuse of funds.

> The duties of this Board would be to receive funds and paying out money to exporters and checking the grain buyers. The estimating of exportable surplus at the beginning of the crop year to be made either by the Department of Agriculture, the Department of Commerce, or preferably both working together.[22]

The article contended that the plan met all objections that were raised against the McNary-Haugen bill and the export bounty plan. In addition it asserted that this was not price-fixing and should overcome the President's prejudices against that type of legislation. It maintained that the market price still remained subject to all the vicissitudes of the open and free market. Admittedly it was indirect price-fixing, but there was no question that "it is impossible to afford farmers any relief except through higher prices for his

[22] *Ibid.*

produce," and for this reason the President and his advisers should give careful consideration to this plan and not object to the indirect price-fixing that it justly imposed.[23]

In an article a month later, *Farm, Stock & Home* looked at the world situation and concluded that Russian and Canadian wheat production would continue to flow heavily into the world market in the years to come. The only answer to this irrevocable trend against the U.S. farmer's participation in the world wheat market was to cut production back to a domestic level. "We see the solution of the problem. Unfortunately we get but little attention," maintained this influential farm editor. He again called for the enactment of the plan, outlined in the February 1 issue of the magazine, to pay the domestic price plus the tariff for home consumption and penalize the growers for the surplus. He did concede that an export corporation might work, but it would have to be coupled with a strong provision of "controlled acreage."[24]

A more elaborate statement of the production control plan appeared the following year in Spillman's book *Balancing the Farm Output: A Statement of the Present Deplorable Conditions of Farming, Its Causes, and Suggested Remedies*. Spillman defined balancing the farm output as adjusting production of farm products to market demand to enable the farmer to get a "fair" price for his products. Spillman came to the Department of Agriculture in 1902. He received his doctor of science degree from the University of Missouri in 1910 and built a reputation in the Department of Agriculture for his interest in scientific agriculture and the broader aspects of agricultural economics before H. C. Wallace successfully established the Bureau of Agricultural Economics. He was chief of the Office of Farm Management from 1915 to 1918.[25]

The Outlook program started under Wallace played a significant role in shaping Spillman's thinking about production control. Estimating allotments would be one way of making the Outlook

[23] *Ibid.*

[24] *Ibid.*, March 1, 1926.

[25] W. S. Spillman, *Balancing the Farm Output: A Statement of the Present Deplorable Conditions of Farming, Its Causes, and Suggested Remedies* (New York: Orange Judd Publishing Co., 1927), p. 11: "By a fair price is meant a price that will on the average meet the expenses of production, return current rates of interest on investment, and pay current wages for the unpaid labor of the farmer and his family"; Taylor Papers, vol. 8, 16.

program effective and profitable for farmers and enable them to cut back production in accordance with estimated market demand. Spillman wanted to carry the Outlook work directly to the local communities. He suggested that county agents might distribute information at committee meetings in the local schoolhouses of the farm community. These schoolhouse locals would attempt to keep farmers informed on the future prices of farm products so they would be able to meet the market and control and stabilize it through planned production.[26]

For the wheat areas, Spillman did not accept the diversification solution. Substitution of other enterprises by wheat growers would not be a permanent solution and would cause a rise in wheat prices that would turn investment away from those enterprises back to wheat. As an example of this Spillman pointed to the rise in the wheat price in 1924 and 1925, which he said touched off a 14 per cent rise in the intentions to plant wheat for the 1926 crop year.[27]

Spillman's book represented a turning point in his thinking about the agricultural question. Previously he had called for diversification in the spring wheat areas. He had been a strong advocate of the Outlook programs, but in his work he recognized the shortcomings of the diversification argument and the inadequacy of the informational programs without proper communication to the countryside and ameliorative actions based on the information provided. This book, like the Owen article, invoked the principle of production control for the purpose of adjusting the farm output. Living through the war cries of "agricultural equality" battles in Washington, Spillman was familiar with the plea to make the tariff effective on farm products. He accepted this as a just goal, but he said any such plan must not cause increases in production and must be a part of a production-control scheme that would make it possible "to sell an exportable surplus at the world price while the remainder of the product sells in this country at a higher price."[28]

Significantly, both Spillman and Wilson worked in the Office of Farm Management in the years 1924 to 1926. O. C. Stine, head

[26] O. C. Stine, COHC; Spillman, *Balancing the Farm Output*, pp. 32–35.

[27] Spillman, *Balancing the Farm Output*, p. 51.

[28] Spillman, "Memorandum for the Assistant Secretary Relating to Agricultural Problems in the Spring Wheat States," Miscellaneous Manuscripts (December 7, 1922), RG 83, NARS; Spillman, *Balancing the Farm Output*, p. 84.

of the Division of Historical Research and Statistical Analysis during the twenties, recalled that there was a "thinking relationship between Spillman's development and Wilson's." Also, Tolley comments, "M. L. and Spillman had lots of contact and M. L. admired him." The importance of this relationship should not be overestimated. The "efficiency" answer for reduction of costs still appealed to Wilson as seen in his continued interest in experimenting with mechanized wheat farms in Montana. In Washington, Wilson had the opportunity to observe the legislative battles in the halls of Congress. Tactics used in the McNary-Haugen fights by his close friend Davis did not escape him. He noted firsthand the practical and political shortcomings of McNary-Haugenism and was exposed to new thinking regarding a farm relief plan that would entail the curtailment of production and possibly meet the chief criticisms aimed at the export surplus plans.[29]

There seemed to be no secret about the production-control thinking inside the Department of Agriculture, although it aroused the anger of some businessmen. One of them, Arnold P. Yerkes of the International Harvester Company, expressed his disapproval in an article he submitted for Wilson's review in 1925. Yerkes criticized the current Department of Agriculture line that efficiency on the farm had only produced a large volume of goods that brought lower prices. He did not understand why the department should be upset that the benefits of lower production costs were being wiped out by lower prices. Deriding the suggestion that farmers should refrain from producing as much as possible for the lowest possible cost, he said that to businessmen this sounded like a "strange doctrine." He continued, "In any other business the producers would fight it out and the losers would get into some other line. . . ."

Yerkes expressed the efficiency ideology of business that seemed to have brought it to the pinnacle of success during the decade. Understandably he could not fit the department's suggestions of limited production into his view of the world. This meant giving up the overseas market in favor of foreign farmers who had learned to produce more and at lower costs, as any smart businessman would do to put his competitors out of business. "Imagine deliberately handing your competitor your market, without trying

[29] Stine, COHC; Tolley, COHC.

to hold it. And imagine trying to increase the prosperity of a country by having its workers produce less efficiency [*sic*]," he concluded.[30]

If the doctrine of restricted production did not impress this businessman, it also did not seem to make a profound impression on Wilson despite his association with the intellectual currents surrounding Spillman. In the summer of 1926 he returned to Montana to continue experiments in low-cost wheat farming along reorganized lines in the Fairway Farms project. His thinking was traditional regarding the primacy of efficiency and low costs on the farm in order to reach some type of fair price-ratio between farm and factory products. On the departure of Wilson from Washington, Tolley remembered, "M. L. felt that he could really do more to influence events in Montana and among the farmers of Montana than he could down here."[31]

A year later, Wilson wrote Davis from Montana that much of his agricultural thinking had changed as he observed the rapid change in the countryside. He had come to the conclusion that fewer farmers would now be needed on the land. The last eight months in Montana, he wrote Davis on March 17, 1927, had demonstrated to him the profound industrial revolution agriculture was undergoing. The result would be far greater output per family farm or producing unit and a much greater capital investment "which will greatly reduce the number of farmers needed but greatly increase the capital required per farm."[32]

A month earlier Wilson had turned down an invitation to testify on the same theme before the Businessmen's Commission on Agriculture because of ill health. In his tentative acceptance in January, Wilson wrote to William Harper Dean, manager of the hearings, outlining his intended discussion. First it was to be devoted to larger-scale family farms such as the Fairway Farms in Montana and especially to what he called the "silent but continuing mechanization of agriculture." This industrial revolution in agriculture gave rise, he contended, to a new type of farm organization different from the units of the past, and presented entirely new problems of financing, tenant-landlord relations, and size of land units.[33]

[30] Yerkes to Wilson (December 17, 1925), Wilson MSS.
[31] Tolley, COHC.
[32] Wilson to Davis (March 17, 1927), Wilson MSS.
[33] Wilson to William Harper Dean (January 22, 1927), Wilson MSS.

In further summarizing this movement, Wilson wrote to John D. Black the following year that because of the tractor, boom farming had been in a constant state of flux ever since the first of December, 1927. He cited the following figures on tractor sales in Montana as dramatic evidence:

1925—1,160	1927—3,607
1926—1,749	1928—4,920

Regarding what Wilson called "harvester threshers or combines," the trend was:

1925—112	1927—968
1926—220	1928—2,800–3,000 (estimated sales)

With some pride he pointed out that mechanical power applied to larger land units gave a lower production cost on each bushel of wheat. Older farmers were absorbing smaller farms abandoned during the Depression and "making a new combination of mechanical farming equipment and land units which under good management are going to give very low cost operation." Wilson said that he understood the tractor movement was going at about the same pace in North Dakota, but the opportunity for expanding the size of farms was not as good there.[34]

Wilson continued his report to Black emphasizing the appeal of mechanical farming to the young people in the community and the tendency of tractor companies to sell a great deal of machinery on very small down payments. From his observations there had been no great movement away from the farms by sons of farmers who had gone into mechanical farming in the last four or five years.

He admitted that Montana farmers had made liberal use of credit, and "if we should have a bad crop we would begin to have some pain in the northwest." This time the "pain" would be mostly in the pockets of eastern manufacturers and those people outside the region who provided credit for the mechanization. In Montana, he reported, the banks had money but were extremely conservative and refused to make the type of loans to tractor farmers that other investors were making. This was a striking reason why any future crisis in wheat

[34] Wilson to Black (April 11, 1928), Wilson MSS; E. A. Starch, "Farm Organization as Affected by Mechanization," *Bulletin No. 278* (May, 1933), Montana State College of Agriculture Experiment Station, Bozeman, Montana, pp. 12–14.

would likely produce more than a regional outcry for a solution to the wheat problem. Eastern capital appeared to be overextending itself and would have a strong interest in the Northwest's recovery in the case of a setback.

On the political scene in 1928, Wilson did not sense among the wheat farmers in Montana any particular interest in McNary-Haugen or other legislation. Conversation simply concerned speculation about the crops that season, the price of equipment, or anything except legislation. But Wilson emphasized, "If we should have a poor crop year or if wheat should go down to about 80 cents, the demand for legislation would, in my judgment, spring up spontaneously." In the spring of 1928, Wilson was under the general impression that state Republicans favored Governor Frank O. Lowden of Illinois. Last year, he related to Black, the farm bureaus of the state circulated a petition without any publicity asking the governor to become a candidate, and secured ten thousand signatures.[35]

In the same vein, Davis wrote Wilson from Washington in May, 1928, saying that Montana Republicans would be wise to avoid backing Hoover and give their support to Lowden. He saw a great anti-Hoover upsurge among midwestern farmers which Montana Republicans should understand before they jumped on the Hoover bandwagon. He concluded Lowden would add more strength to the Republican ticket in the fall against Al Smith than any other candidate. But he did not overlook Prohibition and the religious issues that would work against Smith in the Northwest regardless of who the Republicans nominated.[36]

Just as the Hoover candidacy caused some Republicans discomfort, candidate Smith, despite his claim to support agricultural legislation, would cause great doubts among dry rural Protestant Democrats. How much Smith accentuated the breach between urban and rural Democrats is a subject of disagreement with some historians. Some argue that his origins in New York City, association with Tammany Hall, his anti-Prohibition stand, and his religious allegiance disrupted the Democratic party and made it more difficult for Franklin D. Roosevelt to cement a strong urban-rural alliance in his bid for the presidency in 1932. Others contend that Smith made a significant and somewhat successful appeal to farmers in the

[35] Wilson to Black (April 11, 1928), Wilson MSS.
[36] Davis to Wilson (May 10, 1928), Wilson MSS.

election. Support of McNary-Haugenites like Peek and Davis, who campaigned for him through the Smith Independent Organizations Committee, actually started a Democratic trend in the Midwest that eventually cracked the traditional hold of Republicanism in the area. Raymond Moley, Roosevelt's 1932 campaign manager, watched and studied the Smith campaign in the Midwest. Smith's experience was to serve the Roosevelt campaign well.[37]

The conflict between the Lowden candidacy and the trend for Hoover was a clear indication of the growing split in the personality of northwestern Republicanism. The controversy in the party swirled around Hoover's well-known opposition to export surplus legislation. In no incident is this split better highlighted than in the correspondence of Davis with former Governor Dixon of Montana—both northwestern Republicans. After the defeat of Lowden and the nomination of Hoover, Davis threw his support along with Peek to Smith's campaign. During the fall campaign, Davis wrote Dixon attacking the Republican party and the standard-bearer for their attitudes on agricultural legislation. Davis contended that Smith had supported the principles of the equalization fee in every public statement since the Houston convention and the entire agricultural legislative program for which he had been working since he left Montana. Briefly, he outlined these objectives to Dixon as follows:

> . . . effective control of the sale of agricultural surplus with the object of making the tariff effective to protect the home market of crops of which we produce an exportable surplus and with the costs borne by the marketed units of the commodity benefitted.

Essentially, Hoover opposed these goals as revealed in his West Branch, Iowa, speech, and according to Davis, his maneuvers to defeat the McNary-Haugen bill of 1928 proved it. Furthermore, Hoover's position on the wheat problem was unacceptable. The

---

[37] Gertrude Almy Slichter, "Franklin D. Roosevelt and the Farm Problem, 1929–1932," *Mississippi Valley Historical Review*, XLIII (September, 1956), 238; Fite, "The Agricultural Issue in the Presidential Campaign of 1928," *Mississippi Valley Historical Review*, XXXVII (March, 1951), 669–672, shows that Smith cut into Republican areas in the Midwest by about two million votes over the Democratic total in 1920; Samuel Lubell, *The Future of American Politics* (New York: Harper & Brothers, 1952), pp. 169–170, supports this position with accompanying voting charts; Rexford G. Tugwell, COHC.

only remedy he saw was for American wheat growers to cut down the production of wheat for export. "This is in line with his belief that the American export market should be left exclusively to our industrial manufacturers," which branded Hoover, in Davis's view, as the representative of the industrial interests in the country. Davis could not see how anyone in Montana could become enthusiastic about this policy, which at best, in view of the present wheat conditions, could only be called pro-Canada and pro-Australia.

Since he had left Montana to fight the agricultural battle in Washington, Davis had been increasingly embarrassed by his membership in the Republican party. In Congress he had worked with all parties and factions in promoting the agricultural program. Senator Burton K. Wheeler repeatedly offered his support and gave it whenever requested, but this did not prevent Davis from privately extending his best wishes to Dixon in the contest with Wheeler. The basic political difference between Dixon and Davis was that they did not view Hoover in the same light. But Davis asked his progressive Republican friend to understand how much the political positions in the past six months "have pained me, because that made it inevitable that I should be working for the national ticket to which you are politically opposed." [38]

Likewise, Senator Norris shifted his support to the Democratic candidate in 1928 and urged Dixon not to run against Wheeler in the senatorial race. Norris called Dixon and Wheeler "like-minded progressives," saying that a race against Wheeler would split progressives in Montana. Instead, Norris told Dixon to try for the governorship again, but Norris wanted him to understand that this was only a suggestion made in the cause of progressivism and "not in any way a demand." Whatever the outcome of the election, Davis was hopeful that fall would see the end of his responsibilities in the fight for agricultural legislation. He was looking forward to turning to something else, since he had worked on legislation for a number of years and thought the "time has come when others should carry it on." [39]

[38] Davis to Dixon (September 4, 1928), Davis MSS.

[39] Norris to Dixon (December 31, 1927), Tray 1, Box 6, Norris MSS, Library of Congress; Dixon to Davis (September 4, 1928), Davis MSS.

That spring the McNary-Haugen bill with its equalization provisions had once again passed both houses of Congress and had been returned with a stinging veto message. With the nomination of Hoover in the summer of 1928, it was obvious to Davis that continued efforts for export surplus legislation would never be approved by a Republican administration headed by Hoover. Despite his earlier Republicanism in Montana, he now felt he had to support the Democratic nominee regardless of other issues unrelated to the farm question that might color the political thinking in the Northwest.

John D. Black viewed the recent veto message on the McNary-Haugen bill as "boring" and said it merely replayed the old theme of diversified farming that Secretary Jardine, Secretary Hoover, and President Coolidge had been running into the ground in their various public pronouncements. "At times, this had been carried to the point of suggesting that we ought to cut out most of our exports and try to grow most of our sugar, wool, and even rubber," he wrote disparagingly as he saw the last hope of meaningful reform legislation disappear for that year.

Black attached great political importance to the McNary-Haugen movement. He wrote that "its significance is far more political than economic." As John D. Hicks was to view the earlier Populist revolt as the last effort to save agrarian America from the "devouring jaws" of industrialism, Black saw McNary-Haugenism as "agriculture's stand against the domination of its affairs and the affairs of the country by the commercial and industrial interests." Possibly with an eye to the future, Black observed that labor had never contested this supremacy in the political field. In despair because of the successive defeats of agricultural legislation, Black wrote in June, 1928, that the few successes scored in the halls of Congress by agriculture since 1924 were only permitted in order to head off more radical measures that loomed in the background.[40]

Still, Black was not discouraged to the point where he gave up work on his book, *Agricultural Reform in the United States*, which was designed to spread information and analysis of the agricultural

[40] Black, "The McNary-Haugen Movement," *American Economic Review*, XVIII (September, 1928), 419; John D. Hicks, *The Populist Revolt* (Minneapolis: University of Minnesota Press, 1931), p. 237; Black, "Progress of Farm Relief," p. 266.

situation to help the struggle in the years ahead. Somewhat chagrined that the book did not appear in time to aid in the recent McNary-Haugen fight, Black wrote Peek telling him he hoped that it could be used in the future:

> . . . the book did not appear until after the Farm Relief Bill was in its final agonies. It is now clear that the fight is a long way from finished and that therefore the material in the book is still highly useful. Have you any suggestions as to the way in which it could be made to serve more effectively the cause in which it was written? [41]

Black could not foresee that M. L. Wilson was the man who would make the most effective use of this work in a future campaign for agricultural legislation.

A week later Peek expressed an interest in the writings of another agricultural economist in a letter to Davis. In his letter he included extracts from an article by Rexford Tugwell in the *Political Science Quarterly* for December, 1928, which Governor Lowden had called to his attention. In this article on farm relief, Tugwell expressed admiration for the 1928 McNary-Haugen bill. "As a piece of social legislation it surpasses anything an American Congress ever framed," he wrote. The real question, he felt, was whether six billion dollars of annual loss to the farmers ought to be taken from some other class and given to them. "For this would be the intent of surplus control legislation." The "efficiency" answer to the farm problem, he contended, would dig its own grave because there was nothing contained in its solution to strengthen the farmers' general economic position in relation to the other producing units in the society. He noted that cooperative marketing had been suggested to overcome this disadvantage for the farmer. "There is nothing wrong with this notion," said Tugwell, "except that it does not seem to work very well." These remarks prompted Peek to ask Davis to gather some information on Tugwell and relay it to him. In the meantime the election had opened the door for Hoover to try his particular brand of farm relief. [42]

Tugwell's thinking on "social legislation" paralleled the work begun by H. C. Wallace in this decade of agricultural struggle and

[41] Black to Peek (November 18, 1929), Peek MSS.
[42] Peek to Davis (November 25, 1929), Peek MSS; Rexford G. Tugwell, "Reflections on Farm Relief," *Political Science Quarterly*, XLIII (December, 1928), 491–497.

frustration. Wallace's most thoughtful statement of concern for agriculture in the context of national welfare appeared in his book published in 1925 shortly after his death. He maintained that it was not in the national interest to allow 30 per cent of the population to languish in economic adversity. Holding a basically agricultural fundamentalist viewpoint, he wrote, "But for agriculture there can be no industrial development." Only when agriculture, industry, and commerce worked closely together could rapid development take place. The general thesis of the book was that since agriculture was fundamental to national welfare, its maladies deserved the quick attention of the national government.[43]

Wallace's work in Washington promoted the growth of an intellectual atmosphere dedicated to finding solutions to problems in the light of scientific analysis. In it, Spillman had the freedom to do wide-range thinking about such things as a domestic allotment approach to the overproduction problem. Spillman, Wilson, Tolley, Stine, Taylor, Ezekiel, and others formed a free-swinging academic community untouched by bureaucratic and politically controlled strait-jacket thinking. Although Spillman and Wilson were close associates in the department, Wilson did not appear to be Spillman's intellectual puppet on the subject of controlled production. Evidence suggests that Wilson returned to Montana "because he could do more in Montana," and he was firmly convinced that the answer to winning the cost-price squeeze on the wheat farms lay in the efficiency doctrine of larger family producing units combined with mechanical power. Although he realized the dangers of overcapitalization, his experiments with the Fairway Farms project encouraged his advocacy of this trend in wheat farming.[44] Seeing the disappointment and frustration of Davis's work in Washington for a social and quasi-political solution to agriculture's plight, Wilson returned to resume his work in the college and the countryside of Montana.

[43]   H. C. Wallace, *Our Debt and Duty to the Farmer* (New York: The Century Co., 1925), pp. 11–13.

[44]   M. L. Wilson, "Research Studies in the Economics of Large Scale Farming in Montana," *Agricultural Engineering*, X (January, 1929), 3–12.

CHAPTER FOUR

A Montana Professor
Plans a Campaign

The time is about ready for the breaking loose of a new drive
for farm relief legislation.—John D. Black

In 1928, Republican Governor A. G. Sorlie of North Dakota informed an official of the North Dakota–Montana Wheat Growers Association that the administration's attitude toward the agricultural problem gave little hope for assistance from Washington. Sorlie suggested that wheat growers should be able to solve their own problems by working together through cooperative agencies such as the Wheat Growers Association.[1] This prediction by the north-western governor was partially wrong. Hoover's farm legislation passed Congress in 1929 with little opposition. The Agricultural Marketing Act marked the point where Republicans embraced "Aaron Sapiro-ism" on a national scale, and the longest stride yet taken toward government intervention in the economy of agriculture. Farm economist Mordecai Ezekiel, on hand in Washington when the legislation was passed, recalled:

> When they established the Federal Farm Board to plug coopera-tives on a national scale and stabilize prices with a half a billion dollars in reserve to do it, it was a tremendous departure. I would say that that was really the first real action program of actual government intervention in the process.[2]

[1] Sorlie to Sidney A. Papke (n.d., 1928), North Dakota–Montana Wheat Growers Association Papers, File 2/26, University of North Dakota, Grand Forks.

[2] Mordecai Ezekiel, Columbia Oral History Collection, Columbia University, New York, N.Y.

While important events transpired in Washington, Wilson in Montana made plans for a trip to Russia. The Russians, who were importing American technical know-how in many fields, were developing large factory wheat farms and needed expert advice for the undertaking. Through Harold Ware, an American who spent several years during the twenties working in Russian agriculture, the Soviet trade agency, AMTORG, got in touch with Wilson because of his experience with mechanical wheat farming in the Fairway Farms project. Wilson had some hesitancy about going, but advice from many sources encouraged him to make the trip. Alexander Legge said it would "do 'em good" for Wilson to offer his services to the Russians. L. F. Fletcher, general supervisor of agricultural sales for the Caterpillar Tractor Company, accompanied Wilson on the trip, which lasted from April 15 to September 15, 1929. Wilson's task included estimating size, number, and type of machinery for various land units to be converted into factory collective farms. Of course, Fletcher was eager to take any orders for new machinery that the Russians might place with him in exchange for gold payments. In addition to a close observation of Soviet agriculture, Wilson gained a broad view of the country in his trip home on the Trans-Siberian railroad to Vladivostok.[3]

At first the trip to Russia only intensified Wilson's conviction that American wheat farmers must learn to produce at lower costs in order to stay competitive on the world market. He was impressed by Russia's agricultural potential. While much of the country was primitive, he realized that the Russian government intended to bring large areas under highly advanced cultivation through advice from western experts like himself and the application of mechanical power to the land. Russia was buying some twenty million dollars worth of agricultural machinery a year, and with normal weather conditions, Wilson expected that within the next five years it would begin to place on the European market 300 million bushels of grain.

These facts caused Wilson to do some serious thinking about the future of American wheat production on the world market while he was bedridden with a stomach ulcer after the Russian trip. He wrote to Chester Davis in November, 1929, that he had been very cautious

---

[3] Wilson, COHC; Dana G. Dalrymple, "The American Tractor Comes to Soviet Agriculture: The Transfer of a Technology," *Technology and Culture,* V (Spring, 1964), 205.

in public statements on the situation in Russia: "I did not want to create an alarmist kind of impression." Still, he understood that the increased supplies of grain on the world market would drive prices to new lows. As far as he could now see there was only one recourse for the northwest wheat farmer aside from assistance that might be given by the government: "We must spend every effort at reducing our costs of production to the absolute minimum," he wrote to Davis.

In the same urgent tone, Wilson told Davis that he was trying to raise "somewhere or somehow" a $15,000 research fund for three years to assist in carrying on low-cost wheat research on a five-hundred-acre Fairway Farm. Unfortunately, the Rockefeller representatives felt the money for this undertaking should come from some other source. He wanted Davis's and Peek's opinions on the prospects for obtaining such a research fund for the Fairway experiment in low-cost operation. Also, he solicited Dr. Taylor's opinion and impressed upon Davis that additional funds were imperative in the face of future developments.[4]

Wilson was proud of the experimental work done in Montana on low-cost wheat production. Through various means he publicized its successes and possibilities to Montana farmers. In a letter to C. C. Webber, president of the Deere and Webber Farm Machinery Company in Minneapolis, he told of these efforts the previous winter through the use of special educational trains at meetings along the important wheat-producing points on the Great Northern Railway. A train of fifteen flatcars loaded with experimental equipment for mechanical farming was a main attraction at these "low cost wheat meetings."

At each meeting Wilson and the college extension workers drove home the message that the years ahead would not be easy for the wheat farmer. The first reason cited was based upon the experience of the immediate past. With the erratic weather conditions in Montana, farmers could never be sure of a crop every year. Second, high prices could not be expected in the future with the increased volume of wheat production throughout the world. "Consequently every farmer must make his plan to produce the wheat which he produces at the lowest possible cost," Wilson emphasized, and he "must build up large reserves of cash on good years to take him

[4] Wilson to Davis (November 6, 1929), Peek MSS.

thru the lean years." Such sound business philosophy must have been music in the ears of the businessman from the Twin Cities. Also, Wilson made no secret about the tremendous weeding out of farmers that these hardships were going to produce. He predicted that in Montana those who stayed on the land through that generation would be the rich farmers of the next generation. "Staying on" meant practicing thrift and saving money made in the good years to continue the system of high investment farming through the dry years.

Wilson coupled this sober economic advice with instructions on summer fallow operations and information learned on the tractor experimental farms with reference to intelligent and efficient use of machinery. Clearly Wilson could not confine his advice to purely technical subjects when he talked to the farmers of Montana. Along with facts, figures, and instructions on low-cost mechanical wheat farming, Wilson attached the urgent message about its economic necessity in the light of world conditions and particular hardships under which Montana farmers worked.[5]

Howard Tolley called the new trend in mechanical farming that Wilson saw developing in Montana the "capitalistic family farm."[6] He enumerated three important factors responsible for the development of this style of farming in a speech to the Annual Extension Conference in October, 1929, at Lexington, Kentucky:

1) There are now larger-scale and more effective power units in the form of up-to-date tractors.

2) There are many forms of new machines of high capacity designed primarily to go with these new power units. Conspicuous among these new machines are combined-harvester threshers, mechanical corn pickers, and new, high-capacity tillage machines, such as multiple-row listers, and multiple-bottom plows.

3) The introduction of these new power units and new machines has been accompanied by a significant revolution in tillage and harvest methods, which in many cases has meant a reduction of power and labor inputs per acre, and hence a significant reduction of costs.

[5] Wilson to C. C. Webber (December 27, 1929), Wilson MSS.

[6] Actually he adopted the term from M. L. Wilson's article, "Research Studies in the Economics of Large Scale Farming in Montana," *Agricultural Engineering*, X (January, 1929), 3–12.

According to Tolley the results of these achievements in the increased size of the normal family farm unit, "both in terms of total investment and in total acreage," were most outstanding on the Great Plains from Montana eastward and southward.[7]

Although Wilson patted himself on the back for Montana's achievements in educating its farmers in low-cost mechanical wheat farming, the lot of the Montana farmer seemed to become more difficult. A large farmer from the rich wheat-producing area in the Judith Basin wrote Wilson in November, 1929, of the poor crop that year and the resulting hardships in the community. He said that the merchants were doing a "lot of kicking about collections, which they say are worse than in 1919." The merchants blamed the farmers for the hard times and their insistence upon relying only on wheat for their cash income. They urged more cows, hogs, sheep, and poultry. To support their argument they pointed to the better conditions in Wisconsin, Nebraska, Iowa, and other more diversified farming areas. "They curse the farmers for over buying, and in most cases they themselves are to blame for using 'high pressure salesmanship' to unload the very commodities which are unpaid for," complained this farmer about his friends on Main Street.

A month later this same farmer called on Wilson to direct his efforts toward educating Montana farmers in matters of financing their operations independent of private banking firms. He obviously wanted a more stable and understanding source of credit than the local bankers could provide. "To my mind this is far more important than the question of making two blades of grass grow where one formerly grew, summer tillage, and kindred subjects," he wrote, asking Wilson to subordinate his efforts in technical education to the broader goal of seeking a more liberal source of capital for financing the state's agricultural ventures. He had no suggestion to offer except a farmer-controlled credit facility, and asked Wilson to explore this approach to farm relief.[8]

[7] Howard Tolley, "Large-Scale Farming in the United States," Annual Extension Conference, Lexington, Kentucky, October, 1929 (Howard Tolley Speeches, University of California, Documents Division, Giannini Foundation Library, Berkeley, California).

[8] John A. Wilson to M. L. Wilson (November 23, 1929), and (December 27, 1929), Wilson MSS.

Wilson took time out from the backlog of work left from the Russian trip and his subsequent illness to observe the activities of the Farm Board in Montana. He felt that a "hot spot" in the state at the moment centered in the plan for cooperative wheat marketing. The Farm Board apparently had no intention of favoring competition between cooperatives, and was setting up in Minneapolis a new agency called the Farmers Northwest Grain Cooperative for the purpose of cooperatively marketing wheat in the Northwest. Usually, cooperative marketing had been carried on through elevators of the Farmers Union and the Dakota–Montana Wheat Pool. The entrance of this new competitor in the field fostered by the Farm Board caused disappointment in some circles. "Now you know," Wilson wrote Fletcher, "how so many of the cooperatives are strong for cooperation as long as it is their way." On the local level Wilson saw the beginnings of a hot feud between the old cooperatives and any new organization the government might sponsor for the marketing of wheat.[9]

The problem, as Wilson quickly realized, went deeper than a dispute between old and new cooperatives. No doubt farmers were becoming increasingly critical of the Farm Board, and the campaign for membership in the Northwest Grain Cooperative "was by no means going over like a prairie fire." The high-powered salesmanship for this supposedly time-tested panacea to the Northwest's wheat problem ran into trouble with farmers who resisted the hard-sell and where older cooperatives spread suspicions about this new effort that threatened their position. This was the sea of troubles the Farm Board attempted to calm. The continuing discontent only reflected the basic problem which was in Wilson's words: "Now the whole trouble is that the price is too low."[10]

In the two months from December, 1929, to January, 1930, Wilson's thinking about the future of the American wheat farmer was as uncertain and experimental as the coming decade of agricultural policy. After his experience in Russia, Wilson pursued the establishment of an experimental farm in Montana to do studies in low-cost wheat production through the solicitation of private funds. In early December, Elmer Starch, Wilson's associate and

[9] Wilson to Fletcher (December 28, 1929), Wilson MSS; see also J. W. Brinton, *Wheat and Politics* (Minneapolis: Rand Tower, 1931).

[10] Wilson to Davis (January 29, 1930), Wilson MSS.

assistant professor of agricultural economics at the college, wrote his personal friend, Congressman Victor Christgau of Minnesota, concerning a government-backed program of research in production economics. Starch wrote:

> The trend of the public mind seems to be toward realizing the necessity for approaching some of the agricultural problems thru experimental economic research. I believe a little good leadership would crystalize [*sic*] the movement and do agriculture a lot of good.

He further suggested that as the Farm Board made the cooperatives "going-concerns," the board would become interested in other phases of the agricultural problem, perhaps turning its attention to economic research. For instance, such research in the Northwest could be aimed at investigating production economy rather than the technical problems of production. He explained to Christgau that for too long in North Dakota, South Dakota, and Montana, extension workers had preached the tired doctrines of diversification as the only answer to the region's constant battle with disastrous price fluctuations. In strong words Starch rejected this argument: "I haven't seen a real honest to gosh paying diversified farm west of the Red River and surely not west of the Missouri." Those who argue this point, he contended, did not fully understand the economics of northwest agriculture. The purpose of the letter was to cultivate Christgau's interest in production-economy research that might be obtained through the passage of a bill in Congress. Intent upon obtaining funds for low-cost wheat-production research, Wilson first turned to private sources to finance the research, and now he laid the groundwork for possible government aid in this initial contact with Congressman Christgau. It was a significant change in tactics that once again turned Wilson's eyes back to Washington and the national government.[11]

Wilson's thinking about remedies to agriculture's ills and the wheat problem in particular gradually began to turn on two different approaches, both of which involved action by the national government. During these months he read Black's recently published

[11] Starch to Christgau (December 4, 1929), Wilson MSS; M. L. Wilson, "Experimental Method in Economic Research," *Journal of Farm Economics*, XI (October, 1929), 582–583.

book, *Agricultural Reform in the United States*, and carefully noted the chapter dealing with the domestic allotment plan. The plan provoked his interest, as did a national plan for regional farm adjustments based on comparative cost and advantages in different regions. The latter approach was based on research in the various agricultural regions to determine the most economical crop for the region to produce, size of farm and power units, and future market requirements. The Starch letter to Christgau strongly hinted at these ideas.

According to Black, the domestic allotment plan was most applicable to wheat and cotton. It was not to be advocated for other commodities until tried with these staples. Black introduced his chapter on the domestic allotment plan with the following descriptive capsule:

> The essential principle of the domestic allotment plan is paying producers a free-trade price plus the tariff duty for the part of their crop which is consumed in the United States and this price without the tariff duty for the part of it that is exported, this to be arranged by a system of allotments to individual producers of rights to sell the domestic part of the crop in the domestic market.

An essential difference between this plan and the earlier Owen-Spillman plan was that allotment rights were to be transferable. Farmers with poor crops in a particular year could sell their allotment certificates to offset their losses and provide an insurance guarantee of at least 42 cents a bushel on their domestic production quota. The rights were to be transferable immediately upon issuance and the grower could obtain his money for them at once, possibly at a discount with the local bank. Thus, they became advances to growers before the planting season to finance the growing of crops and initial cash investments. The plan provided not only effective tariff support for the domestic crop, but also crop insurance and production credit.[12]

The annual Farmers' Week program in early February on the campus at Bozeman reflected the current conflicts in agricultural policy. In a letter to the state Farm Bureau president, W. L. Stockton, Wilson outlined some of the discussion topics. The first

[12] John D. Black, *Agricultural Reform in the United States* (New York: McGraw-Hill Book Co., 1929), pp. 271–275.

one centered on the problem of surplus. Does it exist, and if so, "can the Farm Board succeed in placing agriculture on a basis of equality with other industries without production and acreage control?" Wilson wanted the heads of the Montana farm organizations to discuss this question. Elaborating on this theme, he phrased the question in another way that struck at some of the assumptions of cooperative marketing. "Can we have orderly marketing without orderly production?" Wilson indicated that he intended to chair a discussion on the topic "Can wheat production be curtailed or production re-adjusted?" This was to be prefaced by a brief statement on the two approaches to farm relief that he had been considering recently. His introductory statement would refer to the "so-called Black domestic allotment plan"; the other plan that he felt had possibilities called for "National Regional farm adjustments based upon comparative costs and advantages of different regions in the United States." [13]

In a letter to Tolley, now assistant chief of the Bureau of Agricultural Economics, Wilson spoke of formulating a regional adjustment bill for Congress to consider. If Farm Board support for it could not be obtained, he did not think it would have much chance to pass. At this point Wilson showed himself keenly aware of the politics and tactics required to push such a bill through Congress. He told Tolley that ideas like this "have to be pushed out into the fire . . . to talk about for use in building up public sentiment." This is done by attaching a name to them and giving the public something to talk about like the "John Doe Bill." By June, Wilson succeeded in turning the spotlight on his idea by embodying it in the Christgau bill for experiments in regional readjustments.

Wilson believed tremendous support could be gathered from the colleges for this bill. It would provide an opportunity for Extension workers to do something besides devise ways to increase production. This role was coming under heavy attack even by the friends of Extension. The colleges might welcome this bill because they were uneasy about the rumor that Hoover planned to establish a national land-utilization commission to work independently of the colleges and their research agencies. They would then be left without any functions in the future planning of agriculture. For these reasons the time seemed opportune for selling the idea to many of the

[13] Wilson to Stockton (January 22, 1930), Wilson MSS.

forward-looking college people who could help it along by offering much-needed support in the various states.[14]

Wilson's effort to formulate a farm relief bill, plot its course in Congress, and his controversial and pertinent topics for discussion listed on the Farmers' Week agenda reflected the approving attitude of the administration at Montana State College toward these activities and his work in economic education. At the turn of the year, the president of the college, Alfred Atkinson, and Dean F. B. Linfield, both of whom had a broad view of the college's function in the state, urged Wilson to push economic educational programs for the farmers and to devote effort to achieving national legislation that could improve the economic position of Montana agriculture. Wilson's activities also mirrored a growing sentiment among some farmers that the college and Extension people should now point their work away from the technical tasks of increasing production and toward helping farmers gain an understanding of their place in the economic structure of the nation and the world so that they might be better prepared to protect themselves through organization, planning, and sound credit facilities.[15]

From Wilson's discussion with Stockton of the program at Farmers' Week, it appeared that a central question of concern was whether the Farm Board's activities could succeed without a concentrated effort to reduce production in the wheat areas. If reducing production was the key to the answer, could the idea of restricted production be sold to farmers? Indications from the wheat state of Kansas showed that farmers were not going to react favorably to this suggestion. W. E. Grimes, head of the Department of Agricultural Economics at Kansas State College, informed Wilson that one large operator in northwestern Texas planned to produce wheat at a cost of fifty cents a bushel or less. He said that many farmers in Kansas planned to do the same thing and showed no desire to decrease their wheat acreage. Grimes said they were doing this with the conscious knowledge that wheat prices would be lower because of their actions, but he endorsed this competitive approach to the market and called it a fearless philosophy of life, saying ". . . they are ready to take on all comers in the competition of producing wheat economically and efficiently."

[14] Wilson to Tolley (January 29, 1930), Wilson MSS.
[15] Wilson, COHC.

The agricultural economics professor from Kansas, contrary to Wilson's growing conviction, attacked the federal Farm Board and others who urged a reduction in the wheat acreage. He agreed there were those who should reduce their wheat acreage, but, he insisted, they were not on the western edge of the hard winter wheat belt because these farmers were in a position to produce wheat more economically than anyone else in the world. Why should they devote their time to raising any other farm commodity when they can make more money by producing wheat, Grimes asked? "If they can stand the jolt of a crop failure when it does come, they will make more money over a series of years by growing wheat than by devoting their time to anything else," he maintained. Grimes said, "This is our tentative conclusion," on the suggestion to reduce wheat acreage voluntarily. In a short time these views came into conflict with Wilson's developing belief that United States wheat raisers must cut production to the requirements of the domestic market.[16]

Wilson strongly indicated his rising interest in a program of production control in a letter to Black on January 29, 1930. He began by congratulating Black on the publication of his work, *Agricultural Reform in the United States*. "This is, in my judgment," wrote Wilson, "the outstanding economic book of the times." Wilson was so impressed with the book that he initiated an unofficial Extension project at the college in line with his new policy of "economic education" to encourage all the county agents in the state, many of the farm leaders, and "intelligent farmers" to read the book. He announced to Black that presently the northwest country would face conditions nearly as disastrous as in 1921, 1922, and 1923, and laid the cause to existing surpluses. Wilson did not complain about adverse weather conditions, but feared the continuation of "normal conditions" that would aggravate the surplus problem. He felt that early in the fall farmers "warmed up to the Farm Board, but now enthusiasm was waning." The reaction to Legge's appeal for reduced acreage was qualified and about what could be expected, in Wilson's opinion. Farmers said they were willing to reduce acreage if they knew that those who cut back "would not be the goats and the other fellow would get all the benefit."

[16] Grimes to Wilson (January 13, 1930), Wilson MSS.

This subject led to a discussion of the main message in the letter. What Wilson called the Black plan, or the domestic allotment plan, referred to in Chapter 10 of *Agricultural Reform*, possibly could meet these farmers' objections to the workability of a production-control plan. Wilson explained that at every conference he attended that winter the constant complaint was the price on wheat was too low. The next response was what could be done about it? At this point Wilson would reveal the Black plan to his listeners. Their reactions appeared to be favorable: "Every place that I have explained your proposal I have had a very sensible reaction." He was convinced that by "scattering a few firebrands," he could whip up enough sentiment to prompt someone to introduce a bill in Congress for a domestic allotment plan.

Some farmers with recent crop failures were especially interested in the insurance features of the domestic allotment plan. In the high-protein wheat-raising section of northwest Montana it had failed to rain the previous season. With the high investment now required in farm machinery, many farmers in this section "shot all their wad in the 1929 crop and now have almost nothing with which to buy fuel or gas." Wilson pointed out that talk about the Black plan and its crop insurance feature got "100% reaction in about 10 seconds" from these farmers. Such favorable barometer readings encouraged Wilson to press Black for permission to drop the firebrands in Montana to begin a campaign on behalf of the plan. He bluntly asked Black, "If a demand should come from farm organizations in Montana for the introduction of a bill embodying this plan, would you write the bill?" At this point Black was hesitant about giving an unqualified "yes" to this question. Wilson already contemplated asking Republican representative Scott Leavitt from the western district in Montana to introduce the bill.

At local meetings in Montana, Wilson had been able to meet most objections to the plan except on the question surrounding the legality of forcing the miller to buy the allotment certificates. Also the question regarding the honesty of the farmers in reporting their average acreage planted raised some doubts. Most agreed, however, that if these figures were published in the local newspapers and judged by an impartial board in the county the dishonesty could be overcome. Only one month into the decade of the 1930's and Wilson's mind raced ahead on many details and problems to be encountered by this proposed plan. Within three years it would become the first major undertaking of the New Deal in the area of agricultural reform. History would judge whether it would be a permanent fixture in the agricultural economy or an emergency measure.

In this exchange with Black, Wilson moved to a discussion of the regional experimental approach to agricultural problems. He explained that Tolley and he had previously talked of this plan at some length. It involved "coordinated and correlated study of comparative advantages in different types of farming throughout the country, the possibilities of substitution, the effect of mechanical changes, etc." Wilson expressed surprise that the Farm Board had not pushed such a bill, and asked Black his opinion about introducing a bill along these lines in the near future. As Wilson saw it, work could be carried on jointly between the state and the Department of Agriculture. From experimental farms like the Fairway project, improvements for agricultural operations in the various regions could be determined. Wilson indicated that he and Tolley had discussed such a plan when he worked for the Department of Agriculture.

Concluding with his eyes fixed on future developments, Wilson asserted that the psychological time had come "for breaking something loose." By introducing these two bills in Congress, a basis for the awakening of public attention and discussion would at least be formed. Wilson did not care to venture a guess on their chances of passing or of obtaining Farm Board approval, but of one thing he was certain, "both of them would get a whole lot of northwest sentiment rather soon."

In a prompt reply to Wilson's letter, Black wished first of all to attribute the origin of his domestic allotment plan to Dr. Beardsley Ruml of the Rockefeller Memorial Fund who outlined its general idea to him. Dr. H. C. Taylor also advised in the plan's development. Black expressed approval of an attempt to introduce such a bill in Congress. But he revealed his attachment to the export debenture plan when he said that it should be considered simultaneously with the export bill. Despite these obstacles to farm relief legislation, Black agreed with Wilson that the "time is about ready for the breaking loose of a new drive for farm relief legislation." [17]

[17] Wilson to Black (January 29, 1930); Black to Wilson (February 3, 1930), Wilson MSS.

A study of Wilson's activities following his Russian trip reveals a growing interest in experimentation to develop the most suitable crops for the various agricultural regions in the United States and a desire to gear American wheat production to the domestic market. In the process he pushed for expanded experimental farm projects in Montana to study methods of producing wheat at low costs. He broadened this idea to include an experimental farm in each agricultural region of the country to study its regional adjustment problems. Such plans aimed at upgrading efficiency in American agriculture for competition on the world market and at withdrawing marginal lands from production. They were also a step in the direction of planned agricultural production. Wilson's interest in the domestic allotment plan showed his growing disillusionment with the world market and the resulting need to produce only for domestic consumption. His beginning efforts to move for fundamental changes in American agricultural policy by pushing issues into the public eye and into Congress reveal Wilson the tactician as well as the advocate of agricultural relief and reform.

CHAPTER FIVE

1930—Reversal of an Agrarian Tradition

This condition is due partly to . . . the historical emphasis on production rather than on economics and farm management.—Congressman Victor Christgau

By the first month of the new decade, Wilson was considering two paths to agriculture reform. Both involved fundamental changes in American agricultural policy. The Wilson-Tolley plan for "regional readjustments in agricultural production" envisioned planned agricultural production in various regions combined with proper land utilization. Here was recognition that agriculture was an integrated enterprise which required planning, in contrast with the individualism and haphazard use of the land that had characterized the government's longstanding land-alienation process. The Black plan, or the domestic allotment plan, sought to reverse the historical trend toward agricultural expansion by encouraging contracted production.

Both plans shattered the view that agriculture was a highly individualistic enterprise. Each productive unit was closely related to the other, and their collective destinies depended on collective action and planning. There had to be some recognition from government that agriculture was an industry whose problems would have to be dealt with on a collective basis rather than meeting specific short-term needs of individuals. More important, in Wilson's opinion, a successful attack on the growing agricultural problem must come in the area of economic policy. For too long the biological point of view—how to make two blades of grass grow in the place of one—had predominated. Although the Farm Board was a significant intervention of government into the economics of distribution, the undertaking showed itself to be inadequate.

Professor Wilson, a northwestern Republican with a political personality split by the agricultural question, never expressed harsh criticism of Hoover. The attempt to solve the farm problem through the use of the Farm Board and cooperative marketing practices drew his suspicions because of its monopolistic approach to the market. His statements indicated that the board was perhaps faced with the impossible task of trying to revamp the marketing system with too little power and was attacking the problem at the wrong end. Although he expressed disappointment in the actions of the national government, he did not attribute them to any deliberate plot to discriminate against agriculture, but more to an inability to produce creative thinking regarding the problem, not only in the administration, but also in the nation's schools of agricultural economics.

As a professor he did not harbor the attitude of politicians such as Senator Norris who believed that all of President Hoover's efforts were merely pretenses and his words empty promises to American agriculture.[1] Uppermost in Wilson's mind was the continued decline of wheat prices, farmers on marginal lands being driven to despair by periodic droughts, and the Farm Board's seeming inability to strike at the heart of the problem. In all of this he saw no absence of good intentions or lack of desire to remedy the situation. What now must be done was, first, lay the foundation for solutions in the economic education of the American farmer, and second, launch a successful attack on the economic orthodoxy of the business community. Clearly, the task was to formulate new plans. Next they must be exposed to people of power and influence in such a manner that they could be justified in the light of present exigencies and past traditions.

By mid-February, 1930, Wilson had made plans for a Washington trip to confer with Tolley on the regional readjustment bill. Occasionally he referred to it as the "outlook bill." Its goal, of course, was to make the Outlook work effective in the numerous agricultural regions in the United States by discovering the most profitable type of farming to be undertaken. That same month, bills had been introduced in Congress to meet, on an emergency-credit basis, the situation created by the year's drought and low prices in the North-

[1] Norris to Hardy W. Campbell (January 21, 1930), Norris MSS, Library of Congress.

west. Wilson conceded that the drought was largely responsible for the distress that tractor farmers found themselves in, "but low prices are equally responsible." In Montana, Wilson took this opportunity to broadcast among farmers how the crop-insurance feature of the Black domestic allotment plan could take care of such emergencies.

But the Black plan was not Wilson's immediate concern. Foremost in his mind was the drafting of "Outlook bill." Its formal introduction in Congress would provide a vehicle to carry propaganda to the public.

The findings of the Fairway Farms experiments had already given abundant evidence that important information could be obtained from experimental farm projects. But tightening depression budgets suggested sharp curtailments in experimental work, and the Rockefeller Fund made its final allocation in February, 1930. The only possibility for obtaining a continued and expanded program was through the federal government. It was to this end that Wilson and his associates at Montana State College now turned in the formulation of a regional readjustment bill. Facts and figures from the Fairway Farms work were compiled during the winter 1929–1930 to show the benefits of regionally oriented experimental programs. This general information was compiled and published in Montana *Bulletin No. 278*, "Farm Organization as Affected by Mechanization." [2] Obviously the regional readjustment bill was not a piece of legislation dreamed up overnight. Many of its origins lay in the creation and progress of the Fairway Farms experiment. This bill was now to be a vehicle to save that experiment and bring similar benefits to other agricultural regions.

While Wilson planned the trip to Washington, Farm Board member Sam McKelvie toured the Northwest trying to boost farmer confidence in the board. Wilson saw a definite political tint to the visit. The Nebraskan's speeches contained the patent phrases of a man trained in the politics of the Middle West. He berated grain speculation and the Board of Trade mildly but vigorously enough to get applause from farmer audiences. At the Great Falls meeting he tried to explain the government's efforts in setting up the new

[2] E. A. Starch, "Farm Organization as Affected by Mechanization," *Bulletin No. 278* (May, 1933), Montana State College of Agriculture Experiment Station, Bozeman, Montana.

marketing machinery, but when he turned to the problem of stabilization, equality, and control of acreage, "he said that he had consumed too much time in his speech already and wound up by flowery compliments to the good judgment and ability of the American farmer." McKelvie's general message was that prosperity was bound to come to the American farmer who would take care of the matter of acreage adjustments on an individual basis.[3]

When the editor of the *Montana Farmer*, Lester Cole, asked him at a private luncheon about the Black domestic allotment, or transferable rights plan, he said, he had never heard of it and asked for details on the proposal. When it was explained, "he shook his head and said that such a proposal would meet the opposition of consumers and was thoroughly unsound." His reaction to the "Tolley plan for making the outlook effective" was more favorable, but, Wilson said, "I have a hunch that he doesn't hold anything that comes from college professors in very high repute." In the same vein Wilson told Tolley that McKelvie was suspicious of all college professors and "lacks comprehension." The bland acceptance of McKelvie's platitudes in the Northwest reflected, in Wilson's opinion, the dearth of farm leadership which is "right now the poorest that it has been in the last ten years." Philosophically he concluded, "I think that time has to be allowed for some things to soak in."[4]

Sensitive ears in the business community detected more than mild criticism in McKelvie's remarks about the Board of Trade and the grain trade. The Chicago Board of Trade registered complaints with Farm Board Chairman Alexander Legge about press reports on McKelvie's adverse statements regarding private grain dealers. Legge told the Nebraskan that he should avoid using the word "speculator" in a derogatory sense when referring to the grain trade, and cautioned McKelvie by saying:

> I am writing you about it in order to again suggest that you be particularly careful not to create the impression that we are fighting anybody. We will get much further by just going right down the middle of the road and minding our business, regardless of what the other fellows may try to do to us.[5]

[3] Wilson to Black (February 13, 1930), Wilson MSS.

[4] Wilson to Tolley (February 13, 1930); Wilson to Black (February 13, 1930), Wilson MSS.

[5] Legge to McKelvie (February 14, 1930), McKelvie MSS, Nebraska State Historical Society, Lincoln, Nebraska.

This statement revealed the precarious game that the Farm Board played between the producers and the grain trade. Its activities in the marketing arena created suspicions on the Boards of Trade, and if its efforts failed to raise and stabilize grain prices, it quickly lost the favor of producers. The middle-of-the-road position opened the Farm Board to potential enemies on two fronts.

McKelvie's trip to the Northwest temporarily delayed Wilson's trip to Washington on behalf of the Outlook and economic research bill. Trying to pave the way and open doors for Wilson in the capitol city, Starch again wrote Christgau. He told him of the advantages of a regional readjustment bill and said that it would be a feather in Christgau's cap if he could have the opportunity to introduce it. Starch's story to Christgau about McKelvie's reaction to the "research in adjustment bill" was somewhat at variance with Wilson's description of the governor's suspicious reaction to it.

Starch said, "Mr. McKelvie jumped at the idea. . . . He immediately insisted that Mr. Wilson come down and meet with the Farm Board." Obviously hoping to impress Christgau with the possibility that the Farm Board would swing its support to the idea, Starch said he believed that the congressman could get in on the ground floor if he acted now. He concluded with the promise that there would be favorable publicity connected with the legislation. He saw the congressman in an enviable position because he was one of the few people in the business of legislation with a thorough economic background and presumed that he was about the only member of the House with "a midwestern agricultural economic point of view." [6]

In spite of the early communications with Christgau and Wilson's conference with Tolley in February, the Christgau bill for "regional readjustments in agricultural production to assist in preventing undesirable surpluses" did not appear on the floor of the House until late June, 1930. Meanwhile, during the late winter and early spring, Wilson's efforts in publicizing the domestic allotment program gained headway in Montana and with some sectors of the grain trade.

In March, Black informed Wilson that results of his talks in Montana on the domestic allotment plan had reached him in the East. Walter R. McCarthy of the Capital Elevator Company in Duluth, who had heard Wilson's presentation of the plan in Butte, wrote Black asking for permission to distribute reprints of his chapter

[6] Starch to Christgau (February 20, 1930), Wilson MSS.

in *Agricultural Reform* dealing with the domestic allotment plan. The McGraw Hill Book Company had already offered to supply him with copies, if Black would consent. Also Black said that he had recently encouraged Dr. Ruml to write Legge specifically calling his attention to the domestic allotment plan.[7]

By late March, McCarthy possessed large numbers of the reprint of Black's Chapter 10. He was willing to make these available to Wilson for distribution in Montana "in view of the great interest shown at your Farm Week in this plan." He suggested that Wilson might mail them out to the list of farmers who registered that week, and offered as many copies as would be needed. McCarthy explained that the Capital Elevator Company was not actively sponsoring the plan, but was interested in it as a matter of information and discussion. He suggested that Wilson might not want to send the publications from the college because the recipients might think that it was sponsoring the plan. On considering this, he said that the company would be happy to mail them if a list of names of interested people was provided.[8]

Wilson's reply to McCarthy was cautious. It concealed his enthusiasm for the plan and also his future goals for achieving farm relief legislation. Of his and the college's role in such an undertaking, he wrote, "We, of course, at the college do not carry on any wholesale campaigns for legislation of any kind as this is somewhat out of our province. . . ." But Wilson went on to say that it would be all right for the college to mail out the chapter. On the other hand he advised McCarthy that it would be better public relations for the grain trade to do it directly and show farmers that it was concerned with the deteriorating farm situation and was willing to seek remedies and debate on various new proposals.[9]

Toward the last of March, Wilson took the position that the Black plan was far superior to any other plan for farm relief, but emphasized he was not a part of any propaganda move to back it as a legislative program. He told George Campbell, of the Campbell farms operation in Montana, that the Black plan had greater merit than either the previous domestic allotment approach or the debenture plan. He urged him to write for a copy of Black's proposal to

[7] Black to Wilson (March 4, 1930), Wilson MSS.
[8] McCarthy to Wilson (March 22, 1930), Wilson MSS.
[9] Wilson to McCarthy (March 22, 1930), Wilson MSS.

clear up his present objections to the plan, which Wilson thought arose from a misunderstanding. It was at this time also that Wilson openly expressed his opinion to wheat farmers in the state that the Federal Farm Board Act "as it now stands will not completely do the business." He called himself a "believer" in the domestic allotment plan as worked out by Professor Black of Harvard University, and said that the plan's most attractive feature lay in its elevation of prices without causing a corresponding jump in production that would depress the existing market. Also, to local wheat farmers he emphasized that in his opinion "it has the McNary-Haugen and the Debenture Plan beat from all angles." [10]

Black's domestic allotment plan was not the only plan under discussion in the Northwest. Wilson soon learned that W. B. Grobe of the Imperial Elevator Company of Minneapolis was quietly promoting a similar approach to the wheat problem that he called the Grobe plan. This plan provided for direct payment to producers on the basis of the amount of the commodity sold. The rate of price increase would be determined by the world price supplemented by a federal stamp tax on processing. The amount of the anticipated increase in price would, of course, depend on the rate of the federal tax on flour and the total amount sold. There was no special provision to handle the surplus, but by demonstrating that increased production would lessen proportionate payment on the commodity, it might curb excessive planting. In reply to Grobe's suggestions, Wilson agreed that the eventual failure of the Farm Board would create a need for a new plan to help make the tariff effective on commodities like wheat. Wilson diplomatically did not criticize the weaknesses of the Grobe plan, but simply said that something along the line that both Grobe and Professor Black proposed would greatly be needed.

Wilson reiterated that it was not within his province at the college to carry on any educational campaign with reference to legislation. He said he had never done this, but he was becoming more fully convinced that the farmers of the Northwest would be greatly benefited by some arrangement of this kind. "So far as I can see," he wrote, "it is the only arrangement that will do any good." He urged Grobe to keep up his contact on the matter with Congressman

[10] Wilson to George H. Campbell (March 25, 1930); Wilson to J. V. Bennett of Scobey, Montana (March 25, 1930), Wilson MSS.

Thomas Hall of North Dakota. Regarding the coming campaign that he saw shaping up for new agricultural legislation, he remarked that it would be a real opportunity for the Minneapolis Chamber of Commerce to win back the good will and support of farmers if it would "look with favor, not necessarily actively participate in a legislative campaign, but would look with favor on a measure of this kind." Wilson could not end his communication with Grobe without inserting a plug for the regional readjustment plan. He felt that any new legislation should carry with it a plan or bill for regional readjustment to assist in the adjustment of agriculture throughout the country. "You will recall I explained this somewhat at Farmers Week at Bozeman and I think a bill embodying this idea will be introduced in this Congress." Wilson failed to mention that he was a prime mover along with Tolley in the creation and promotion of this legislation.[11]

The last day in March, Wilson wrote to the presidents of the Montana State Farm Bureau and the Farmers' Union pointing out the advantages of the Black domestic allotment plan. He told Stockton that the old McNary-Haugen forces should turn to this proposal because he believed McNary-Haugenism was a dead letter. To J. T. Kelly, president of the Montana Farmers' Union, he explained that he had formerly been an advocate of the McNary-Haugen plan, but he had abandoned that effort in favor of the Black plan because "it would make the tariff effective without causing an increase of acreage to follow because of this increase in price." In closing he urged the Farm Union president to write to Walter McCarthy in Duluth for a copy of Black's chapter on the plan. Perhaps more important than a favorable reaction from either of these organization leaders was a pledge from Lester Cole that he would

---

[11] Wilson to Grobe (March 27, 1930), Wilson MSS. There seems to be some disagreement in published sources over the origin of the Regional Readjustment Bill. Roy E. Huffman asserts that it was a product of Starch's thinking at Montana and his friendship with Congressman Christgau, "Montana's Contribution to New Deal Farm Policy," *Agricultural History*, XXXIII (October, 1959), 164–167; Richard S. Kirkendall in a later article, "Howard Tolley and Agricultural Planning in the 1930's," *Agricultural History*, XXXIX (January, 1965), 25–33, asserts that his research shows that Wilson and Tolley were the key men in the formation of the bill. My research appears to confirm Kirkendall's position. A recent communication from Starch to the author (May, 1967), suggests that Huffman probably made his claim on the basis of an oral interview with Wilson, who modestly directed all of the credit for the bill to Starch.

continue discussion of the domestic allotment plan in the *Montana Farmer*.[12]

While Wilson cultivated good relations with the farm organizations, he was assured of his good standing with the grain trade by Ray B. Bowden, secretary of the Northwest Country Elevator Association in Minneapolis. This association promoted the interests of the small rural elevators who were not affiliated with large government subsidized cooperatives. Bowden wanted Wilson to know that if he approved of the Tolley plan for regional readjustments, he would get whatever support he needed from the grain trade. "Without trying to pass on any blah," Bowden wrote to Wilson, "I want to tell you that the grain trade leaders here have more faith in your judgment than in any other man they have mentioned." The friendly attitude of the grain trade toward Wilson later was to open him to the charge that he was allied with big business and eastern interests in the campaign for the domestic allotment plan.[13]

Concerning the Grobe plan, with which Bowden had become familiar, Wilson wrote that he objected to it on practical political grounds and not on its failure to meet the requirements of good economic sense. It would never survive in Congress because it proposed to apply to wheat only. In Wilson's opinion, any plan that expected to go through Congress must include at least one other major commodity and better if it pertained to all three—cotton, pork, and wheat. He also felt the plan provided inadequate controls against the growth of surpluses. This would be contrary to his view on what a national farm plan should accomplish: "elevate the price to producers without the attendant stimulation of acreage taking place." Again, Wilson showed insight into the political requirements of a successful farm bill. It must not only appeal to the wheat men, but also to the corn-hog and the cotton people.

As talk of new farm relief legislation continued, resentment against

[12] Wilson to Stockton (March 31, 1930), and Wilson to J. T. Kelly (March 31, 1930), Wilson MSS; actually Wilson did not believe the farm organizations carried any weight in Montana, so it was very much a matter of courtesy for him to consult them. He remarks in COHC that the farm organizations in Montana "never amounted to much"; Cole to Wilson (April 1, 1930), Wilson MSS.

[13] Wilson to E. J. Bell (May 24, 1930); J. A. Simpson to W. R. Ronald (September 8, 1932), Wilson MSS; Gilbert C. Fite, "John A. Simpson: The Southwest's Militant Farm Leader," *Mississippi Valley Historical Review*, XXXV (March, 1949), 576.

the Farm Board mounted in the Northwest. In the spring of 1930, Wilson thought that conditions were going to be as binding as they had ever been before in Montana. Many farmers the previous fall, who did not have storage space, sold their grain for a low price. With the proceeds, they paid their debts and invested what was left in options on stored wheat. Eventually they intended to convert the options into cash to finance operations in the coming season. The Farm Board had repeatedly said that the price of wheat was too low and intimated that through its loan policies it would not be permitted to go below the so-called loan value. Of course, businessmen and advisers to farmers told them they would be safe in buying options because the board would prevent wheat from sinking lower; if it went higher they would be able to sell their options and accomplish the same end as if they had followed the original advice of the board and held their wheat for higher prices. When the board's loan policies failed to stem the downward movement of prices, farmers suffered huge losses. "The banks up in Sheridan County alone claim that this action caused the farmers in the county to lose a million dollars," wrote Wilson.

Suffering this loss, the majority of farmers did not have the funds for gasoline and summer fallow operations. In addition, the banks shut off credit to most wheat farmers. Wilson said that there was a story being circulated, which he did not believe, that this action was in response to a request from the federal Farm Board to the chain banks. Such action, it was reasoned, could force a reduction in acreage and bring about the situation that the board had been advocating. These ideas were prevalent among farmers and in the Twin Cities. "I do not think that this is anything to be alarmed about just now, but it will bear watching during the year," cautioned Wilson.[14]

Wilson would have readily acknowledged the charge that he was friendly to the grain trade. He believed that the organized and existing channels of the trade rendered an important and valuable economic service to farmers and was "sorry for" the existing breach between the two. As the agricultural crisis of the thirties deepened, Wilson revealed himself as a man asking for unity on farm relief legislation in the entire agricultural community— producers, landlords and tenants, distributors in the grain trade,

[14] Wilson to Bowden (April 10, 1930), Wilson MSS.

and eastern credit interests. His general approach to the different segments in the American economy was to abhor conflict and emphasize cooperation among producers, distributors, and the consuming public. In a real sense he emerged as an advocate of the "community of interest doctrine," which simply meant that different groups in the economy had more to gain by recognizing their interdependence rather than their continuing conflict.[15]

He felt that the antipathy of the farmers to the grain trade stemmed in large measure from the trade's active campaigns in the past against farmer-supported and -sponsored plans that were designed to give "equality for agriculture." In particular, "the active hostility of the Minneapolis Grain Exchange to the McNary-Haugen bill has produced in the minds of many farmers a sore which will not quickly heal." In Wilson's opinion nothing could do as much to heal this sore and "produce a friendly cooperative spirit . . . beneficial to all phases and divisions of any industry," than if the grain people would try and view the problem, at least in some aspects, from the farmers' standpoint. The first step in this direction, said Wilson, would be for the grain trade to stand behind some proposal like the Grobe plan or Black's domestic allotment plan.[16]

What the grain trade needed was a carefully planned good-will program among the farmers. In many ways the hostility to this channel of trade was a mystery to Wilson, but it was a cold fact that he encountered daily. "Any one could start in and damn the Chamber of Commerce as grain speculators and more or less get by with it," said Wilson. A couple of decades earlier this was the

[15] Admittedly this was an optimistic view of the possibilities of the American economy. It was also held by nineteenth-century American economists Mathew and Henry Carey who saw a "harmony of interests" and minimized conflict in an economy of increasing abundance, George Soule, *Ideas of the Great Economists* (New York: The Viking Press, 1952), pp. 105–109; Rexford G. Tugwell, *The Democratic Roosevelt* (Garden City, N.Y.: Doubleday & Company, Inc., 1957), p. 230: "This concept, described several times as 'concert of interests' and referred to sometimes as 'interdependence' and finally worked into legal language as 'parity' or 'fair trade practice,' would be one idea brought to Franklin by the Brains Trust which he would never quite let go. It was responsible for agricultural 'adjustment,' and also for the 'codes of fair practice' of the NRA"; Arthur M. Schlesinger, Jr., in *The Age of Roosevelt: The Crisis of the Old Order, 1919–1933* (Boston: Houghton Mifflin Company, 1957), pp. 182–183, connects these ideas to the concept of a planned economy.

[16] Wilson to Grobe (April 17, 1930), Wilson MSS.

case with railroads and corporations. With reference to the cooperatives, he believed that they would continue to be a factor in grain marketing and distribution, "but likely not a predominating factor." He believed that the best thing for the cooperatives was intelligent competition. "If they grow they must grow because of being able to render to their members direct or indirect benefits . . . thru the regular organized system of grain trade." The Montana professor showed himself as much opposed to market monopolies as the older Populists had been opposed to industrial monopolies. Open and fair competition tested the merit of any organization to survive.[17]

Wilson always made it clear that his position prevented active participation in any legislative enterprise. As a college professor, he said, "I, of course, have no active interest in politics whatsoever, but as a citizen of the United States I have always been a Republican." If the Farm Board was all that the Republicans intended to do in offering equality for agriculture, he wrote, ". . . we will have radical re-action up in this northwest country that will make a situation, and I expect over the whole United States, that will not do anybody any good." Throughout this period Wilson constantly showed his fear of radical reaction and the conflicts that might result if the situation were permitted to drift unattended. Radicalism would produce a situation based on conflict. In it there would be no room for the growth of a "community of interest" and the search for answers through the cooperation of the entire community.[18]

Wilson was somewhat amused at the reaction in the Northwest to the Farm Board's attempt to convince farmers to reduce their acreage in wheat. The whole effort ran contrary to the barrage of propaganda that had been drummed into the region in the past years about the best wheat in the world being produced in Montana. He said he had repeatedly heard the question, Why should the Farm Board ask the Montana farmers to reduce their acreage when they are producing the finest in the world? Here the indisputable fact of overproduction was brought home to the local level.[19]

While surpluses, low prices, and drought caused despair in Montana, Wilson continued his letter writing in behalf of a regional readjustment bill. In a long letter briefing Henry A. Wallace on the

[17] Wilson to Bowden (August 20, 1930), Wilson MSS.
[18] Wilson to Grobe (April 17, 1930), Wilson MSS.
[19] Wilson to E. J. Bell (April 18, 1930), Wilson MSS.

proposal, he explained that research funds would provide for state and federal agencies to work out fifteen hundred or more distinct farming areas in the United States. Economists and farm management men would determine the competitive position of commodities in each area, consider changes in techniques of production, marketing, and farm organization. This would ultimately lead to what Ezekiel called "orderly retreat of agriculture from sub-marginal regions." It would also form a scientific and objective basis for adjustments in crop acreages and livestock production. This could be done on the sound basis of comparative advantage in each region's specialty rather than the across-the-board reductions that the Farm Board was calling for throughout the country.

Research work would be carried on in a regional way and "compel the State Experiment Stations to function in regional research rather [than] independently as is now the case." This is one of the first instances in which Wilson admitted that a significant feature of this plan was the retirement of submarginal lands that served no purpose except to produce surplus harmful to the general price level. Thus, the first step in an effective agricultural relief program of enduring significance was a reversal of traditional land policies in the United States, which had centered on the alienation of the public lands into productive use. Now Wilson saw the need and the possibility of success in removing at least some of these lands from production. A long-held precept of American land policy now stood outmoded in his view; the tradition of agrarian expansion had to be reversed.[20]

O. C. Stine commented that the ideas in the regional readjustment bill largely grew out of Spillman's development of the Outlook program and the role it could play in making crop allotment plans successful. Stine drew this conclusion in part from reading Spillman's book, *Balancing the Farm Output*. The Outlook work, of course, hoped to make accurate estimations of types and quantity of crops to be planted for future market demands and distribute these estimates to farmers. Tolley, in Stine's opinion, pursued this

[20] Wilson to Wallace (April 21, 1930), Wilson MSS; Herbert Hoover had advocated "some device for return of marginal lands to pastures: with payments to be made for the readjustment to farmers after the war," Herbert Hoover, *The Memoirs of Herbert Hoover, the Cabinet, and the Presidency, 1920–1933* (New York: The Macmillan Company, 1952), II, 110–111.

line of thinking. The results emerged in the Christgau bill, "which was to make local and regional planning effective from an Outlook standpoint." As has been noted, Wilson on several occasions referred to the Christgau regional readjustment bill as the Outlook bill.[21]

While Wilson shored up backing for the readjustment bill, the Farm Board's policy that spring produced confusion in many circles. The ending of the board's loan policy on wheat during the last week in April caused mistrust on all sides. Farmers' elevators holding futures options suffered heavy losses. Apparently many considerations entered into the board's decision. The upcoming meeting of the National Chamber of Commerce, it was rumored, loomed large in the picture because a central question of their discussion was to focus on competition of the government with private business. Terminating the loan policy as of May 1, 1930, would enable them to go before the chamber and declare they were no longer competing, and possibly this could forestall resolutions or demands from the chamber that they get out of the grain market. The announced reason for stopping the loans was that the loan on the 1929 crop ended on this date and that most of the wheat was now out of the farmers hands, ". . . the last not being exactly true."[22]

At the annual meeting of the Chamber of Commerce of the United States on April 30, 1930, the Farm Board came under heavy fire. Businessmen at the meeting denounced the activities of the board because it placed government in competition with industry, undermined private initiative, and operated contrary to economic law. In reply Legge took the floor at the meeting and lambasted the chamber and its business membership for failing to take action "to improve the farm situation after voting overwhelmingly in favor of the principle of cooperative marketing." Daniel Millet, a Denver stockman and banker, echoed the general sentiments of the gathering when he accused the Farm Board of entertaining "a fantastic dream of stabilization." Secretary of Agriculture Arthur Hyde unexpectedly broke his silence during the exchange and asked members of the chamber to "take a look at the wild men over in the Senate and view the rising tide of discontent" before they destroyed the entire

[21] Wilson to Black (February 13, 1930), Wilson MSS; O. C. Stine, Columbia Oral History Collection, Columbia University, New York, N.Y.

[22] Bowden to Wilson (April 26, 1930), Wilson MSS.

structure and accomplishments of the Farm Board. He implied it might be replaced with something far more offensive to them. Despite this warning, the chamber passed a resolution asking for drastic restriction of Farm Board activities.[23]

Bowden in Minneapolis said that grain people seemed to have no idea what the board was trying to accomplish or what it actually intended to do with or about the present grain trade. It was also his opinion that that uncertainty surrounding future policies of the board toward country elevators prevented the construction of much new elevator space. Another contact of Wilson's engaged in the Duluth grain trade, Walter MacCarthy, said in Washington that the Farm Board ruined the business of the independent grain merchant and was "unfair and un-American." Regarding the Chamber of Commerce's criticism of the board, Wilson said that as far as he could determine, the chamber's action guaranteed the Farm Board's existence for years to come. It was about ready to die because of the farmers' indifference, but now the attack transformed apathy into an entirely different psychology in favor of the board.[24]

A month later Wilson saw convincing evidence that the tussle between the Farm Board and the National Chamber of Commerce had been to the advantage of the board. "Everyone with whom I talk about the Farm Board–National Chamber of Commerce scrap thinks that old Alex Legge came off the big winner," wrote Wilson. When farmers seemed most disgusted with the board this event bolstered their confidence in it. "Some way or another they [the farmers] all seemed to know about it and seem to feel good over the affair." Despite this opposition by many farmers to the Chamber of Commerce, Wilson was happy to announce that he had been appointed to the Agricultural Committee of the National Chamber of Commerce. This presented an opportunity for him to publicize the regional readjustment bill and, in his words, "to do some good on the Tolley hill."[25]

Wilson's friend in Minneapolis saw the Farm Board's call for acreage reduction very much at cross-purposes with the agricultural education as carried on in the state colleges. Bowden wanted to

[23] *Washington Post*, May 1 and 2, 1930.

[24] Bowden to Wilson (April 26, 1930); Wilson to Bowden (May 13, 1930), Wilson MSS.

[25] Wilson to Bowden (June 5, 1930), Wilson MSS.

know if the Farm Board was asking college men to abandon their program of increasing quantity and quality per acre. In the light of the goal of most agricultural education, the Farm Board's effort seemed "silly and inefficient." He wondered why some of the colleges did not "call" the board on "this inconsistency between their program and the average county agents' program."

From Bowden, Wilson received a confidential report on the attitude of weekly newspapers in four northwestern states toward the Farm Board. The report proved, Bowden said, what he had suspected for a long time. Despite the huge propaganda effort to sign farmers up for cooperatives, the movement failed to capture the enthusiasm of the weekly press. The report showed that approximately 65 per cent of the weekly papers took no stand on the Farm Board program and were classed "indifferent"; 20 per cent were classed sympathetic or in support of Farm Board policies; and 15 per cent were classed as hostile to the Farm Board program. This percentage breakdown generally held true for Montana east of the Rocky Mountains, although the high line—counties in north central Montana— showed a number of papers actively favoring it. Bowden noted with interest that only in northeastern Montana and northwestern North Dakota were papers "noisily favoring the non-co-operative plans." This was the battleground of the old Nonpartisan League.

Several conflicts stirred in North Dakota. Bowden openly admitted that the Nonpartisans were about to make a new bid for power in the state. The Independent Voters Association was in real trouble and it was generally felt that it would not be able to hold the line against the mounting tide of Nonpartisan revival. In signing farmers up in cooperatives, the Farmers' Union showed a clear lead in North Dakota and Montana with the Northwest Grain Cooperative second. The rivalry between these two cooperatives showed itself in Farm Union President M. W. Thatcher's public attacks on A. B. Kuhrt, director of the Northwest Grain Cooperative. This was all very amusing from Bowden's position in the private grain trade when he wrote to Wilson, "They have started a merry little war right in Mr. Legge's family group." Far from producing a cooperative and harmonious spirit among the northwest farmers, the Farm Board served to create political conflict and destructive competition among the cooperatives in what was supposed to be the orderly marketing of wheat.[26]

[26] Bowden to Wilson (June 9, 1930), Wilson MSS.

Amidst the growing unrest in the Northwest over Farm Board policies, the cooperative battles, and the reawakening of the Non-partisans, Wilson and Tolley worked quietly to ready their agricultural readjustment bill for introduction on the floor of the Congress. By June 18, Wilson was able to announce that he and Tolley had put the finishing touches on the readjustment bill and had sent it off to Congressman Christgau to be introduced on the floor later in the week.[27]

On June 20, 1930, Wilson dispatched a long and instructive letter to Christgau suggesting preliminary steps before the bill's introduction. A central figure in the eventual passage of the bill would be the Secretary of Agriculture. Wilson wanted Christgau to write the secretary and phrase the letter in such a way "that he cannot register against the bill." He thought the congressman could explain that he had given the bill a great deal of thought and with the aid of a few agricultural economists had formulated his conclusions about the correct approach to the agricultural problem in the form of this bill. Uppermost in his argument to the secretary, he should mention that the proposal of across-the-board adjustment, such as proposed by the Farm Board, had met with stiff opposition. Still, adjustments had to come, and this bill would provide a scientific basis for withdrawing lands from production in a manner that would not be haphazard and uneconomic. It should be made clear to the secretary that Christgau introduced the bill late in the session in order that it might receive the benefits of discussion and suggestion before the next session of Congress. Wilson emphasized that the congressman should be careful not to ask for a flat endorsement of the bill, but rather confine his request to suggestions that the secretary might make to strengthen and improve it. In Washington, Christgau should contact Eric Englund, assistant chief of the Bureau of Agricultural Economics, at his home, and "by all means stay away from him in the department or officially" for further suggestions on how to word the letter and proceed with the secretary.

Wilson also expressed concern at the bill's standing with the farm organizations. He felt that Christgau had an excellent entree to the National Farm Bureau through Eric Olson, president of the Minnesota bureau. Olson had formerly been an agricultural teacher in a Montana high school and later a county agent under Wilson. On the basis of this acquaintance, Wilson also intended to write

[27] Wilson to Bowden (June 18, 1930), Wilson MSS.

Olson informing him of Christgau's high standing among the agricultural economists of the country and that for some time agricultural economists had been aware that Christgau was interested in agricultural relief legislation. As a result they had been in correspondence with him and offered suggestions that were contained in this bill. Now Wilson struggled with a problem that confronted him throughout all of his efforts to obtain agricultural legislation—to stay free from the political infighting and accusations of political meddling. He plainly told Christgau:

> I think from now on we must always have our wires straight on this point, that you have taken the initiative and that you have asked assistance and consultation from some of the agricultural economists, that this is your bill and not somebody else's.

Also Olson's attention could be drawn to the constructive service he would be performing, if he influenced the national organization to support it. Already the support of the Montana state bureau was assured.

From Chester Davis, Wilson expected to obtain the good will and support of the McNary-Haugen group and the various organizations they represented. He also hoped that some of the big cooperative groups would swing their support behind it, as well as C. E. Huff, national president of the Farmers' Union. He urged Christgau to send Henry Wallace a copy of the bill and have a talk with Dan Wallace when he returned to Minnesota. "I think that Henry Wallace can be quite a factor in the development and support or something favorable thereto," said Wilson, with an eye to where power lay in the agricultural community.

As Wilson well knew from defeats in the twenties, power did not lie entirely in the agricultural community when it came to passing bills in the Congress. Through his new position on the Agricultural Committee of the National Chamber of Commerce he hoped to convince the chamber and business interests to support the bill. "My acceptance of a place on their committee was made largely with this in view," he told Christgau. His contacts with the grain exchanges revealed that they too sought a sound program to back that would not be inimical to them. He thought both of these power groups could swing a great deal of influence in favor of the bill, but cautioned, "We will have to be diplomatic in this regard and keep them in the background rather than in the foreground."

A bill that received too much enthusiasm from business sources would immediately be suspected by the agricultural community.[28]

On June 30, 1930, Congressman Christgau introduced H.R. 13275, "To aid farmers in making regional readjustments in agricultural production to assist in preventing undesirable surpluses." In his introductory remarks, he asserted that farm production was difficult to control. Restating the Outlook philosophy, he said much could be done through dissemination of information among farmers, ". . . advising them of trends in world production and changes in world demand for their products." The goal of the bill is best summed up in the following paragraph:

> The gradual mechanization of agriculture in certain areas has resulted in great differences in the costs of production of a certain commodity as between different areas or regions. That some regions are better adapted for the production of certain farm commodities than others has become more apparent during the last few years. One of the purposes of the bill is to aid the farmers in certain regions to determine what commodities they can produce to their greatest advantage in view of actual and potential competition with other regions in this country and also in competition with producers of agricultural commodities in other countries.[29]

The work envisioned in economic research would be carried on in cooperation with the United States Department of Agriculture and the state agricultural colleges and experiment stations. From this would result a program of farm readjustment and farm reorganization which would encourage farmers to take advantage of the changing economic conditions arising from improved techniques. Hopefully this would aid systematic substitution of other enterprises for surplus-producing enterprises, "especially where certain farm enterprises are now carried on in high-cost production regions." The bill admitted to reversing a historical trend in American agriculture. Until this time the public had given little attention to the problem of overproduction in many sectors of agriculture. "This condition is due partly to lack of available funds to research institutions and the historical emphasis on production rather than on economics and farm management," this unique piece of agricultural legislation announced to the nation.[30]

[28] Wilson to Christgau (June 20, 1930), Wilson MSS.
[29] *Congressional Record*, 71st Cong., 2d sess., June 30, 1930, 12120.
[30] *Ibid.*, 12121.

The initial step of introducing the bill in Congress had been accomplished. Now Wilson turned to the task of bringing it to the attention of the various groups that could aid in its acceptance and passage. He felt that the "first and most important and most diplomatic job" was selling the idea to the land-grant-college administrators and Extension directors. This presented certain difficulties, because, in Wilson's opinion, "these people, in general, do not think in economic terms and there is a tendency for them to overemphasize the biological point of view." By this, of course, he meant that their minds were occupied with the "historical emphasis on production" and caught up in the technical problems that obstructed this goal. If managed correctly, Wilson was convinced that the proposition could be sold to them and their support could be counted on in the next session of Congress. He foresaw that they would immediately question the regional approach to the problem and the establishment of regional research councils operated in conjunction with experimental farming aimed at discovering the particular needs of a region for suggested readjustments. The state officials might view this as the creation of a new level of action that would supersede and threaten their positions.

With this delicate situation well in mind, Wilson already planned strategy to bolster the regional readjustment bill at the annual convention of the Association of Land-Grant Colleges and Universities to be held in Washington, D.C., November 17–19, 1930. Dean and Director Linfield of Montana State College, whom Wilson called "economic minded," had read the bill and was sympathetic to it. Fortunately for Wilson's sales campaign, Director Linfield was to be chairman of the experiment station section at the convention and was responsible for the preparation of a program dealing with some important problem in agriculture. Wilson revealed that Linfield had confidentially authorized him to prepare a suggested program centering on a present problem in agriculture, which Wilson chose to be "Regional Adjustments in Agricultural Production."

On the program, Wilson planned for Tolley to read first a paper giving the economic and philosophical background of the need for economic research for regional production adjustments. Following Tolley, either BAE chief Nils Olsen, or Eric Englund would be asked to speak on changes in foreign demand and general economic changes that necessitated adjustments in production, techniques, machinery, and output per man. They would present the background for the next important question, which would be, What is the most constructive thing that the land-grant colleges can do ? In the speech he suggested that the congressman pay compliments to the deans and directors for the work of the agricultural institutions and "pat them very much on the back for the chemical and biological research." After making them "feel good in this respect," the congressman could then move to economic matters and explain the proposals contained in the bill. The bill should not be referred to as the final answer, but rather the best thing that he could put together from his own knowledge and from consultations with a number of agricultural economists. Again Wilson reiterated, "I think it is very important that you take the responsibility for the bill and keep the Department of Agriculture, state people, and Tolley and myself in particular in the background from this time on."[31]

True to the plan outlined in the summer, the program for the annual convention of the Association of Land-Grant Colleges and Universities listed speeches by Tolley, Englund, and Christgau. In the Joint Session of the Sub-section on Agriculture, chaired by Linfield of Montana, first Tolley spoke on "Economic Readjustment of American Agriculture"; second Englund, on "Researches to Aid Readjustments in Agriculture"; followed by Christgau on "Legislation Needed to Bring About Readjustments in Agriculture."[32]

Before Wilson confirmed Englund's place on the program, he sounded him out carefully about his attitude on the Christgau bill. He wished to make it clear to Englund that if he could not support the ideas contained in the bill, he hoped he would decline Chairman Linfield's invitation to deliver a paper along these lines at the committee meeting. If the assistant chief of the Bureau of Agricultural Economics felt that the situation within the Department of Agriculture conflicted from the standpoint of policy, or if this did not square with his own intellectual honesty, he should withdraw

[31] Wilson to Christgau (June 20, 1930), Wilson MSS.
[32] *Proceedings of the Forty-Fourth Annual Convention of the Association of Land-Grant Colleges and Universities*, Washington, D.C., November 17–19, 1930, ed. Charles A. McCue (Burlington, Vt.: Free Press Printing Co., 1931), pp. 108–130.

his name from the program. Wilson explained that the "rights of agricultural politics" decreed that he and Tolley should have complete support in this program or complete silence from Englund:

> I hope that you will feel that you can head it 100 per cent. . . . I know you realize the feeling of Tolley and myself in this matter . . . the Gods someway decreed that we have the control of this program and we, therefore, feel that by the rights of agricultural politics we should see that our control amounts to 100 per cent party discipline.

Also, since the bill arose principally from the efforts of Tolley and Wilson, he did not want any moves to amend it or reshape it from other sources, at least not at this juncture. Englund endorsed Wilson's efforts in his speech to the November convention. [33]

While Wilson continued his high-level maneuvering on the Christgau bill, talk about a new farm relief bill raced through the Northwest. In July, Legge in North Dakota noticed a reviving interest in the McNary-Haugen idea and made a special attempt to point out why the McNary-Haugen type of relief could not function under present world conditions. It was a difficult task to meet the new wave of McNary-Haugenism when all he had to offer in its place was an appeal for reduced acreage to wheat farmers. [34]

By August the chairman of the Farm Board admitted the failure of the campaign, but he blamed failure on Kansas farmers who produced 25 per cent over their quota. President Stockton of the Montana Farm Bureau told Legge that more drastic action than requests for acreage reduction was needed. He said that Legge instructed Montana farmers last fall to reduce their acreage by 10 per cent for a higher price at marketing time. Normal production in Montana was fifty million bushels, but because of adverse conditions less than thirty-five million bushels went to market. Still, the price turned out to be the lowest in years in spite of the fact that much of the nation was hit by severe drought. "Is this not positive proof that a solution of the Farm Problem requires more drastic action than traveling over the country telling the farmers that if wheat was scarce the price would probably be higher?" asked Stockton. The Montanan suggested that Legge consider the Black

---

[33] Wilson to Englund (August 19, 1930), Wilson MSS.
[34] Bowden to Wilson (July 18, 1930), Wilson MSS.

plan or any others with similar merit. "I can only implore you, for the good of the Agricultural Industry, for the good of the nation, and for the good of the Republican party," of which Stockton admitted that he was a member, "to try out some one of the schemes that have the ear marks of producing results." [35]

Still, Wilson was ambivalent about the production-control philosophy. In October, 1930, he told the editor of the *Montana Farmer* that with larger family farms, intelligent use of machinery, and present land values, American wheat farmers could still compete with the world. One of the few certainties in the Northwest during the fall of 1930 was general disillusionment with the Farm Board. During the previous summer, in observer Bowden's opinion, Legge had been the personal hero of many North Dakota farmers because of his bout with the National Chamber of Commerce. "Today there is . . . a personal bitterness against Mr. Legge and the International Harvester Co." Two months ago, he continued, farmers were saying that the "Farm Board should be given a chance to prove itself." Now there was mounting conviction that the "Farm Board has definitely not only failed to help their position but made it worse." Everywhere, Bowden met the demand that trained scientists "should get busy and do something" about the situation. This indicated a favorable reception to the Christgau bill if it could be brought into the public eye soon. But Bowden expressed fears that if it were not put into the spotlight soon, there would be another movement toward McNary-Haugenism. He expressed this fear to Wilson:

> I am afraid you will think I am frothing at the mouth in my excitement over the present situation, but really few men understand the tremendous change in opinion that has swung into the agricultural districts in the past two months. If ever there was an opportune time to do good work it is right now.

Bowden assured Wilson that without direct reference he was trying to build sentiment in favor of the regional readjustment bill. [36]

In Montana, Wilson saw no startling positive or negative reaction: "I find the farmers more or less like sheep blinded and drifting

[35] Stockton to Legge (August 15, 1930), Wilson MSS.

[36] Wilson to Cole (October 5, 1930); Bowden to Wilson (October 24, 1930), Wilson MSS.

before a storm." Congressman Leavitt's usually substantial majority, however, fell noticeably in the election and reflected an awakening protest. Leavitt made the mistake of centering his campaign on the tariff, supporting the administration, the Farm Board, and prosperity around the corner. A platform of open sympathy for the farmer's plight would have been much more successful, in Wilson's opinion, than repeated speeches about the tariff.[37]

Although Wilson could only see a stunned and apathetic reaction in Montana to the worsening farm situation, Henry Wallace in the corn belt heard the rumblings of a new fight for "agricultural equality." In mid-November he wrote Peek saying that there had been much talk about reviving both the debenture plan and equalization fee, as well as lowering the tariff on industrial products. But Wallace said that he had little faith in a fight for the debenture plan or equalization fee, "unless there is some one stationed in Washington with will power and intelligence such as is possessed by you and Chester Davis." Peek replied that there was no sense in starting the battle with Hoover in the White House. A victory in Congress would only mean a Presidential veto. At the moment, Peek felt energies should be directed toward the eventual election of a sympathetic President: "Would it not be better to put forth an effort to elect a president who will sign a bill when it has been passed by Congress?"[38]

Some Hoover stalwarts saw the threatening political future and urged a more forceful and precedent-breaking farm policy. Sydney Anderson, former representative from Minnesota, who had chaired the Committee for Agricultural Inquiry in 1921 and was presently vice-president of General Mills, tried to persuade the administration to meet the problem through a coordinated plan for intelligent land utilization which involved the retirement of marginal lands. The Farm Board's appeals had involved "too much exhortation and not enough exposition," he contended. Any plan for reduction of acreage must be accompanied by an exposition of methods by which this reduction can be achieved. This must include an increase in price to the farmer without the reduction of net farm income with which the recent appeal of the Farm Board threatened every farmer.

[37] Wilson to Bowden (November 8, 1930), Wilson MSS.

[38] Wallace to Peek (November 19, 1930); Peek to Wallace (November 21, 1930), Peek MSS.

His concluding inquiry came close to suggesting moves that resembled the contents of the Christgau bill:

> I am just wondering if the time is not pretty nearly here when
> the necessary set-up should be made to accomplish consideration
> of a plan of better land utilization including the retirement of
> those marginal lands which continue to be a menace not only from
> the production point of view but from the point of view of their
> influence upon the financial condition in rural sections.

Also Anderson took note that three of the annual reports of cabinet
members suggested the necessity for a coordinated plan for land
utilization. The moorings of the established agricultural policy
began to weaken even in the citadel of their faith.[39]

[39] Sydney Anderson to Walter H. Newton, secretary to the President
(December 19, 1930), RG16, National Archives and Records Service, Washington, D.C.

CHAPTER SIX

Agricultural Planning : Long-Range and Short-Run Goals

What is the use of Chairman Legge advising farmers to reduce acreage—each fellow for himself. Why haven't you proposed some plan for doing it.—Washington State Senator F. J. Wilmer

For two years hopes for higher grain prices had rested in the cooperatives and on the Farm Board's activities in the market. Market operations alone failed to stabilize the wheat situation, and the search for stabilization now turned to other areas. With the quest for solutions ranging beyond the performance of the Farm Board, the Department of Agriculture once again began to assert its leadership along a broad front of possible new approaches to the problem. Pleas from the Farm Board for acreage reduction turned the attention of business-oriented minds in high circles of the Republican party to the productive plant of agriculture. Perhaps the cause for agriculture's inability to obtain equality in the economic community was an improper utilization of its productive plant. In agriculture this involved the land and its use. An uneconomical use of the land might lie at the root of the industry's problems.

Much attention began to focus on the question of land reform. But this was not a land reform directed at placing more land in the hands of small proprietors or at breaking up large landholdings as is the goal of many twentieth-century agrarian reform projects. The immediate question about the land in the American countryside was more economic than social in the early 1930's. Those lands that produced only after a high investment of capital stood on the marginal fringes of economic return. Through their contribution to the market surplus, they depressed prices at a time when their production and use could best be eliminated. As far as any business mind was concerned, this was improper use of productive resources.

M. L. Wilson was also abreast of this shift in thinking toward the problem of land and its utilization. Throughout 1931 he devoted time to organizing an important meeting of land-grant-college and agricultural leaders to discuss land policy at a conference to be held in September, 1931, at the University of Chicago. Of course, these activities provided a convenient sounding board for advertising the pending Christgau bill and its particular approach to land reform, which was not too far afield from the growing demand that sub-marginal lands be removed from production. While directing his attention to the question of land policy, Wilson still had the domestic allotment plan tucked under his arm ready for discussion. At this point he had doubts about the plan ever receiving serious consideration because of its complicated nature.[1]

In a move to draw the spotlight away from the Farm Board and bring the Department of Agriculture back into the farm relief picture, Secretary Arthur Hyde in the fall of 1930 turned to the pressing question of land policy. In a letter dated January 6, 1931, Hyde wrote to all senators, representatives, farm organizations, and editors of farm papers stating that a sound policy of land utilization was basic to agricultural prosperity. "I think there is need for a new and vigorous approach to the whole question," he wrote and hoped that farm leaders, editors, and all others working for agricultural improvement would put their minds to this fundamental question. "The formulation of a land policy is a big task; we need all the cooperation and help we can get," he declared.[2]

Alex Legge, in a letter to Dr. C. W. Warburton, director of Extension Service in the Department of Agriculture, explained that the Farm Board, besides conducting stabilization operations in the market, was on a campaign with farmers to encourage "a gradual readjustment downward to bring their wheat production within the limits of domestic consumption." He said that American wheat growers drifted into their present position without fully realizing

---

[1] Wilson to A. S. Goss, master, Washington State Grange (January 28, 1931), Wilson MSS.

[2] Arthur Hyde (January 6, 1931), Land Policy folder 1931, RG16, National Archives and Records Service, Washington, D.C.

it and now must be made to realize that to free themselves of the present depressed world prices they must reduce production to domestic levels in order to make the tariff effective on wheat. Legge emphasized that the current campaign was designed to put these facts before the farmer, and "from there on the action is up to them." If the wheat farmers decided to fight it out on the basis of the survival of the fittest until a sufficient number of them were eliminated to bring production below the demand level, "that is their privilege," said Legge. The Farm Board could analyze the situation and suggest voluntary actions for acreage reduction, but was powerless to take action beyond its words of advice to the farmer.[3]

The imminent failure of the Farm Board touched off new searches for solutions as well as a variety of theories as to why Hoover's agricultural policy had backfired. In a statement on "Hoover and Agriculture," Senator Norris said, "Of course I am opposed to the renomination of President Hoover." Norris aimed his attack at the Hoover tariff policies. He said the President signed a tariff bill that burdened agriculture and contradicted his promises to place agriculture on an equal basis with other lines of business through a revision of the tariff. In a letter to the economist for the Grain Section of the Farm Board, Wilson declared that sentiment toward acreage reduction among Montana farmers had reversed itself from the opposition of a year ago to a serious consideration of it. The new interest in acreage reduction, however, arose out of an atmosphere of despair in Montana produced by the general feeling that the 1931 drought would continue, and even if it did not, a good crop would only bring prices of a little over twenty-five cents a bushel. In any event the Montana wheat farmer had little optimism in his outlook for the coming year.[4]

In a letter to the new president of the Montana State Farm Bureau, Wilson explained the need for a revised land policy that aimed at retiring submarginal land from production to shift people off the poorer range and dry-farming lands. The bleak price situation in wheat for the future held only despair for families in the plains

---

[3] Legge to Warburton (February 2, 1931), RG 16, NARS.

[4] Norris, "Hoover and Agriculture" (February 3, 1931), Tray 1, Box 6, Norris MSS, Library of Congress; Wilson to Bell (March 6, 1931), and (March 14, 1931), Wilson MSS.

region of Montana, "which because of soil or rainfall will not be sufficiently productive to give them anything except the most extreme poverty during the period of anticipated low prices." In Wilson's opinion the plains section of Montana was one of the most undesirable places in the country for poor people. He felt, "If we are to have people struggling for an existence I feel confident that there are many other places where life could be made much more attractive to them. . . ." Here they had no timber for fuel during the harsh winters, distance made schooling opportunities difficult, and the frequent dry season even prevented the cultivation of gardens. A sensible land utilization program would not only be correct from an economic point of view, but "human welfare would be promoted by assisting in shifting these people to other districts." This argument nicely squared human needs with what was developing into economic realities. [5]

Others reviewed the results of the campaign to reduce acreage on a voluntary basis. A Chicago conference to consider acreage reductions, surplus control, and related subjects held April 7, 8, and 9, 1931, with representatives from the Farm Board, Department of Agriculture, cooperatives, and other interested parties made a searching analysis of these questions. Eric Englund sent Wilson an extensive memorandum on the minutes of the meeting marked "confidential." In the course of the remarks, C. C. Talbott of the North Dakota Farmers' Union Co-op pointed out that the charts revealed that spring wheat growers responded to the campaign for reduced wheat acreage while winter wheat growers continued at high production levels. He suggested that any plan for acreage reduction "should reward the fellow that reduces and punish him who doesn't." Sam McKelvie voiced the "utter impossibility of continuing stabilization" operations by the Farm Board in the wheat market and pointed out that by the next July about one-half of the revolving fund would be tied up in wheat. He called for farmers to adjust acreage, not under an agency of the government, "but under the leadership of farmers themselves, with the support of the Farm Board." [6]

[5] Wilson to W. S. McCormick (March 20, 1931), Wilson MSS.

[6] "Memorandum on a Meeting to Consider Acreage Reductions, Surplus Control, Related Subjects," Chicago, April 7, 8, 9, 1931, Wilson MSS.

It was suggested that unless immediate action occurred the country faced a political revolution, and indicative of the unrest was the convening of the Corn Belt Conference in Des Moines on May 6. "That is the outfit that started all the hell six or eight years ago," injected McKelvie. State Senator F. J. Wilmer of Washington presented a plan that called for a one-fourth reduction in the wheat crop, and said the farmer should be informed that he could get more money for three bushels than for four. Under the plan the Secretary of Agriculture should allocate to each county the amount it could market. The senator from the eastern Washington wheat country criticized the recent appeals of the Farm Board for acreage reduction: "What is the use of Chairman Legge advising farmers to reduce acreage—each fellow for himself. Why haven't you proposed some plan for doing it." Senator Wilmer elaborated on his Whitman County Plan. It would reduce acreage 25 per cent in 1932 if 75 per cent of the wheat acreage in the country were signed up. Not later than September 1, the Secretary of Agriculture would designate the amount of wheat each county would be allowed to grow. On the basis of this estimate each would be issued "production rights." Any wheat produced above this, the farmer would agree not to market, and a fine of forty-two cents would be levied on each bushel marketed in violation of the contract.

The large number of cooperative leaders present urged that the revolving fund of the Farm Board be kept intact for the development of cooperatives. The board hinted that continued stabilization operations in 1931 would dissipate the fund, and "everyone recognized that Congress probably would not advance another dollar." Talbott and others said it would be useless to go to the farmers with an appeal to curtail acreage in 1932 unless there was some assurance that an effective way would be devised for handling the surplus of 1931. They wanted to bargain with the board for surplus control in 1931 in exchange for acreage reduction in 1932. It was generally agreed that the board could not buy the 1931 surplus. Then discussion turned to withholding production on the farm to about one-fourth of the 1931 crop.

Talbott termed the withholding propositions as out of the question. "No farmer in North Dakota," he said, "would sit by and watch the sheriff sell out his farm for debt and taxes and watch his children go without shoes if he had wheat on the farm that could be sold at any price." This would only be inviting the bootlegging of grain that would destroy the plan. "There is already enough of it bootlegged in bottles," was his concluding argument.

Another proposition called for one bushel out of every four to be turned over to the Farmers' National, the Grain Stabilization Corporation, or any other organization set up by the Farm Board. The farmer would receive a certificate for the bushels that guaranteed to pay him for the wheat when it was disposed of and after deducting the cost of handling it. This, of course, was moving in the direction of the domestic allotment plan. Ultimately the meeting proposed that the Farm Board consider this approach to the surplus problem. Englund attacked these plans in a speech before the conference on the grounds that it would be impossible to force farmers to live up to the contracts in wheat acreage reduction. He suggested that a better alternative would be to strengthen the Outlook work, and efforts should be made to reduce costs as far as possible by improved technique, more suitable size of farms, and crop substitutes for wheat. Although he did not name the Christgau bill, his speech embodied its proposals. In a final swipe at reduced acreage plans, he said, "Flat acreage reduction may sound spectacular, but in my judgment it is futile."[7]

Meanwhile with the land-retirement idea under increasing discussion, Wilson kept prodding Christgau in Washington to bring his bill to the attention of prominent people in the Department of Agriculture. Dr. L. C. Gray, chief of the Division of Land Economics, was one of the essential contacts in the department who should be informed about the bill. Wilson encouraged Christgau to use "a lot of diplomacy" in talking with him and to keep himself and Tolley in the background. Gray, according to Wilson, should be approached as though his advice was needed in order to enlist his support. "I think he feels just a little bit slighted that he has not been consulted more in the preparation of your plan," and therefore needs to be handled with care, for "he can be quite influential if he cares to in the future," said Wilson. Overall, Wilson thought that the congressman would find the people in the Department of Agriculture a little "gun-shy" in talking about this proposal. This is why it should be explained to them that they were only being consulted in an unofficial manner and that their names would not

[7] *Ibid.*

be used to embarrass them if anything should develop on the bill.[8]

Wilson also kept the regional readjustment bill alive in his wide correspondence. M. S. Winder, executive secretary of the American Farm Bureau Federation, expressed "a great deal of interest" in the proposal that Extension should now teach farmers to plan effectively to produce to the best advantage on a restricted area, thus eliminating from production much of the submarginal land. This, he agreed, could be done through the establishment of a consistent land policy. In such a policy he saw the government promoting the retirement of lands, "just as in times past the government has helped to bring new areas under cultivation." He made it clear, however, that he was not in favor of a direct subsidy to the farmer for the removal of these lands from production, but ". . . an intelligent program of re-forestation, or re-vegetation, of grazing areas might be carried through."[9]

Although Wilson looked to Extension to play a major role in a land-readjustment program, he saw a growing resentment against these officials as the economic situation tightened in rural areas. On his trips into the state he heard the faculties of the state institutions and many public employees criticized and "put almost in the class of crooks and criminals." Yet the Montana professor recognized this as a normal reaction of the public mind to officials drawing salaries from tax funds. In the Judith Basin, county commissioners had recently decided that the Extension service could not be continued for the county without a referendum from the taxpayers. The service survived the test, but the vote was close enough to suggest that Extension's future in the county was doubtful. In Nebraska, North Dakota, and South Dakota, Extension services were being curtailed in many counties as local communities voted against the continuation of the service.[10]

On the national front, Wilson was happy to announce that the National Chamber of Commerce had approved the Christgau bill. Now he felt that the next move was to swing the support of a

[8] Wilson to Christgau (April 2, 1931), Wilson MSS.

[9] Winder to Wilson (April 8, 1931), Wilson MSS.

[10] Wilson to Bowden (April 16, 1931), Wilson MSS; Annual Extension Reports for Nebraska, South Dakota, North Dakota, and Montana located in the respective state agricultural colleges at Lincoln, Nebraska; Brookings, South Dakota; Fargo, North Dakota; and Bozeman, Montana.

national farm organization behind the bill. The one that was most likely to be persuaded, he thought, was the American Farm Bureau. After such a commitment was made to the bill, "then we want all of the guns of war turned loose," he said. With his ear attuned to public opinion, Wilson said that he felt that the "general public is sort of sick and tired of much of the farm relief talk that we have had," and he was convinced the "public psychology is ready to take up the idea of national planning in relation to agriculture."[11]

In Montana, Wilson grew much less optimistic than he had been a year earlier about the ability of the dry-land wheat farmers to stay on the land in the face of persistent drought and depression. C. L. Holmes, in charge of the Division of Farm Management and Costs, reported to BAE Chief Olsen that Professor Wilson said the drought in the state was unbroken and that over 50 per cent of the winter wheat was gone. Although this may have been desirable from the Farm Board's point of view in the acreage reduction campaign, it dashed many of Wilson's hopes for large, economical dry-land-farming operations. At the same time it reinforced his belief in a readjustment of agriculture away from the marginal lands.[12]

By mid-May, Wilson laid plans for a national conference on land planning to be held in the late summer. He hoped to bring together a group of outstanding people in agriculture who were thinking along planning lines and "who might make collectively a valuable contribution to the philosophy and methodology of the planning idea as related to agriculture." The meeting, he hoped, would help crystallize thinking on the subject at a time when the idea was still nebulous. The proceedings of such a conference could be printed and circulated among the agricultural colleges and other interested and influential people. Wilson told George Soule, editor of *The New Republic* that Tolley and Congressman Christgau had also been corresponding with various people on the possibility of an agricultural planning conference and wanted his reaction to the idea. Wilson explained there would be no money available for the conference, and they would have to depend upon people who were willing to contribute their time and travel.[13]

[11] Wilson to Bowden (May 13, 1931), Wilson MSS.
[12] Holmes to Olsen (May 5, 1931), "Memorandum on Past and Possible Future Shifts in Wheat Acreage in the United States in Relation to Farm Population and to Certain Livestock Enterprises," RG 83, NARS.
[13] Wilson to Soule (May 14, 1931), Wilson MSS.

Capitalizing on the current discussion about land planning, Wilson did not hesitate to mention to Montana congressmen that the Christgau bill provided a basis for agricultural planning in the United States. To Democratic Congressman John M. Evans from Missoula, Wilson noted that Christgau was an agricultural economist and had almost completed his doctor's degree at the University of Minnesota before going to Congress. His bill had received wide acclaim among agricultural economists and had been endorsed by the Montana Farm Bureau Federation at its meeting the previous winter.[14] While pushing the Christgau bill and land-planning idea among congressmen, Wilson also moved to put the projected Land Planning Conference onto the calendar of events at the University of Chicago in the late summer of 1931.

As the summer progressed, he became the prime mover in organizing the conference and persuaded his former Montana associate, Professor E. A. Duddy of the University of Chicago School of Commerce and Administration, to issue invitations. In a letter of invitation to C. L. Holmes in the Bureau of Agricultural Economics, Duddy explained that those who attended were asked to come as individuals and not as representatives of any organization to which they might belong. He told Holmes that the conference was to be kept small to facilitate free and open exchanges of opinion, and also that it was not a publicity stunt. Uncertain as to the exact object of the conference, Duddy said that discussion topics were to be broad with the intent that leaders would open up specific problems involved. "If I interpret correctly," said Duddy, "the purpose of the conference is to find what ideas must be dealt with, what problems are of significance, what methods of working out plans may be useful in adjusting agriculture on some rational basis." Although Duddy sent out invitations, it was clear that he was somewhat confused on what ultimately was to develop from the conference.[15]

Economist Black responded cautiously to Duddy's invitation because he thought the University of Chicago professor had made the conference too large for any real accomplishment. Black wrote Wilson, "I am sorry that Duddy has made such a mess of your perfectly good idea." He wanted to be "absolutely certain" that

[14] Wilson to Evans (July 23, 1931), Wilson MSS.

[15] Duddy to Holmes (July 9, 1931), RG 83 NARS; Howard Tolley, Columbia Oral History Collection, Columbia University, New York, N.Y.

Wilson was going to attend the Chicago meeting because he did not want to take time out to go to Chicago and "listen to a bunch of papers in which various people will say certain things which they have already said before." Black proposed that Wilson select about fifteen people to be asked quietly during the conference to stay over for one or two additional days and shape a definite program of action to put up to Congress, the state legislatures, and the federal Farm Board in the ensuing year. "I nominate you as Chairman of this Committee," wrote Black to Wilson, and he suggested that it be known as the Committee of Fifteen. He warned that it must be made up entirely of people outside of the Bureau of Agricultural Economics and the federal Farm Board. The Department of Agriculture would help the committee behind the scenes.[16]

Farmers in the Northwest were rapidly losing hope of help from any source as drought ravaged the Dakotas and Montana. Like Wilson in Montana, Bowden noticed a receding of radical sentiment instead of a new outburst as conditions worsened in North Dakota. The farmer was too numbed by the "unspeakable drought conditions" and could not find words to make his voice heard in politics as he had in the years before. The weather conditions seemed to have subdued him to the point that he could not waste the effort in "forensic exercises" blaming the government, the grain trade, or Russia for his predicament. His first concern was to make it through the coming winter with food and shelter for his family.[17]

In South Dakota, Sherman E. Johnson, head of the Department of Agricultural Economics at South Dakota State College in Brookings, estimated that nearly half of the counties in the state would need outside aid to survive the winter. "The state and county governments are in a pretty sad financial condition and the only way out which I can see is for federal aid," he wrote Wilson. President C. W. Pugsley of the South Dakota State College suggested to Secretary Hyde that the Farm Board use some of its surplus wheat in loans, gifts, or sales for livestock and human food in drought- and grasshopper-stricken sections of the Northwest. Referring to the growing disillusionment with the Farm Board, Pugsley wrote, "I am certain that nothing would do more to clear the atmosphere here concerning the Farm Board and at the same time do a needed

[16] Black to Wilson (July 20, 1931), Wilson MSS.
[17] Bowden to Wilson (June 23, 1931), Wilson MSS.

and useful service." Hyde replied that the Farm Board could not make gifts under the terms of the law and it would take authorization from Congress.[18]

Montanans also planned to make a bid for outside help. Wilson explained that the strategy would involve a tour by himself and Montana Governor John E. Erikson of all the drought counties in the state. Spokesmen in these counties would present their stories of woe to the state committee in open meetings. Hopefully this would develop the belief that the state government was putting forth its best efforts, and in reply the governor and college officials planned to outline the establishment of a state relief committee to gather all possible funds in the state and from county committees. The organization would resemble the one established during the war and later distress period. In other words, said Wilson, "We want to convince the outside world, both the Red Cross and the government that we are bleeding ourselves right in state support before we are asking outside aid." After this accomplishment they intended to spring a large number of specific proposals to aid the situation in the state through outside help. Wilson admitted that most of his work in the summer and fall would have to be devoted to relief work in the drought areas. In July he foresaw five to six thousand families receiving public aid by the winter, but asked that these figures not be discussed publicly.[19]

Northern Nebraska also felt the whiplash of drought and grasshoppers in the summer of 1931. Governor Charles Bryan responded in characteristic fashion by declaring that Nebraskans would aid Nebraskans in the crisis without help from outside. During the winter of 1931–1932 the "more favored sections of Nebraska" sent 437 carloads of livestock feed and other supplies to the stricken areas of the states. Others in Nebraska felt these measures were inadequate. Glen B. Eastburn, Secretary of the Omaha Chamber of Commerce, wrote Senator Norris informing him that the board of directors recommended that Congress give consideration to agricultural rehabilitation in the territory of northern Nebraska. He said that the Red Cross and special committees set up by Governor Bryan

[18] Johnson to Wilson (July 28, 1931), Wilson MSS; Pugsley to Hyde (August 18, 1931); Hyde to Pugsley (August 25, 1931), RG 16, NARS.

[19] Wilson to Johnson (August 1, 1931); Wilson to Bowden (July 10, 1931), Wilson MSS.

were caring for the personal needs of the people, but no adequate steps, either federal or state, were planned for the rehabilitation of agriculture in the affected areas. "This is not only true of Nebraska but also South Dakota and some of the other western states," he said, making his plea for aid to Nebraska on a regional basis.[20]

In mid-July, Wilson reported to Black that a radical debt-repudiation movement was sweeping over North Dakota and was expected to hit Montana soon. He described the conditions in the two states as the "worst situation imaginable" resulting from the drought and the low prices which portend the "complete cave-in of agriculture." Hand in hand with increasing dimensions of the disaster came the brief flourishing of a blatantly Communistic movement on the northern plains. In June, Bowden reported from North Dakota that a Communist organization was gaining rapid headway in the northwest part of the state. By October, he said, the organization, called the United Farmers League, had 5,250 paid members in Sheridan, Daniels, and Roosevelt counties in Montana, and four northwest North Dakota counties. The league seemed to be gaining many of its members from people who were dropping from the ranks of the Farmers' Union.[21]

Wilson said that he did not detect any sweeping radical movement in Montana. A tremendous slump in morale during the past two months had not only hit the farmer but was perhaps worse with the businessmen, for they were "just as down in the mouth as farmers," wrote Wilson. Most Montanans remained in a dazed condition about the turn of events, but Wilson told of his recent visit to Plentywood, Montana, where the Communists were concentrating their efforts. He barely missed a demonstration and parade by the Communists on a visit to the northeast Montana town, but he was told there had been about two hundred and eighty in the parade. Many carried banners such as "No unemployment in Russia." Children bore signs reading "We do not want cast-off clothes from the Red Cross or charity," and others, "How are we

[20] *Nebraska Farmer*, February 20, 1932 (Lincoln, Nebraska); Eastburn to Norris (December 10, 1931), Tray 5, Box 2, Norris MSS, Library of Congress.

[21] Wilson to Black (July 15, 1931); Bowden to Wilson (June 29, 1931), and (October 16, 1931), Wilson MSS; John L. Shover, *Cornbelt Rebellion: The Farmers' Holiday Association* (Urbana: University of Illinois Press, 1965), pp. 69, 176–178.

going to have our candy for Christmas?" But businessmen in Plentywood reassured Wilson that they did not expect that "this movement of red flags will get very far." Wilson also observed that the Farmers' Union had come in for the greatest abuse from the new movement. By late October, Wilson had revised his figures on the number of families dependent on Red Cross aid upward to ten thousand over his estimate of five to six thousand previously. The bright spot that Wilson saw in the stunned and helpless atmosphere in Montana was a growing interest in the development of a national plan for land utilization.

This hopeful conclusion no doubt helped Wilson justify taking time out from the emergency programs in the state to work on plans for the Land Planning Conference in Chicago through correspondence with Tolley, Black, Duddy, and others. He told Tolley that he was happy that the meeting was to be held at the University of Chicago and would not be under the watchful eye of the land-grant-college officials. Both he and Tolley agreed that they should cooperate with the land-grant-college men, but Wilson said, "Personally I am glad to see this thing developing outside of the Land Grant College bunch." This opinion reflected Wilson's view that the land-grant agricultural economists were too conservative and afraid of their superiors to take any positive action in working out and endorsing a comprehensive plan for national land planning. On August 25, Wilson informed Black that he would definitely attend the conference to be held September 7, 8, and 9, 1931.[22]

O. C. Stine recalled that from the outset there was confusion about the purpose of the conference. Was the conference to outline an agricultural policy? Or was it to consider how to develop a national agricultural policy? The meeting was not entirely composed of land-grant-college economists. John R. Commons, Henry A. Wallace, Rex Tugwell, and John Simpson of the Farmers' Union were also present. At the meeting Simpson voiced the opinion that he disapproved of "economists" gathering to formulate agricultural policy. He insisted that farmers should develop policy. Duddy explained that the idea for the conference grew out of the recent discussions on regional planning of agricultural production conducted by Tolley, Wilson, Black, and Englund. The conferees

[22] Wilson to Bowden (October 31, 1931); Wilson to Tolley (August 26, 1931); Wilson to Black (August 25, 1931), Wilson MSS.

heard papers on national agricultural policy, beginning with Black's paper on "The Problem of Determining an Economic Policy for American Agriculture," and ten papers later, concluding with Tolley's delivery on "Regional Planning for Agriculture."[23]

The official meeting, however, was not Wilson's central concern. During the meeting steps had been taken to ask a select number of those present to remain for a session the day after the formal adjournment of the conference. Later, Wilson made a confidential report on the session of "vigilantes" to Black, who was not in attendance. From the list of those asked to the meeting it appeared that only agricultural economists made up the committee. They included Edwin Nourse of the Brookings Institution, B. H. Hibbard of Cornell, W. E. Grimes of Kansas, Charles Stewart of Illinois, O. B. Jesness of Minnesota, Rex Willard of Washington State, H. C. Filley of Nebraska, W. G. Patton of Michigan, J. W. Tapp from the Bureau of Agricultural Economics, C. E. Bonnan from Texas, A. G. Black of Iowa State, and, of course, Wilson and Tolley. Wilson opened the discussion, which was held in a committee room of the LaSalle Hotel, by giving his views on the need and function of such a committee. He proposed that this be a permanent organization, and a motion was carried to that effect.

Discussion then turned to the function of the committee. Jesness suggested that it should be independently active, but should function in conjunction with the deans and the Land-Grant College Association. Wilson did not like the direction of this discussion because he and Tolley favored a more progressive committee completely independent from the restrictions of the Land-Grant College Association. He quickly cut off discussion and turned to other topics. On this point, however, he was keenly disappointed that Nourse and some others did not argue strongly for an independent committee. In a talk with Jesness afterward, Wilson detected that he was afraid to do anything without talking with Dean W. C. Coffee of the Minnesota school. Most of the others, with the possible exception of Hibbard and A. G. Black, had reservations about acting without consulting with their respective deans. Still, Wilson hoped that through correspondence in the future the consent of the committee

[23] Stine, COHC; Tolley, COHC; *Conference on Economic Policy for American Agriculture*, ed. Edward A. Duddy (Chicago: University of Chicago Press, 1932).

could be secured on propositions developed and put before them without the undue conservative influence of the deans' intervening to paralyze the committee's effectiveness.

Charles Stewart tried to dominate discussion with the subject of export debenture, but Wilson and Tolley successfully sidetracked him and switched attention to Tolley's proposal for planning and the Christgau bill. Grimes thought experimental farming and experimental research foundations should be struck from the bill. Tolley replied supporting this measure with as much modesty and grace as possible regarding his own proposal. Wilson said he also came to its support without, as chairman, becoming a propagandist. The group was even less responsive on this subject than on the land question, and Wilson said, "I doubt if many in that group really have much conception of the significance of the readjustment proposal."

The meeting turned attention to the Outlook program, whose funds had been greatly curtailed by the administration in the last year. Protest against this action was not nearly as vigorous as Wilson expected "from a group of this kind meeting as a committee of vigilantes." It was agreed that a specific Outlook bill should be drafted that would contain definite authority and funds for Outlook operations on a permanent basis. Wilson closed his communication to Black with a second request for suggestions on the two land bills to be drafted and for any suggestions on strategy in eventually achieving the legislation. In summation, Wilson felt that the Chicago conference had been worth the effort, but "was a little disappointed that the committee of fourteen didn't have more pep." Wilson's group of "vigilantes" turned out to be little more than a group of cautious academics.[24]

In reviewing the work of the committee for Tolley, Wilson relayed John R. Commons' opinion, which had been expressed to Wilson, "that the difficulty with this bunch of agricultural economists is that their salaries come from the public and therefore, they lack the snap and drive to do something." Commons also said that such a group had little conception of strategy and accomplishment. Intellectually, Commons believed that the Chicago gathering would rate high, but he could not escape the conclusion that there was not much action in them. Tolley and Wilson were in agreement on this point and felt they were afraid of their deans and the Land-Grant

[24] Wilson to Black (September 16, 1931), Wilson MSS.

College Association. Wilson expressed a similar belief to Eric Englund regarding the members of the vigilante group and the "distinct fear complex with reference to their superiors." [25]

Although the conference at the University of Chicago put forth elaborate theories about land reform, Wilson was interested in translating theory into practical accomplishments through legislative action. From the do-nothing atmosphere of agricultural economist circles, he turned to the farm organizations. By the first of November, Wilson informed Grimes that he had made encouraging contacts with the executive committee of the National Grange. Wilson's friend, A. S. Goss, Master of the Washington State Grange and "one of the most able members of the executive committee," told him that the Grange had been thinking along the line of land planning also and was interested in obtaining sound advice from economists in forming a bill on the subject. Goss said they had thought about asking the economists in the large eastern universities but had overlooked the agricultural economists in the state colleges. Both he and L. J. Taber, Grand Master of the National Grange, said they were sorry they had been unable to attend the Chicago conference. Goss became enthusiastic about a connection between the grange and the agricultural economists. Wilson quoted what Goss outlined to him as a pattern of action for the economists to pursue through the farm organizations. Goss said:

> I think that you are very scientific and technical men, but the power for action resides with the farm organizations and the farmers and I think that we can take your material and put it through to the dirt farmers in a way which will translate itself into national policy.

Wilson also indicated to Grimes that despite forewarnings against it, he was going to contact the Farmers' Union for support of a new land policy bill. In his judgment the Farmers' Union played an important role in representing the left wing of the agricultural community. Although Wilson feared the union's policies on many issues, he was not as prejudiced against it as some officials in the state colleges, because "I think if they should go out of existence something else would replace them by another name." In

[25] Wilson to Tolley (September 17, 1931); Wilson to Englund (September 17, 1931), Wilson MSS.

northeastern Montana and northwestern North Dakota the organization of the other name was the United Farmers League that showed ominous signs of success where the union's membership dropped. Grimes concurred with Wilson's apprehensions about the Farmers' Union and hoped that the present leadership would soon be ousted by the challenge of H. G. Keeney of Nebraska and his supporters from Kansas.[26]

In a belated report to editor Soule of the *New Republic* on the actions of the committee that met after the Chicago conference, Wilson said that the first recommendation was the formation of a bill to repeal the Homestead Act. Although land fit for homesteading no longer existed, the bill would serve to attract publicity and create national discussion as a forerunner for a land policy bill to follow. "Also the passage of such a bill would automatically close one period of land policy as far as this country is concerned," Wilson emphasized. In addition it was decided to make the Christgau bill much narrower in scope by cutting out many of the appropriation features on the assumption that nothing requiring appropriations could be approved by Congress. Still, the planning aspect through the establishment of regional planning boards and the cooperation of the state colleges was retained.

Most important in pushing land planning, the committee decided to stay undercover and out of the public eye. They preferred to sell themselves and ideas to farm organizations such as the federal Farm Bureau, the National Grange, and possibly the National Farmers' Union, and work as specialists in conjunction with them. This plan would require them to keep in the background and be heard only through these organizations. Wilson said that he had discussed the matter with members of the executive committee of the Farm Bureau and the Grange, and "I am in hopes that we will be able a little later on to effect a kind of arrangement which will be very satisfactory to us." He concluded by saying that he was certain that any editorial comments on agriculture by Soule in the *New Republic* would bring support to the "program of the Agricultural Economists."[27]

[26] Wilson to Grimes (November 2, 1931); Grimes to Wilson (November 10, 1931), Wilson MSS.

[27] Wilson to Soule (November 3, 1931), Wilson MSS.

Wilson lost no time in gaining the cooperation of the Montana State Farm Bureau as a vehicle for action at the national level. From the college he wrote to W. L. Stockton, now vice-president of the Montana organization, asking him to sign a letter written by Wilson to the Secretary of Agriculture. The letter urged the secretary to restore slashed funds to the Outlook and agricultural forecasting service in the department. Confidentially Wilson wrote to Stockton, "Our engineer friend in the White House has shut out the department from carrying out this work." He said they wanted to bring pressure on the Secretary of Agriculture and were therefore asking Stockton to rewrite the attached letter on his letterhead and sign it as vice-president of the Montana Farm Bureau Federation. Wilson concluded his request by saying that Stockton should not do this if he was not in agreement with the contents of the letter. This communication with Stockton marks the beginning of a long series of letters drafted by Wilson and sent to Stockton for the state Farm Bureau letterhead and Stockton's signature. In the following months these letters spread information and gathered opinions regarding the domestic allotment plan.[28]

Wilson's contact with the Farm Bureau extended beyond the Montana organization. In December, 1931, he was billed as a principal speaker at the annual meeting of the National Federation of American Farm Bureaus in Chicago. His speech to two hundred and fifty delegates dealt with land planning, but he was certain that the ideas "went over the heads of half or perhaps two-thirds of the listeners." The new president of the bureau, Edward O'Neal, made favorable comments on the subject of a revised land policy, but also laid emphasis on the equalization fee and the immediate elevation of the price level. Henry Wallace, who attended the meeting, also complimented Wilson on his speech, but beyond this Wilson was convinced that he had not reached many at the meeting with his message.[29]

While Wilson pursued a reform in the country's land policy through the summer and fall, he also continued a subtle propaganda campaign for the domestic allotment plan. In response to a communication from Wilson on the domestic allotment proposal, I. M.

[28] Wilson to Stockton (November 3, 1931), Wilson MSS.
[29] Wilson to Tolley (December 12, 1931), Wilson MSS.

Branjord, Commissioner of Lands in Montana, said that if present prices lasted for a few more years, the wheat growers of the Northwest would be ruined and with them every other line of business. "It is up to the northwest to see to it that something fundamental is done in regard to the price of grain," he said. Branjord said he had always looked to the agricultural college "as the source of salvation of our agriculture," and was glad that Wilson had some faith in the domestic allotment plan. But the Northwest must move solidly behind one relief plan or face paralysis, he advised Wilson.[30]

Stockton also drafted letters in behalf of the Black plan explaining to his friends in the Farm Bureau why he now supported it instead of the previous equalization fee. In a letter to the secretary of the American Farm Bureau Federation, he maintained that the Black plan was far superior to the equalization fee because of the present depressed conditions of the world market. If foreign countries would not buy American wheat, it was impossible to achieve results through the equalization fee, he contended. Also he did not think opposition to the Black plan from the President would be as predetermined as with the equalization fee. He concentrated on these two arguments: (1) world conditions made the abandonment of the equalization fee imperative, and (2) the Black plan would be more palatable to the opposition. "If they objected to the Black plan, it would simply mean they were coming out in the open and saying that the farmer was not expected to get the benefit of the tariff," was Stockton's analysis of the situation.[31]

Despite reservations, Wilson did not neglect to present the plan to John A. Simpson. In his letter to Simpson, Wilson attributed the plan's origin to Dr. Spillman's work in the Department of Agriculture and avoided playing up the role of the Harvard economist Black in its further development. "I have never understood why it was," said Wilson, "that the farm organizations have not at least given some thought and study to Dr. Spillman's proposals." The plan, he explained to Simpson, accomplished the same end as the export debenture or the equalization fee, but at the same time acreage would not increase because of higher prices under this plan. Wilson emphasized Spillman's role and attempted to justify his

[30] Branjord to Wilson (August 14, 1931), Wilson MSS.
[31] Stockton to Winder (August 15, 1931), Wilson MSS.

propagandizing the plan because of his earlier close association with Spillman:

> I went over the plan many times with Dr. Spillman, who was at one time my superior officer and I, therefore, think I am as well qualified as any living person now to know what was in his mind.

Wilson obviously knew that Simpson would raise suspicious questions about his advocacy of the plan and about interest groups who were prompting Wilson to bring this to the attention of farm leaders and the general public. He therefore took this opportunity to point out his close association with Spillman and to portray himself as the intellectual heir of the plan after Spillman's death in early 1931.[32]

Although Wilson had opened the avenues of communication on the domestic allotment plan with the Grange, the Farmers' Union, and the Farm Bureau, he feared that they would revert to sponsoring various forms of the export debenture and the equalization fee. If they did this, he was convinced "that nothing will come out of the whole affair." He thought the three organizations should compromise on the domestic allotment, and "if they put up a united front, I think there is considerable chance that they might be able to get it over at this session of Congress." On this hopeful note Wilson asked Stockton to write Winder again about the issue, but cautioned Stockton not to mention Wilson, "because I do not want Winder to become too suspicious that I am a propagandist on the domestic allotment."[33]

Before the year ended, the domestic allotment plan received an unexpected boost from an influential source. In late November Henry I. Harriman, president-elect of the National Chamber of Commerce and New England hydro-electric magnate, disclosed his support of the domestic allotment for agriculture to Wilson. In extensive conferences with Professor Black and talks with Wilson on the Agricultural Committee of the National Chamber of Commerce, Harriman became convinced that there must be government interference to balance the supply and demand of the market forces. If

[32] Wilson to Simpson (September 14, 1931), Wilson MSS.
[33] Wilson to Stockton (September 14, 1931), Wilson MSS.

this must occur for agriculture, he believed that the domestic allotment was "probably the wisest course and comes quite near doing for agriculture what the tariff does for industry." Harriman's declared support of the domestic allotment would prove invaluable for Wilson's use in the coming year as he corresponded with business interests throughout the country for a sympathetic consideration of this new farm recovery plan.[34]

The year 1931 witnessed activity in agriculture on two fronts. One movement visualized land reform as a long-range solution, especially through the elimination of marginal wheat areas. The other was a search for a more immediate measure of relief from low prices through the device of a domestic allotment plan. These two levels of action that were to characterize many of the New Deal programs—one aimed at immediate relief and recovery and the other at broad reforms in the system that had unwittingly led to disaster—already took shape before the formal attempts by the Roosevelt administration. As the emergency in the country heightened, interest shifted from the broader goals of institutionalized reform to the more immediate demands that required an available and viable relief plan. In foreshadowing these two levels of action in the New Deal, Wilson now turned more of his efforts to the relief promised by the domestic allotment.

[34] Harriman to Wilson (November 24, 1931), Wilson MSS.

CHAPTER SEVEN

M. L. Wilson: Apostle of the Domestic Allotment

It is a finished product and not something which has just bobbed up out of the Montana sagebrush.—M. L. Wilson

An apostle has been defined as one who first advocates a great moral reform. Theodore Saloutos has used this term regarding M. L. Wilson's role in promoting the domestic allotment plan in the months leading up to the 1932 presidential campaign.[1] Wilson was a reformer, but he did not regard the domestic allotment plan as a reform in the same sense as he viewed a fundamental alteration of the nation's land policy. The Montana professor in 1931 did not give the domestic allotment plan the priority he attached to a land readjustment policy. The domestic allotment plan commanded his complete attention only when it became apparent that a broad land reform could not pass Congress and would not meet the emergency situation. Now the domestic allotment program moved to the forefront of his interests, but not as a reform. It was an emergency measure designed to achieve in a speedy manner the ultimate goals of a studied land reform policy. Wilson's ideas on American agricultural policy and rural life were too broad-gauged to be satisfied with the achievement of an emergency measure for agricultural relief. There is little wonder that at the beginning of 1932 the question of a new land policy still lay heavily on his mind.

In early January of the new year Wilson learned from John M. Evans, the new Democratic chairman of the House Committee on Public Lands, that he did not believe there would be any legislation with reference to land matters in the present session of Congress.

[1] Theodore Saloutos, "William A. Hirth: Middle Western Agrarian," *Mississippi Valley Historical Review*, XXXVIII (September, 1951), 229.

The congressman felt there were such wide differences of opinion in western states regarding land policy that "nothing will come out of it." Wilson described Evans as a "kind of Jacksonian democrat and as a matter of principal [*sic*] . . . opposed to most kinds of governmental activity." On this basis he would be opposed to a bill calling for government purchase of land, but he informed Wilson that should Governor Roosevelt make it a cornerstone of Democratic party policy, "he might modify this view a great deal" and become a Democratic politician first and a man of principle second. This event began to emphasize the important role that Roosevelt's personality and attitudes would play in shaping any future agricultural legislation, if he became the Democratic candidate.[2]

Reacting to the general antiappropriations sentiment in Congress, Wilson entered into correspondence with Tolley to revise the Christgau bill along lines of less appropriation requirements. "It is my judgment it should be made a planning measure without much appropriation attached thereto," said Wilson. Winder of the Farm Bureau reported that the organization's support for the bill would be forthcoming as soon as they began action on their secondary legislation. The bureau intended to concentrate front-line efforts in this session of Congress on monetary stabilization, equalization fee, and support of the Farm Board. After this they would turn attention to land policy and planning. Wilson also looked forward to a session with National Farm Bureau President Edward O'Neal in Bozeman later in the month.[3]

Black, too, devoted some thought to a revision of the Christgau bill to avoid asking Congress for extensive appropriations. He told Wilson that a considerable part of what the bill proposed could be accomplished without special legislation. This could be done through cooperation between various state and federal agencies and interested semiprivate and private agencies in the regions. For example, Black said, "Why should you not set about establishing in the spring wheat area of the United States a regional readjustment committee." It could be composed of representatives of the land-grant colleges, leading bankers, leading farm editors, railroad executives, and probably some of the central marketing interests handling spring wheat in the territory. One of the first jobs of the

[2] Wilson to Black (January 8, 1932), Wilson MSS.
[3] *Ibid.*

agency would be to divide the spring wheat area into types-of-farming areas. Then meetings could be held in each of the type-of-farming areas to work out the readjustments that seemed to be most promising under the particular set of conditions prevailing in the different areas. These results would then be used as a basis for some of the Outlook and Extension programs in the territory. After a season's experience along this line, said Black, the regional readjustment committee could meet and carry forth work for larger programs, "including recommendations for changes in land utilization and programs to carry it out." The larger problems could also include details for a plan of production control in the area.[4]

In response to the Black suggestion of voluntary regional councils, Wilson replied that he had considered voluntary schemes for three years and "we have made three voluntary attempts and each have failed." Wilson explained that from 1926 to 1929 there had been a four-state regional range livestock project involving cooperation among North Dakota, South Dakota, Wyoming, and Montana. It failed because of the inability of both economists and administrative officers to see the regional economic unity of this problem and overlook state lines. A similar failure occurred in 1931 when Frank E. Murphy, publisher of the *Minneapolis Tribune*, invited the deans, directors, and upon Wilson's suggestion, the agricultural economists of the four states to spend two days at his summer estate near Detroit Lakes for the discussion of common problems in the states. At the conference Wilson suggested that the economists of the four states meet in the near future to work out a readjustment program for the spring wheat areas, "but the proposition didn't get to first base."[5]

Dean W. C. Coffey of Minnesota said his state could not participate because it was not in the wheat belt. Dean Christian Larsen for South Dakota said, "South Dakota had no business being in the spring wheat belt and . . . should go into dairying." Director P. F. Trowbridge for North Dakota was favorably disposed, but thought the undertaking was too great, according to Wilson. The only agreement that could be achieved was on a suggestion from Dean Coffey that all present should think about it and that they could discuss it at a conference in the following years. "Now it is

[4] Black to Wilson (January 12, 1932), Wilson MSS.
[5] Wilson to Black (January 30, 1932), Wilson MSS.

because of these kind of discouragements that I am pretty conservative on the proposal," said Wilson in reference to Black's earlier proposal for voluntary regional councils, "and have come to the conclusion that but little progress will be made until this kind of thing is financed from a definite specific source and there is definite machinery to help it along." Later Black replied that Wilson had convinced him that voluntary organization of a spring wheat regional readjustment committee would be impossible without outside leadership and financing.[6]

Wilson was already at work planning new tactics to reintroduce the Christgau bill in Congress. He wrote Christgau in mid-January suggesting three steps for him to follow that involved streamlining the original bill and the introduction of two new bills. First, Wilson called for a bill to repeal the Homestead and Public Land Alienation Act in a grandstand play to capture publicity. Second, he envisioned a new land policy bill that would provide for the acquisition of public lands through the purchase of marginal lands by the federal government. Third, he planned the introduction of a new Christgau bill following these moves. Wilson admitted to Christgau that there had been much indecision in his mind on whether to reintroduce the bill as a production readjustment bill or "whether we should be frank about it and call it a bill to provide for national agricultural planning." The regional research councils would then be called agricultural planning councils and work under a general national agricultural planning council. The real issue, as far as Wilson was concerned, was reintroduction with the experimental farming sections deleted and consequent lower request for funds or a recasting of the bill as a purely agricultural planning measure. In the West, Wilson expected opposition to any planning program for agriculture when he said, "There will be some kick back on this from the west but it is good medicine, nevertheless."[7]

To his friends in the business world, Wilson also had to defend his planning ideas about American agriculture. Fletcher charged that such a concept was similar to what they had witnessed in Russian

[6] *Ibid.*; Black to Wilson (February 6, 1932), Wilson MSS; The regional problem approach came into use later in 1936 when the Great Plains Council was organized with representatives from ten colleges and other agencies participating.

[7] Wilson to Christgau (January 19, 1932), Wilson MSS.

agriculture. But Wilson answered that he did not see any connection between the kind of planning that he stood for and that was being developed in the American economy, and the Russian system with its kind of planning. "They are entirely two different things," Wilson emphasized to this businessman who was fearful of government intervention into the economy. [8]

By this time Wilson was sufficiently involved in agricultural legislation for the wheat areas that political representatives from the cotton South deemed him important enough to contact for support of a proposed cotton relief bill. Senator John Bankhead of Alabama submitted his cotton bill to Wilson for study and pointed out that it set up machinery for cotton producers to agree by vote upon the quantity of cotton to be marketed each year with accompanying enforcement provisions. Bankhead said that the solution to cotton's problems hinged on the reduction of the surplus which could only be handled by national action rather than state attempts at uniform acreage-reduction programs. He hoped to prompt action on the bill in time to govern that year's cotton crop and urged Wilson and his friends to write their senators and congressmen in support of the Bankhead cotton bill. Wilson, however, did not stand in a good position to convert such senators as Burton K. Wheeler to production control. Ezekiel reported from Washington, "Your Wheeler is dead against acreage reduction—doesn't think it will work. Can you get some farmer to write him in favor of it?" These requests indicate that Wilson's name was associated with those groups advocating restricted production to improve the market for American agricultural goods. [9]

Similarly, Harriman of the National Chamber of Commerce and Gerard Swope, president of the General Electric Company, advocated restricted production for industry in hearings before the LaFollette Committee on the establishment of a National Economic Council. LaFollette attacked Harriman for proposing the establishment of monopoly prices in the market. Wilson did not believe this was the Harriman position, but thought that the businessman's response to the economic crisis was "a reaction both of idealism and fear" and that these proposals were based on the "greatest

[8] Wilson to Fletcher (January 18, 1932), Wilson MSS.

[9] Bankhead to Wilson (January 23, 1932); Ezekiel to Wilson (January 25, 1932), Wilson MSS.

good for the greatest number and not in terms of restricted monopolistic markets." Wilson did draw some satisfaction from LaFollette's railings against Harriman: "In a way I am glad that LaFollette is attacking Harriman because this will be prima facie evidence that the Harriman report is not radical stuff." This preserved the usefulness of Harriman's name when Wilson mentioned him as a strong supporter of the domestic allotment plan to conservative businessmen.[10]

In turning his attention to the domestic allotment plan Wilson scanned carefully the role that the Montana State Farm Bureau could play in a future promotional campaign. He could be sure of vice-president Stockton's support, but he knew that president W. S. McCormick would at best be indifferent to such a complicated proposal. In its annual January meeting, however, the Montana State Farm Bureau, after a presentation of the domestic allotment plan, passed a resolution asking the National Farm Bureau to investigate the merits of the plan as a compromise between the equalization fee and the debenture. At this same meeting Ed O'Neal, president of the National Farm Bureau Federation, told Wilson frankly that the bureau now had no intention of backing readjustments in production, planning, or purchase of lands by the government while their program for winning approval of the equalization fee or debenture was pending. In his speech to the state meeting O'Neal stated that there was no surplus production of either wheat or cotton and the only problem in American agriculture was in making the tariff effective on exportable commodities.

Privately O'Neal apologized for the "rawness with which he made these statements," but said he could not consistently support the debenture or equalization fee as a solution on the one hand and acreage adjustment on the other. Wilson observed that he felt O'Neal was totally politically minded and did not have the understanding or philosophy of Winder, secretary of the National Farm Bureau. O'Neal did admit that "our ideas about acreage adjustment, planning . . . were not so bad but as far as the Washington strategy of the Farm Bureau was concerned they would have to come after the

[10] Wilson to J. S. Crutchfield, president of the American Fruit Growers Association, Pittsburgh, Pennsylvania (January 15, 1932), Wilson MSS; *Senate Hearings*, Subcommittee of the Committee on Manufactures, 72d Cong., 1st sess. S. 6215, pp. 172–173.

main show." Under close questioning O'Neal showed himself almost completely ignorant of the provisions of the domestic allotment plan. After some embarrassment, he confessed that he had never discussed the plan intelligently with anyone before the meeting in Montana. He requested five copies of the chapter reprint from *Agricultural Reform* for a special study committee and told Wilson before he boarded the train that "it really sounded pretty good to him" after thinking it over during the day. Before parting Wilson argued that agricultural planning would have to go hand in hand with any scheme of this kind. In addition Wilson told him bluntly that "he would not get very far with the equalization fee or debenture, in case they passed, until he would have to get over into the planning aspects." Attendance at the state meeting showed that the strength of the bureau in the state had dwindled. There were only about six or seven counties represented and at no time was any statement made about the number of paid members.[11]

Somewhat appalled at O'Neal's ignorance of the domestic allotment plan and the planning approach to agriculture, Wilson wrote Grimes proposing the creation of a small committee of economists to analyze, criticize, and "report from an economics point of view on national programs" to the Farm Bureau and the Grange. In strict confidence Wilson told Grimes that one of the national officers of these organizations had informed him that there was great need for economic education among the small group of men who ran these two organizations. "Economic education is not exactly the word to use," said Wilson, "rather it is education of these men to the point of view of agricultural economics towards their problems." This particular farm organization man, however, expressed disappointment in his contacts with agricultural economists and "said in general they were quite academic and not much in sympathy with the rough and tumble state of affairs in the realistic farm organization world." Wilson said that he had given the matter some thought since the Chicago meeting in September and had come to the conclusion that a small group of five to ten economists should be formed to carry on aggressive contacts with the national organizations "to get together and formulate a platform." Grimes replied that he agreed that a small committee of

[11] Wilson to Stockton (January 13, 1932); Wilson to Black (January 30, 1932); Wilson to Bowden (January 30, 1932), Wilson MSS.

economists could work well with the national farm organizations and said, "It is encouraging to know that you think there is a possibility that this could be done." [12]

Meanwhile, businessman Harriman wanted immediate action from the farm economists. "I think it is high time that the farm economists developed the Domestic Allotment plan into a simple bill," he wrote Wilson in mid-February. He believed that Congress was eager to find a way out and feared they would blunder into adopting the export debenture or the equalization fee, "if you people who have been thinking straight on this matter don't formulate your plan in the very near future," he warned Wilson. Harriman pledged his support, but qualified it by saying, "I cannot pretend to know half as much about the subject as do the rest of you." Wilson returned the compliment to the business community by objecting to Senator Robert LaFollette's current attack on the chamber's planning board bill. LaFollette contended that it was fundamentally an attempt to limit production in order to maintain profits to investors. According to Wilson this was neither here nor there, and he said: "It is my judgement that the best managerial brains of the country are in business and that progress has to be predicated upon these managerial brains rather than visionary idealistic schemes." He felt that the report of the chamber's committee on national planning represented a new attitude on the part of business leaders throughout the country and "I further have the feeling that it is possible to inject . . . this point of view into agriculture." [13]

In a few days Wilson began an active campaign for the domestic allotment plan with the Farm Bureau organizations of the Midwest and Far West. He undertook the promotional drive in an anonymous fashion, however. The letters that he wrote were mailed out bearing the letterhead of the Montana State Farm Bureau and the signature of W. L. Stockton, vice-president of the state organization. The letters went to the following officials in state organizations: Charles E. Hearst, president, Iowa State Farm Bureau; Ralph Snyder, president, Kansas Farm Bureau; R. W. Blackburn, president, California Farm Bureau; George Stalling, president, Utah Farm Bureau; Earl

[12] Wilson to Grimes (February 5, 1932); Grimes to Wilson (February 10, 1932), Wilson MSS.

[13] Harriman to Wilson (February 16, 1932); Wilson to Harriman (February 18, 1932), Wilson MSS.

C. Smith, president, Illinois Agricultural Association; Troy Lindley, president, Washington Farm Bureau; William Taylor, vice-president, Indiana Farm Bureau; L. B. Palmer, president, Ohio State Farm Bureau; R. W. Brown, president, Missouri State Farm Bureau; Frank P. First, president, Texas State Farm Bureau; P. P. Cedar, president, Nebraska State Farm Bureau; William Settle, president, Indiana Farm Bureau.[14]

To his friend Louis Clarke, who was director of the Kolke Investment Company in Omaha and active in the farm mortgage business, Wilson wrote that it was necessary "to keep the farm element in the forefront on this move otherwise we are in danger of getting a flare-up from the farm organizations." Wilson had a great deal of faith in this gesture and believed the organizations would soon see the futility of working for the equalization and the debenture plans and felt that the domestic allotment was "an excellent means of getting together a compromise." But Wilson was also aware that businessmen as well as farmers would be needed to support the plan. The first was George L. Holmes, president of the First National Bank in Lincoln and also a member of the Chamber of Commerce Agricultural Committee. The second was A. J. Tabb, president of the South Omaha Livestock Exchange. Wilson wanted his name left unmentioned in contacting these men because they might question Wilson's place on the Chamber of Commerce Agricultural Committee if they knew he was carrying on a promotional campaign.[15]

In early March, Wilson already envisioned a national meeting of the supporters of the domestic allotment to be held by the first of April. For the moment the urgency of the domestic allotment plan apparently had eclipsed land planning in Wilson's mind. To Harriman, Wilson explained that he had done the groundwork for such a conference with the farm organization people through correspondence, "particularly in the northwest." He cautioned Harriman that businessmen must not be too aggressive in their support of the domestic allotment plan, for "they would be apt to develop an intense animosity on the part of the farm groups, who are essential if there is to be any legislation." Always eager to find a consensus, Wilson

[14] Wilson to Black (February 20, 1932); Wilson to Stockton (February 25, 1932), Wilson MSS.

[15] Wilson to Clarke (March 5, 1932); Wilson to Clarke (February 23, 1932), Wilson MSS.

also saw support for the allotment developing among many agrarian fundamentalists. William Hirth of Columbia, Missouri, editor of the *Missouri Farmer*, head of the Missouri Farmers Association and formerly one of the "irreconcilables" on the McNary-Haugen issue, came out "flat footedly for the allotment plan," said Wilson. The National Farmers' Union, which Wilson called "a pretty wild crowd," was preaching an allotment gospel mixed with greenbacks, public ownership, and "a lot of other populism." Nevertheless they were condemning the Farm Board's stabilization attempts and suggesting that the allotment might work. "The significance of this," Wilson wrote Harriman, "is that if our plan could be pushed into the ring I do not believe that the National organization would fight us." In more conservative circles, he felt considerable support could be drawn from the state mortgage bankers associations.

Wilson named Chicago as the possible place for a meeting to be held within thirty days on the domestic allotment plan. He suggested that some officers and people from the farm organizations should be present, a few agriculturalists, some of the old McNary-Haugen endorsers, and a few businessmen who might be interested also. Wilson said that in his correspondence he was not as yet mentioning Harriman as a supporter of the plan, but only said that a number of men from the industrial world were interested in attending a meeting to discuss the feasibility of a domestic allotment bill. Wilson was greatly encouraged and said, "times are just getting right for our proposition which can be put over if there are enough of us who can unite by putting our shoulders to the wheel." [16]

Still Wilson toyed with the idea of creating a federal farm-land reserve through the withdrawal of submarginal lands from production. This had also been a proposal of James F. Bell, president of General Mills. In reference to Bell's proposal Wilson wrote him directing his attention to Black's domestic allotment plan. He pointed to the large number of supporters it was now attracting, especially among businessmen of the country, and to the real possibility that it would be introduced into Congress as a substitute for either the equalization fee or the debenture, "in which case it will attract national attention." A proposal in connection with this plan, which Wilson thought might be of special interest to Bell, was the proposal that the excise tax should be used for the purchasing and renting

[16] Wilson to Harriman (March 5, 1932), Wilson MSS.

of marginal or submarginal wheatland. As Wilson explained it, the proposal resembled closely Bell's original idea of a federal farm reserve that called for the productive lands of the United States to be contracted and particularly the wheatlands restricted. Elaborating on the philosophy of the domestic allotment approach, Wilson said that it rested, as far as wheat growers were concerned, on the philosophy underlying the trade association and antitrust law modifications.[17]

This approach, of course, called for a revision of the cutthroat competition that had always prevailed among agricultural producers. To other businessmen, like grain elevator man Walter McCarthy of Duluth, the land-purchasing scheme was the worst possible approach to aid agriculture. He said:

> I do not believe that merely because a business becomes unprofitable, it is necessary for the United States Government to buy the plant and put it out of production. If this were an equitable way of handling all businesses, Uncle Sam now would be the proud possessor of a lot of breweries, to say nothing of carriage and bustle factories.[18]

It was no secret that Governor Roosevelt's agricultural policy in New York State also involved the withdrawal of submarginal lands from production. The governor had talked of this approach to the agricultural problem in his speech before the annual Conference of Governors in 1931 at French Lick, Indiana. The speech attracted Wilson's attention in Montana, and in the spring of 1932 he requested copies of the text for a land economics seminar composed of representatives from different departments in the State government, organizations such as the Bankers' Association, State Farm Bureau, State Chamber of Commerce, and Range and Livestock Associations, which met four times a year for discussion of land utilization within the state. Before the meeting Wilson hoped to supply each representative with the best material on land utilization, and he requested copies of the governor's speech, entitled "Acres Fit and Unfit." He called the speech "a classic in its line" and also asked that a copy be sent to every county agricultural Extension agent in Montana. Concluding his letter of request, Wilson informed

[17] Wilson to James F. Bell (March 10, 1932), Wilson MSS.
[18] McCarthy to Wilson (March 19, 1932), Wilson MSS.

Roosevelt that he was held in the highest regard by the citizens of Montana.[19]

Outside of government in private enterprise Wilson attempted to convince businessmen of the wisdom of shifting American farm production to a purely domestic basis. He agreed the American commercial farmer could compete with all the world, but a state of free competition in the world markets did not exist and made it necessary to retreat to the domestic market. "No doubt we could compete with the world if we had a free and open field," he said. Wilson's belief in the efficiency doctrine had been shattered by the growth of nationalism in Europe, which he felt had changed the rules of the competitive game. It would be very difficult to compete effectively and be required to penetrate tariff walls of eighty cents on the bushel. This would require super-efficiency, in Wilson's opinion. Taking a hardheaded realistic approach that he thought would appeal to businessmen and advocates of the efficiency doctrine for solving the farm problem, Wilson said that like it or not the high tariff walls constituted the present political situation in European countries, and it was likely to continue for some time.

This was Wilson's argument against free competition and the efficiency doctrine on the international scene. In the domestic market he had come to the conclusion that free competition did not prevail either. Those who called for an unrestrictive, highly competitive agricultural society ignored the conditions in other sectors of the economy which certainly did not reflect a state of perfect competition. If the rest of the economic field was as individualistic and as highly competitive as agriculture, the strict efficiency doctrine might apply to agriculture. But, Wilson explained, "What we are getting is a controlled society in the industrial field and an uncontrolled competitive society in agriculture which is resulting in great agricultural impoverishment." As an example he pointed to figures showing that during the Depression, raw-material prices from competitive fields such as agricultural production declined far more than other fixed-price commodities. He criticized some business views on the present economic crisis because they overlooked what Wilson

[19] Franklin D. Roosevelt Library, Record Group 12, M. L. Wilson to Roosevelt (March 11, 1932); see also Gertrude Almy Slichter, "Franklin D. Roosevelt and the Farm Problem, 1929–1932," *Mississippi Valley Historical Review*, XLIII (September, 1956), 238–258; Bernard Bellush, *Franklin D. Roosevelt as Governor of New York* (New York: Columbia University Press, 1955), p. 84.

called perfect competition in the field of agriculture and the state of limited competition that existed in industry. In this light, he predicted continued social and political disturbances in agriculture until another temporary balance was achieved.[20]

While Wilson carried on these highly theoretical arguments with some of his business friends, he was also taking practical and concrete steps toward bringing the domestic allotment to the attention of influential men in agricultural politics. Through Stockton he carried on a large correspondence and sent out invitations for a projected Chicago conference on the domestic allotment plan in mid-April. He was particularly happy to have a contact with the insurance and mortgage dealer, Clarke, in Omaha. He told Clarke, "I think you are in a very strategic position as far as the insurance companies and the mortgage groups is concerned and also as far as the middle west is concerned."[21]

A week later, on March 22, 1932, Clarke wrote George Peek calling his attention to the domestic allotment plan and requesting Peek's comments on the proposal. Earlier, Clarke had written R. R. Rogers, head of the Prudential Farm Mortgage Department, requesting his attendance at the Chicago domestic allotment conference. Clarke also expected to have a meeting soon with the manager of Hearst's *Omaha Bee-News*. He hoped to interest him in the allotment plan and in turn have the manager plug the plan with Hearst. Clarke said that if Hearst could be sold on the proposition, "It would be a grand thing, because, believe me, he has power, with all his papers, and when he is sold on a proposition he certainly keeps hammering away each and every day."[22]

Chester Davis, the old McNary-Haugen warhorse, felt that the domestic allotment plan looked better than any of the other proposals, but he said he was a "little bit skeptical of getting much steam behind any farm relief proposal in the light of the Farm Board fiasco." Davis did suggest that if Wilson were going to go through with the domestic allotment conference that it would be wise to prepare a short and simple statement of the plan and how it would work. This statement should be distributed before the meeting and would induce more to come to the meeting if they felt they knew

[20] Wilson to Fletcher (March 11, 1932), Wilson MSS.
[21] Wilson to Clarke (March 15, 1932), Wilson MSS.
[22] Clarke to Peek (March 22, 1932), Peek MSS; Clarke to Wilson (March 14, 1932); Clarke to Wilson (March 22, 1932), Wilson MSS.

something of what it was about. Although the leaders of the Farm Bureau were going to put up a sham battle for the equalization fee or the debenture plan, Davis questioned the political wisdom of holding a domestic allotment conference without inviting them if they were to be lined up for the proposition later.[23]

Wilson also did not ignore Senator Bankhead's earlier communication regarding the cotton control bill. He told the senator from Alabama he appreciated receiving the information on a bill designed to control agricultural surplus production. He emphasized that he thought a great deal of the proposal and that coincidentally a number of people in Montana had been thinking along the same line regarding wheat. After this introduction, Wilson said he was taking the liberty of sending the senator a copy of a proposal called the domestic allotment plan which was gaining considerable headway in the spring wheat country, and he felt the fundamental thinking underlying this plan paralleled the senator's proposal. This was a tacit suggestion that perhaps at some point in the future cotton and wheat producers should conclude an alliance on a general farm program stressing production control.[24]

By the last of March, Wilson was in a position to write Clarke an extensive letter outlining the plans for the April conference in Chicago and general tactics in the next month. Wilson reported that the "latest dope on Domestic Allotment matters" was the planned meeting in Chicago at the LaSalle Hotel on either April 15 or 16. The official call for the meeting was going out over the signature of W. L. Stockton, vice-president of the Montana Farm Bureau Federation. Wilson thought Clarke would agree that the movement should ostensibly be launched by a farm group. He described Stockton as a graduate of the University of Nebraska in electrical engineering in the 1890's and talked of his twenty-year service with General Electric Company under Gerard Swope. About fifteen years earlier he had moved to Montana to operate a thousand-acre wheat ranch owned by Swope and had been president of the Montana Farm Bureau Federation for several years until he retired in 1968 to become vice-president.

Stockton was one of the original McNary-Haugen "enthusiasts" and fought for the idea from 1924 to its defeat in 1928. As a lifelong

[23] Davis to Wilson (March 15, 1932), Wilson MSS.
[24] Wilson to Bankhead (March 16, 1932), Wilson MSS.

Republican he left the party in 1928 and followed the McNary-Haugen group in their support of Smith. Wilson said that he was recounting this for Clarke because it had considerable bearing on the farm psychology that was to play an important part in the formation and successful passage of future farm legislation. In other words, he was showing that Stockton's history of participation in the McNary-Haugen struggles put him in good standing with the equalization-fee backers and the National Farm Bureau, and "they do not consider him as a traitor to their cause." With this background he made a good pivotal man around which to plan the domestic allotment meeting. The similarity between the allotment plan and the proposals for continuity and stability in business made by Swope and the United States Chamber of Commerce did not escape Wilson, and he admitted the business connection between Stockton and Swope might prove a delicate problem if some groups hostile to the domestic allotment got wind of the relationship.

Stockton's ranch was about sixty miles from Bozeman and he usually visited with Wilson once a week, during which time Wilson would submit letters for Stockton to sign and send out in support of the domestic allotment. Wilson hoped that others would understand that a "college professor can go about so far in such matters but it is unwise for him to get out to the point where he attempts to influence legislation." For this reason everything done in a public way for the domestic allotment conference would be done through the leadership or over the name of Stockton. "Confidentially, we have a perfect understanding and agreement with regard to this," Wilson told Clarke.[25]

To another party Wilson explained that Stockton asked the "College for my services in preparation of the bill with the understanding that the bill is the Farm Bureau bill and not the college bill." Wilson justified this by saying, "They [the Farm Bureau] are calling on the Economics Department for this assistance just the same as a farm organization might call upon the soils department or horticultural department for assistance with some problem within their field."[26]

[25] Robert George Raymer, *Montana: The Land and the People* (Chicago: The Lewis Publishing Company, 1930), II, 27–28; Wilson to Clarke (March 25, 1932); Wilson to John Lee Coulter (March 25, 1932), Wilson MSS.

[26] Wilson to DeLos L. James, assistant manager, Agricultural Service Department, National Chamber of Commerce (April 1, 1932), Wilson MSS.

Since there was no money to pay for travel to the Chicago conference, the date April 15 had been tentatively set because Wilson was scheduled to be in Chicago at the expense of the National Broadcasting Company that weekend to conduct a program for the National Advisory Council on Radio Education. These were Saturday evening programs on aspects of the Depression and the way out. The subject of his talk on April 16 was to be "Land Utilization," but he also intended to mention the domestic allotment plan. Wilson doubted whether Stockton would be able to attend the Chicago conference, but said, "Of course, I will represent him." Others invited would be Walter R. McCarthy of the Capital Elevator Company of Duluth; Henry I. Harriman of the National Chamber of Commerce; and Henry A. Wallace, who had not yet agreed to be present but whom Wilson thought would come. Wilson hoped that Clarke could persuade people from other mortgage banker associations or insurance companies to attend. He also wanted Clarke to contact Mark Woods of Lincoln, whom Wilson felt was a very dynamic person and could show much interest in the domestic allotment. While Wilson encouraged Clarke to make more contacts among businessmen, he said, "I am concerned about getting more farmers; am working on it and will do all that I can." [27]

Invitations had also gone from Stockton to the following persons: Burton Peek of Moline, Illinois; Professor E. A. Duddy of Chicago; M. S. Rukeyser, School of Journalism at Columbia University; Orlando F. Webber, president of Allied Chemical and Dye Corporation New York; Hickman Price of Texas; George A. Starring, executive secretary of the South Dakota Bankers Association, Huron, South Dakota; Dean Beardsley S. Ruml, Spielman Foundation of New York; M. S. Winder, secretary of the American Farm Bureau Federation; L. J. Taber, Master, National Grange, Columbus, Ohio; Charles E. Hurst, president of the Iowa Farm Bureau Federation, Des Moines, Iowa; Clifford B. Gregory, editor of the *Prairie Farmer* in Chicago; Earl C. Smith, president of the Illinois Agricultural Association, Chicago; William Settle, president of the Indiana Farm Bureau, Indianapolis; Robin Hood, secretary-treasurer of the National Cooperative Council, Washington, D.C.; W. R. Ronald, editor of the *Mitchell Republican* of Mitchell, South Dakota; Harry Owen, editor of the *Farmer*, St. Paul, Minnesota;

[27] Wilson to Clarke (March 25, 1932), Wilson MSS.

Charles Holman, National Milk Producers Federation, Washington, D.C.; C. O. Moser, American Cotton Cooperative Association, New Orleans, Louisiana; James Hill, president, Eastern Oregon Wheat League, Pendleton, Oregon; E. A. O'Neal, president of the American Farm Bureau Federation; R. B. Lusk, editor, *Evening Huronite*, Huron, South Dakota; W. C. Lusk, *Yankton Press and Dakotan*, Yankton, South Dakota; Fred W. Sargeant, president of Northwestern Railroad, Chicago, Illinois; Ralph W. Reynolds, agricultural department of the Chicago, Milwaukee and St. Paul Railroad, Chicago; Charles Brand of the American Fertilizer Association, Washington, D.C.; Governor J. E. Erickson of Montana; A. G. Black, chief of Agricultural Economics Sections, Iowa State College, Ames, Iowa. The names on these lists suggest that a wide range of interest groups were to be represented at Chicago, and they extended far beyond the narrow interests of wheat men on the northern plains.[28]

Wilson hoped to bring James Bell of General Mills to the conference, but he did not want too many men from the grain trade because they had fought the Farm Board so bitterly. "I think bringing them into the picture would excite suspicion," he said, adding, "Our strategy just now is to edge along getting as many friends as we can and not creating any enemies." Wilson revealed that a rough draft of an allotment bill was in the mill and would soon be made public. It started with the suggestion that when a certain percentage of the producers of a commodity petitioned the Farm Board, the board could take a vote of all of the producers of that commodity, and if the proposition carried by a certain percentage, the allotment on the commodity could be put into effect.

Hopefully these voluntary aspects of the bill would rally public opinion and the good will of the farmers to the plan. It had to have local support because if it did not strike farmers in the correct psychological manner, "it simply wouldn't work," said Wilson. This approach would result in a meeting in schoolhouses in every township in which wheat is raised in the United States. There the plan could be explained and argued pro and con before the farmers and with their participation. Wilson hoped for two results. "I think it would work up a tremendous public sentiment among them in favor of the proposition and the second thing, they would understand it and have a part in it and a responsibility in its administration."

[28] Stockton file (April, 1932), Wilson MSS.

At some point during this period Wilson abandoned his emphasis on land-purchase schemes and immediate action to retire sub-marginal lands. He now aimed directly at formulating an allotment bill without reference to marginal lands. He did suggest that a later amendment could be prepared that would require one-third of the allotment fee collected to be devoted to a fund for the purchase and retirement of land. Although "these side issues" tremendously interested Wilson, he felt that any bill now should be shaped on a straight allotment basis. In discussing the background of the allotment with Clarke, Wilson admitted that the original idea of production control through the allotment plan had not been his. He attributed the "germ idea" to the fertile mind of Dr. W. J. Spillman, who had been for many years chief of the Office of Farm Management in the Department of Agriculture. Spillman had been fired by Secretary D. F. Houston during the war because he fought for higher fixed prices on hogs and wheat under wartime controls, according to Wilson. During the twenties he came back into the department, but because of his age did not resume an administrative responsibility. While Wilson was in charge of the Division of Farm Management and Cost of Production in the Bureau of Agricultural Economics, Spillman served under him in a research capacity from 1924 to 1926. When the McNary-Haugen clamor was at a high pitch, Spillman introduced Wilson to the allotment idea. Wilson told him, "Lay off from what you are doing and try to work it out." He and Wilson conferred together each day for some time and Spillman produced a short book called *Balancing the Agricultural Output.* During the uproar about McNary-Haugen, the book attracted very little attention and sold few copies.

As he related the background of the allotment proposal for Clarke's edification, Wilson explained that later the Laura Spielman Rocke-feller Foundation in New York, of which Dr. Beardsley Ruml was head, gave the Harvard University Department of Agricultural Economics ten thousand dollars to make a study of farm relief proposals. It was reasoned that Harvard should be in a position to make an impartial study without carrying the prejudices of the farmers on the one side and the commercial interests on the other. Dr. Ruml, himself an Iowa farm boy, arrived at the allotment idea independently through his own thinking about the problem and talked about it with some of his Wall Street friends who pronounced the idea sound. He also suggested the idea to Dr. Black, author of the Harvard study, without knowing of Dr. Spillman's work. Of Black's study in relation to the allotment plan, Wilson wrote Clarke:

> If you read Dr. Black's book on Agricultural Reform in the United States you will find there, in an academic way, he hit both the Equalization Fee and the Debenture squarely under the belt and knocks them out, and while he does it in a smooth, academic way, he nevertheless, comes to the conclusion that he believes of all the proposals the allotment is the best.

As soon as the plan was published in book form, Wilson said that he began "in the language of the street, raising a little hell on that plan and have been after it ever since." Extending a compliment to Clarke, Wilson said that the seed had fallen on stony ground until he and Harriman began to push the plan. As he looked forward to the coming domestic allotment conference in April, Wilson expressed his confidence in putting the plan into the national arena and was willing to bet that something was going to spring from it. "I may be kidding myself but I believe that we are actually making history right now," he wrote Clarke, and promised to keep him posted on developments and to have an official letter of invitation to the conference from Stockton sent to him in early April.[29]

Wilson often returned to his theme that any farm plan must include the participation of farmers on the local level. This was one of his main objections to the equalization fee, the debenture, and the Farm Board's operations where everyone seemed to be passing the buck to the federal government. Plans that promised to remedy the situation and at the same time required little adjustment or effort on the part of the individual left Wilson skeptical about their workability. The local community had to rise to the crisis in cooperation with strong leadership from above. Effective reform and relief could not come simply through orders or plans imposed from a higher governmental echelon. Another important benefit that would arise from the discussion of the allotment, in addition to focusing attention on readjustments, would be a renewed interest on the part of the individual farmer in the economics of his operation. Wilson's conviction that the local community had to show an interest and play a significant role in the process of any national

[29] Wilson to Clarke (March 25, 1932), Wilson MSS.

planning persisted throughout his career with the New Deal administration.[30]

To Black, Wilson confided that, in general, reaction to the allotment plan in the current correspondence had been enthusiastic, but it was believed that it never could be made to operate with hundreds of thousands of wheat farmers. For example, Rex E. Willard, Washington State College agricultural economist, said, "The detail problem of getting a few million independent farmers, first to subscribe to some program such as the allotment plan or any other and then stick to it, seems to me futile of accomplishment." Businessmen charged that it would create the largest bureaucracy that the government had ever attempted. "Also I have heard them say," said Wilson, "that there is not an office building in Washington that would begin to hold the clerks that would be required to administer it and the whole thing would break down because of the cost of administering it." Wilson attacked this argument by speaking in terms of decentralization, local responsibility, county committees, state committees, and supervision by the federal Farm Board. Wilson said he frequently had to answer questions about dishonest farmers "who would be apt to fudge and endeavor to increase the allotments per county."

Wilson's answer to this question—"At least I always get by with it," he said—was the following: Railroads knew almost to the bushel the amount of wheat or flour in counties where there were flour mills which shipped from local stations for at least the past five years. From this information, the amount of wheat sold and moved out of the county for a five-year period could be calculated to arrive at an average allotment for every county. "With such a check," he said, "the state allotment committee could prevent any county committee from playing hookey." From his experience in meeting with farmers' groups during the winter, Wilson said that he was convinced that "this talk about its being so unwieldy, etc. is the greatest strength it has. I am not the least afraid of that." Most essential, the inclusion of a local referendum in deciding the acceptance of the plan would help develop a favorable public psychology necessary for success.[31]

[30] Wilson to Grimes (March 23, 1932), files of the Economic and Statistical Analysis Division of the Economic Research Service, USDA, Washington, D.C.

[31] Willard to Wilson (April 15, 1932); Wilson to Black (April 6, 1932), Wilson MSS.

In addition to the many letters sent out over Stockton's signature calling attention to the domestic allotment and the upcoming Chicago conference, Wilson carried on a frank correspondence with many contacts to whom he felt safe in revealing his role in the campaign for the domestic allotment. To Sherman E. Johnson, head of the Agricultural Economics Department at South Dakota State College in Brookings, he openly acknowledged Stockton's role in calling the Chicago conference and his own moving force behind the scenes. "It is all right for you to smile when you read this statement in this letter, but for Heaven's sake don't smile out in public," Wilson told Johnson regarding his work in calling the Chicago conference.[32]

Wilson wrote directly to the bishop of Great Falls, Montana, Edwin B. O'Hara, for an entree to Dr. John A. Ryan, Catholic social reformer and professor of economics at Catholic University in Washington, D.C. He hoped to introduce the domestic allotment plan to Dr. Ryan and explain to him the work that was going on in behalf of the plan in Montana and hear his judgments and reactions to the plan. At the same time he recited the history of the domestic allotment plan to the bishop, and said that it was widely talked of in the cotton, tobacco, and wheat-producing sections of the country at the moment and was receiving favorable reaction from both labor and business groups. Wilson said that he would be happy to receive the bishop's comments on the plan and that he had given a brief history of the plan to show that "it is a finished product and not something which has just bobbed up out of the Montana sagebrush."[33]

With the flurry of communications increasing rapidly, prospects for the plan's success grew brighter. Some of the replies to Stockton's letters indicated to Wilson that progress had been made with the farm organizations, especially the Farm Bureau leadership. In a March 24, 1932, letter the leader of the National Farm Bureau, O'Neal, told Stockton that the organization agreed with the objectives of the plan, but thought that it could not be administered practically. But O'Neal did say, "There seems, however, to be some possibility of our getting together on a plan somewhat akin to the allotment plan, without the complicated machinery." After reading the letter to Stockton, Wilson underlined this last sentence and noted in the margin, "We are under this darn cuss's skin."

[32] Wilson to Johnson (March 25, 1932), Wilson MSS.
[33] Wilson to O'Hara (March 25, 1932), Wilson MSS.

The political infighting and persuasion techniques reminded Wilson of the battles of the McNary-Haugen days in Washington and Montana. He told Chester Davis that Stockton had been in Bozeman a couple of days ago and they had "mixed a great lot of medicine which was of the same brand as was mixed in 1924" for the Equalization Fee League of Montana, the official paper organization that launched the propaganda for the McNary-Haugen idea. Wilson said that Stockton and he had commented on the similarity of the situation today and regretted the absence of Davis "as a participant in the plot."

Wilson felt it was a significant sign that spontaneous outbursts of the allotment idea appeared throughout the country. He reported that he had one from South Dakota, another from Oklahoma, and a third from Kansas. They were "purely farmer things which come from the soil," according to Wilson, "and of course they do not have much economics in them but the philosophy and central core is exactly that of the allotment proposal." Generally, Wilson was disappointed at the muddled replies received from most of the officials and presidents of the state farm bureaus regarding the domestic allotment plan. "We have a motley set of replies . . . which indicates to me that the great mass of farm leaders have no conception as to what this is all about." He told Black that the replies gave evidence of the chaos and confusion in the thinking of the so-called farm leaders.[34]

Plotting the preconference details, Wilson hoped Harriman would invite and bring prominent businessmen who would add prestige to the Chicago meeting. Also it was important that Harriman forward such names to Montana so that they would receive Stockton's invitation. The strategy was to keep the Montana State Farm Bureau in the foreground. This would give it the appearance of a farmer movement that was attracting the support of the business element in the country.[35]

Wilson was fully aware that many businessmen would come to the meeting opposed to the basic philosophy of the domestic allotment plan. On the other hand many would understand some action had to be taken to meet the present emergency. One of these men

[34] Wilson to Davis (March 26, 1932); Wilson to Tolley (March 26, 1932); Wilson to Black (March 26, 1932), Wilson MSS.
[35] Wilson to Harriman (March 26, 1932), Wilson MSS.

was James Bell of General Mills who earlier had proposed a federal farm-land reserve, and now said he could not endorse the principles of the domestic allotment and was in theory opposed to his own proposal for a farm reserve maintained by the government. "Frankly, I am not in favor of any plan, not even the Federal Farm Reserve," he wrote Wilson. Ideally he believed in the free play of supply and demand in an unrestricted market. "We cannot legislate our way out of the present depression and we cannot change the operation of the fundamental economic laws," he maintained. But he conceded, "If public psychology is not to be satisfied short of some attempt in this direction, then I still believe that the Federal Reserve Plan is the best . . . with the least possible harm." [36]

On the question of bringing more businessmen into the meeting, Harriman later replied to Wilson that he would only invite George W. Holmes of Lincoln, Nebraska, president of the First National Bank of that city. But he believed that at the moment other business-men should be left off the invitation list to this first meeting because "their natural attitude will be antagonistic on the grounds that it means more government in business. . . ." Time would be needed to convince them that this plan was simply an extension of the tariff protection or its equivalent to the farm. This was Harriman's strategy. He would win over orthodox businessmen who objected to the domestic allotment plan because it meant too much govern-ment in the economy by convincing them to accept a broadening of the traditionally supported business policies on tariffs. Upon receiving this word on Holmes from Harriman, Wilson contacted Clarke in Omaha telling him that Holmes was the only businessman that Harriman intended to invite and said, "It is absolutely essential that we make a Christian of Holmes before he comes to the meeting. If you have not seen him will you please tend to this?" [37]

Because Wilson was striving to gather a number of men at Chicago who could talk calmly on the problem and avoid too many heated arguments, he and Stockton had decided against bringing William Hirth of the *Missouri Farmer* to the meeting. He explained that Hirth had "blood in his eye and wants to fight the Farm Board," and there was no need to fight old battles at this meeting. Wilson

[36] Bell to Wilson (March 26, 1932), Wilson MSS.
[37] Harriman to Wilson (March 30, 1932); Wilson to Clarke (April 5, 1932), Wilson MSS.

also had doubts about inviting A. W. Ricker, editor of the *Farmers'
Union Herald* in St. Paul. He wanted to "find out something about
which side of the fence these people are going to be on" before they
came to the conference. He knew that the *Herald* had quite a wide
circulation in the Northwest and "the thing that we do not want is
to have the farmers formulate an opinion of our plan before they
know something about it." Since letters had been sent to Kelly
of the Montana Union and Talbott of the North Dakota Union, the
Farmers' Union group had not been ignored in the Northwest.
Also, since these two gentlemen appeared to be fairly favorable, it
might be wise to ask them to write Ricker on behalf of the plan,
reasoned Wilson.[38]

Various replies to the suggested meeting on the domestic allotment plan brought fresh discussion topics and advice on strategy in
the developing campaign. Charles L. Stewart, head of the Department of Agricultural Economics at the University of Illinois and
supporter of the debenture plan, pointed out that the domestic
allotment might win more support in the submarginal agricultural
regions in order to force restriction of production on the more
established agricultural sections of the country. If this did become
apparent, he felt that efforts to push the domestic allotment at that
time would drive a wedge between eastern and western agriculture.
This would be unfortunate from the standpoint of agrarian unity on
a farm program. Because of this he felt that the allotment idea
should only be given "honorable mention" instead of trying to shape
it in the form of a legislative bill. An attempt to give it the same
degree of consideration as the equalization fee or export debenture
would force its complete elimination, warned Stewart. Peek said
that if the domestic allotment plan met the principles of an American
price for American consumption independent of the world price
for surplus, "it is immaterial to me whether the result is achieved
through one plan or another." But he felt that no such legislation
stood any chance "with the same crowd in control of the administration that has directed our policies since the termination of the
war."[39]

[38] Wilson to Davis (March 26, 1932); Wilson to Stockton (April 2, 1932),
Wilson MSS.

[39] Stewart to Wilson (April 5, 1932); Peek to Clarke (April 4, 1932), Wilson
MSS. Actually the allotment, as Wilson later discovered, would discriminate

Peek offered a word of caution to the people involved in the domestic allotment campaign: "Do not let yourself get in a position of going around the farm organizations. On the other hand, work through and with them to the fullest extent." In response to this warning Clarke assured Peek that Wilson wanted to work through the farm organizations as much as possible and pointed to the fact that invitations for the Chicago meeting were sent out by one of Montana's highest ranking Farm Bureau officials. Peek reminded Clarke that the allotment plan was not new. It had been around for at least ten years through Dr. Spillman's work in the Department of Agriculture. This was a subtle way of telling domestic allotment enthusiasts such as Clarke that they were not the first people to fight for a farm relief plan. Also Clarke informed Peek that Harriman, contrary to Peek's view, was of the opinion that Congress and the administration were eager to find a solution to the present crisis and that they might accept the domestic allotment plan.[40]

Through Sherman Johnson, Wilson learned that a chain of South Dakota newspapers representing the currently out-of-power faction in the state had taken up the cause of the domestic allotment plan in the state. The papers at Huron, Mitchell, Rapid City, and Yankton were owned by the Lusks, who were critical of the present Republican administration in the state, and there had been some talk that the elder Lusk would run for governor that year. His son, Robert Lusk, editor of the Huron paper and a graduate of the University of Missouri School of Journalism, had done considerable thinking along the lines of farm relief. In the previous year he developed a plan that Johnson had reviewed. A conference was held in Huron during the winter on this so-called Hand County Plan of Farm Relief, at which George A. Starring of the South Dakota Bankers Association and Lusk became interested in the domestic allotment plan. Starring had already written Wilson about the Hand County plan which resembled the domestic allotment but was much more rigid in its provisions. The editor of the *Mitchell*

---

against submarginal areas that had suffered severe drought, for the allotment would be based on the past five-year production average. The requirement also would hurt farmers who let portions of their lands lie fallow each year in accordance with wise and prudent dry-farming techniques.

[40] Peek to Clarke (April 14, 1932); Clarke to Peek (April 15, 1932), Peek MSS.

Republican in the Lusk newspaper chain, W. R. Ronald, caught the attention of Wilson through a highly complimentary editorial on the domestic allotment plan. Wilson requested a copy of the editorial for use at the Chicago conference and had Stockton send a formal invitation to Ronald to attend the conference. In the next months Ronald was to become one of Wilson's most aggressive lieutenants in pushing the domestic allotment plan both in South Dakota and in Washington through his connection with Senator Norbeck.[41]

Norbeck encouraged Ronald's attendance at the Chicago conference and requested a report on its proceedings. The South Dakota senator saw dim prospects for new McNary-Haugen legislation and was willing to consider the domestic allotment as a viable alternative. Norbeck understood that the domestic allotment was intended to avert what he called the "imaginary danger of overproduction," but he appeared ready to experiment with production control if it could place farm prices on a par with other industries. He admitted the Black plan would not be easy to administer, but felt the underlying features were sound. Despite reservations, by August, Norbeck agreed to join Ronald in writing an article for the *Farm Journal* of Philadelphia extolling the advantages of the domestic allotment.[42]

In urging Ralph Budd, president of the Chicago, Burlington, and Quincy Railroad, to attend the Chicago conference, Wilson pointed to the distress sweeping the wheat and cotton farms of the country and said that it would soon be as bad in the corn belt. In Wilson's judgment the situation demanded that a constructive farm recovery program be put before the farmers of the country or "they are going to turn on a very radical tangent and if the populous [sic] days repeat themselves we will see them leaning towards very uneconomic and non-constructive proposals. . . ." In this regard he mentioned Senator Lynn Frazier's plan for the government to take over all the farm indebtedness of the country. Wilson mentioned to Budd some of the prominent people who would be in attendance at the conference, such as H. A. Wallace; Clifford B. Gregory,

[41] Johnson to Wilson (April 9, 1932); Wilson to Ronald (April 12, 1932), Wilson MSS.

[42] Norbeck to Ronald (April 18, 1932); Norbeck to Robert Lusk (April 1, 1932), Norbeck Papers, Vermillion, South Dakota; Peter Norbeck, "The Voluntary Allotment," *Farm Journal*, LVI (October, 1932), 5–6.

editor of the *Prairie Farmer*; and Henry I. Harriman, president of the National Chamber of Commerce and chairman of the U.S. Chamber of Commerce Committee on Continuity and Stability in Business. "Mr. Harriman now owns the largest cattle ranch in Montana at Miles City and has his hands enough in agriculture to feel the pinch," was Wilson's brief explanation for Harriman's interest in the domestic allotment meeting.

Other names he thought might impress the president of the Chicago, Burlington, and Quincy Railroad were L. S. Clarke, president of the Nebraska Mortgage Bankers Association; Walter R. McCarthy of the Capital Elevator Company in Duluth; Chester C. Davis, president of the Maizewood Corporation of Chicago; Burton Peek, vice-president of the John Deere Company; Hickman Price, Amarillo, Texas, largest wheat farmer in the United States; and R. R. Rogers of the Prudential Life Insurance Company. At the meeting, Wilson explained, a plan embodying the principles of Black's original proposal would be submitted and it would call for the use of one-third of the income derived from the excise tax on flour for the purchase by the government of submarginal lands. This could be seen as a basic change in the land policy of the United States and a movement toward readjustment of land in the productive plant with some reference to agricultural planning, Wilson asserted. Apparently the Montana professor was not entirely sacrificing his ideas about land planning and readjustment in favor of the allotment.[43]

In Wilson's radio broadcast on April 16, 1932, his chief topic was "Land Utilization," but he wove the domestic allotment plan carefully into the text at several points. He spoke of American farming facing peasantry if the nation did not adopt a system of planned land use. In his fifteen-minute talk Wilson outlined six steps that he regarded as essential to a land-use-planning program: "First, Congress should immediately repeal the Homestead Act, together with other free-land laws and enact a new national land-policy bill." This would close the epoch of free land and limitless agricultural expansion. "Second, each state should immediately classify its lands, develop a state land-use plan, and institute a program of action." In this regard he pointed to the New York State program. The third step should endeavor to remove poor lands

[43] Wilson to Budd (April 14, 1932), Wilson MSS.

from farm production. In support of this point he quoted from the 1930 report of the Secretary of Agriculture:

> It should be an essential aim of our agricultural policy to facilitate the withdrawal from agriculture areas that seem likely to remain unprofitable. Public provisions should be made for the utilization of this land for purposes other than farming. Public ownership of land that cannot possibly be farmed would in many areas mean a better economic use of the lands in question and also do something to relieve the pressure of unneeded production upon our markets.

The fourth step suggested was that land taxes should be reduced and, where necessary, local rural government reorganized. The fifth step would be a reduction of surplus production on the good lands. This was to be achieved under the domestic allotment plan where a farmer grew only a certain number of acres according to the alloted number of his domestic production quota. "He would be at liberty to grow more but this would be without tariff benefit." The last step that Wilson recommended was part-time farming and decentralization of industry. This program looked to resettling families from poor lands into small agricultural communities around towns and small cities.[44]

As had been foreseen, Stockton failed to attend the Chicago conference, which finally convened April 19, three days after Wilson's radio talk. He did address a long letter, probably written by Wilson, "To the Group Meeting in Chicago to Frame Legislation Embodying the Principle of the Domestic Allotment Proposal." In the text Stockton pointed to his previous support of the McNary-Haugen bill and said, "I remained absolutely loyal to this proposal to the bitter end." Presently, with the different world situation, he felt that the nationalistic policies of the European countries made any export plan impossible. As early as 1929, with the publication of Black's book *Agricultural Reform*, he had been interested in the domestic allotment plan, and during the last ninety days he had carried on a wide farm correspondence about it that brought interested inquiries from many parts of the country asking why the plan was not worked over into a legislative proposal and intro-

[44] M. L. Wilson, "Land Utilization," Economic Series Lecture no. 25, April 16, 1932 (Chicago: University of Chicago Press, 1932).

duced into Congress. To this end he hoped that the conference would devote itself to writing an allotment bill based upon the plan set forth by Dr. Black with modifications and amendments that the group deemed necessary. Stockton said that his move in behalf of the domestic allotment plan was not designed to cause friction with the farm organizations, but he believed it superior to either the equalization fee or the export debenture plan. He thought it could be put before Congress without any embarrassment to the farm organizations. Finally, he said, should questions arise at the conference concerning his views on the plan, "You can depend upon Mr. Wilson giving my views accurately and concisely." [45]

In the conference Wilson observed the amazement on George Peek's face at the important people who attended the meeting. W. R. Ronald spoke in praise of the McNary-Haugen bills, but said that he had always harbored grave doubts about their workability, but the new plan seemed to overcome these doubts. This type of approach Wilson thought did not offend people like Peek who had given a great deal to the McNary-Haugen struggle. Also, Wilson noticed Wallace "warming up to the plan" and asking perceptive questions. But Peek could not accept reduced production. According to Wilson it was obvious that he did not like plans from college professors and economists. "He probably thought that this was just another damn farm plan—and there were so many of them in the air at that time," said Wilson. But it was reasoned that it was better to have Peek at the meeting rather than to make an immediate enemy of him by leaving him out of the initial plans for the proposal. [46]

The conference decided to appoint a permanent committee to promote the domestic allotment plan. The committee, called the Voluntary Domestic Allotment Plan Committee, was composed of M. L. Wilson, H. I. Harriman, R. R. Rogers, H. A. Wallace, Louis Clarke, and W. R. Ronald. The word "voluntary" was placed in the committee's title to distinguish its domestic allotment plan from that of the Farmers' Union plan that was currently under

[45] Stockton to the Group Meeting in Chicago to Frame Legislation Embodying the Principle of the Domestic Allotment Proposal (April 14, 1932), Wilson MSS.

[46] Wilson, Columbia Oral History Collection, Columbia University, New York, N.Y.

discussion in the form of the Thomas-Swank bill in Congress. The Farm Union plan called for a fixed domestic price on bushels grown for domestic consumption with no provisions for limiting the total production. The surplus was to be disposed of on the foreign market.[47]

Before the Chicago conference, Wilson had already planned ahead to a second conference on agricultural policy and planning to be held June 23 to 25 at the University of Chicago. Wilson, Tolley, and Joseph S. Davis of the Food Research Institute at Stanford, and Professor Duddy of the University of Chicago were currently planning the program. Wilson especially wanted Rex Tugwell of Columbia University to receive an invitation. This move was to prove decisive in obtaining an interview for Wilson with Governor Roosevelt in Albany in July shortly after the June meeting.[48]

On the day of his Chicago broadcast Wilson received an important telegram in his hotel room in the LaSalle. It came from James C. Stone, chairman of the Farm Board and read: "Come to Washington our Expense to discuss plan with Board." This request resulted from a memorandum delivered to Stone by Farm Board economist Mordecai Ezekiel on April 15 on "Mr. M. L. Wilson's Proposal," which was an analysis of a Wilson letter to Stone on April 9. Ezekiel outlined the history of the domestic allotment idea to Stone and the recent steps taken in behalf of the plan that led up to the Chicago conference. He expected that Montana groups had already drafted legislation which was to be polished in the Chicago meeting and shortly introduced into Congress. With this in mind, Ezekiel suggested that it would be wise for the board to go over the proposed legislation in advance of its introduction to Congress and call attention to features that the board would not want included in case the bill became law and the board was charged with its administration. Ezekiel ventured the opinion that there was considerable chance this plan would meet with success in Congress. For this reason he suggested "that Mr. Wilson, who is better qualified than

[47] These names are found in Wilson's handwriting in the files of the Economic and Statistical Analysis Division of the Economic Research Service, "Domestic Allotment Proposals," USDA; William R. Johnson, "National Farm Organizations and the Reshaping of Agricultural Policy in 1932," *Agricultural History*, XXXVII (January, 1963), 37.

[48] Wilson to Soule (April 12, 1932), Wilson MSS.

any other person to explain the plan and point out its merits, should be invited to come to Washington from Chicago, at our expense, to discuss the plan with the Board." [49]

Stone's invitation brought Wilson to Washington directly after the Chicago meeting. While in Washington he also succeeded in interesting Senator Norbeck in the domestic allotment. The senator suggested that he testify before the hearings in the Senate Committee on Agriculture and Forestry, which was then considering changes in the Farm Board Act and the Farm Loan Act with reference to farm relief. This marked one of the first congressional discussions of the domestic allotment proposal. Ronald encouraged Wilson to keep close to Senator Norbeck. He pointed out that Norbeck had received the endorsement of the three farm organizations in South Dakota for renomination and re-election. Ronald believed this was an indication that the senator would be a powerful force in farm relief legislation. Wilson also spoke to Congressmen Clifford Hope of southwestern Kansas and Marvin Jones of Texas. They were both from wheat districts that almost bordered each other but for the panhandle of Oklahoma. Hope said he was aware of the domestic allotment plan but had not talked about it with anyone. He took a copy of Black's book from his desk drawer and asked Wilson if he had read it. Hope thought it was the best piece he had read on the agricultural problem. [50]

Besides keeping Peek well informed on events concerning the domestic allotment campaign, Wilson told long-time agrarian politician Charles L. McNary of the progress and that he hoped to confer with him on the coming trip to Washington. Peek also talked about the domestic allotment among his band of cohorts who had fought for the equalization and the debenture in the twenties. He wrote Governor Lowden he thought the plan would work but might be

[49] Stone to Wilson (April 16, 1932), Wilson MSS; Ezekiel to Stone (April 15, 1932), files of the Economic and Statistical Analysis Division of the Economic Research Service, "Domestic Allotment Proposals," USDA.

[50] Ezekiel to Tugwell (October 20, 1939), files of the Economic and Statistical Analysis Division of the Economic Research Service, "Domestic Allotment Proposals," USDA; U.S. Senate, 72d Cong., 1st sess., Committee on Agriculture and Forestry, April, 1932, pp. 55–61; Gilbert C. Fite, *Peter Norbeck: Prairie Statesman*, University of Missouri Studies, XXII (Columbia: University of Missouri Press, 1948), 164; Ronald to Wilson (April 30, 1932), Wilson MSS; Wilson, COHC.

more cumbersome than the equalization plan. Still, the essential principle of equalizing the lower world price on the surplus over the whole crop was preserved. In reply to a communication from Peek on the plan, Earl Smith said he did not question the principles of the plan and agreed that the "principle of the equalization fee is embodied in the plan, but the machinery of its operation is very much more cumbersome." He quoted Peek's phrase back in the letter. Although he had no disagreement with the plan in principle, he could see no benefit from the new plan at this time. "It will only operate to bring forth more confusion rather than the much needed crystallization of sincere thought behind the equalization fee," Smith said. Peek replied that he did not agree with the statement that "it will only operate to bring forth more confusion," and thought that something could be accomplished in Washington "by whipping this proposal into understandable shape."[51]

Wallace cautioned Wilson to go slow on introducing legislation. He feared that if Wilson provoked people to look prematurely into the details of the plan, "I am afraid that the whole thing is sunk." He did not mean to question the practicality of the plan, especially in the light of what he believed would be the country's destiny in the next few years. "I think," he said, "it can be made practical if we are really going the route of state socialism. And I am very much inclined to think that we really are going that route." Nevertheless, he believed that if Wilson induced a large number of people to concentrate on the details of the domestic allotment plan, the movement would get bogged down in needless confusion at the moment when perhaps at a later date it would be much easier to have the plan accepted. He urged Wilson to assure both Democrats and Republicans that his intentions as a professor were not political and he was not pushing the plan to help either party. Make it clear, Wallace said, that the present emergency made it necessary "to forget all about party considerations and consider this in a realistic rather than a political way."[52]

Secretary of Agriculture Hyde could not endorse the domestic allotment plan as explained by Black, but he did endorse the move-

[51] Wilson to McNary (April 20, 1932), Wilson MSS; Peek to Lowden (April 22, 1932); Smith to Peek (April 21, 1932); Peek to Smith (April 25, 1932), Peek MSS.

[52] Wallace to Wilson (April 20, 1932), Wilson MSS.

ment to curtail production. It was his opinion that this plan or a plan for the purchasing of submarginal lands would be impossible to force through Congress at the moment. Englund, assistant chief of the Bureau of Agricultural Economics, also thought that the plan had no political chance to become law because the urban representatives would never agree to an excise tax on flour that would be used to buy up land in Montana, Kansas, and North Dakota. The farm editor Harry N. Owen, who had called for a domestic allotment approach to the farm problem as early as 1926 in his publication *Farm, Stock, and Home,* expressed complete disillusionment with all plans to achieve a domestic price for wheat plus the tariff. Such plans, he said, "leave me cold, because I feel that the administrative features of any plan are of such a complicated nature as to preclude their working in a commercial way." [53]

Evidence in the Peek correspondence points to his growing interest in the plan. At the end of April he volunteered a suggestion on the administration of the plan to Wilson. He suggested a tax on the commodity to pay the cost of administering the plan, particularly local administration. This could be accomplished by the local buyer deducting from the equalization certificate a fixed tax on wheat and depositing it to cover the costs of local administration. Peek conveyed this idea to Wilson because he had heard that O'Neal and others did not understand the degree to which local administration was to play in the plan and feared the creation of a large body of government employees paid by the federal government. Wilson thanked Peek for the suggestion to emphasize local administration of the plan and said this might help with the farm organizations. [54]

In early May, Wilson traveled from Washington to New York to confer with R. R. Rogers and other insurance men with investments in western agriculture. They impressed him generally as men who had supported Hoover and opposed McNary-Haugenism down the line. Most, however, were aware of the present desperate situation, and Wilson told them that sometimes things must be attempted

[53] Hyde to Clarke (April 20, 1932), files of the Economic and Statistical Analysis Division of the Economic Research Service, "Domestic Allotment Proposals," USDA; Englund to Wilson (April 16, 1932); Owen to Stockton (April 21,1932), Wilson MSS.
[54] Peek to Wilson (April 25, 1932); Wilson to Peek (April 27, 1932), Peek MSS.

whether or not they conflict with ideas about how things should work. When Wilson mentioned that the president of the National Chamber of Commerce, H. I. Harriman, supported his plan, "That just helped like sixty—that just helped like sixty" with these people, Wilson repeated. While in New York he made a special effort to meet with Tugwell at Columbia University and then returned to Washington to confer with Beardsley Ruml. Ruml acknowledged that he had given Black the germ of the idea for the chapter in *Agricultural Reform*. After the Washington meeting he again returned to New York and met with Rogers, who talked about raising money from his business friends for Wilson's expenses in the campaign. From New York, Wilson flew to Chicago and then boarded a train for Bozeman. On the way he stopped over in Mitchell, South Dakota, and held "a regular Domestic Allotment meeting" with Ronald and many farmers from around the state.[55]

After Wilson had met with the Farm Board on the domestic allotment, Stone instructed Ezekiel to make a study of the proposal and draft a sample bill that would include the provisions which seemed essential to make it as feasible as possible from an administrative standpoint to achieve the results which Wilson said could be obtained. Upon his return to Montana, Wilson asked Ezekiel to stay in touch with the Senate drafting room on the legislation and be able to explain to them any minor details of the bill which were not clear. Ezekiel made it clear to Wilson that he was "acting in this matter more as a personal friend . . . than as an official representative of the Board. . . ." He assured Stone that Wilson was aware the board was only studying the plan's possibilities along with other proposed agricultural relief measures. Ezekiel went on to suggest in his lengthy memorandum that in order to avoid embarrassment to the board that it would be well to have in the files a written instruction from Stone to himself authorizing work with Wilson as a technical adviser without committing the board in the process. As like-minded agricultural planners, Wilson and Ezekiel were developing a close relationship in working for this first foothold in the door leading to planning in agriculture and proper land utilization. One result was that Ezekiel prepared a series of favorable memoranda on Wilson's domestic allotment proposal during the months of May and June, 1932, for the members of the Farm Board.

[55] Wilson, COHC.

One of these memoranda listed nine advantages of the Wilson proposal:

1. No government appropriation needed.
2. No stimulation to increased production.
3. A definite method for limiting or reducing production.
4. No retaliation by foreign governments.
5. Decentralized administration and local responsibility for allotment benefits.
6. No compulsion on individual farmers.
7. No disturbance of markets or marketing agencies.
8. No price fixing.
9. Definitely secures tariff protection on domestic consumption of exportable products.

Ezekiel admitted the plan had been severely criticized from an administrative angle, but although difficult, "it would not be more difficult than jobs already successfully handled by the Federal Farm Board." [56]

Ahead of Wilson lay a long summer of extensive travel and conferences on the domestic allotment. His efforts eventually led him to the State House in Albany where he had a successful and encouraging interchange with Governor Roosevelt on the plan. The fruits of this meeting would soon be realized in the Democratic candidate's conduct of the campaign in the agricultural Midwest.

[56] Ezekiel to Stone, "Confidential Memorandum" (May 18, 1932); Ezekiel to Stone, "Memorandum: Further Comments on the Wilson Plan" (May 10, 1932), files of the Economic and Statistical Analysis Division of the Economic Research Service, "Domestic Allotment Proposals," USDA.

CHAPTER EIGHT

Mr. Wilson Takes His Plan to Albany

What we were looking for was a way of controlling production which would be politically feasible.—Rex Tugwell

The campaign for the domestic allotment did not lead directly to the capitol steps in Albany. Early in the spring Wilson brought it to the attention of the Republican hierarchy through the Farm Board, leading conservative businessmen, and Republicans Peter Norbeck and Clifford Hope. Through Rex Tugwell, Wilson gained access to what were to be the high councils of power after the fall elections. Tugwell's interest in the domestic allotment and its democratic administrative features prompted him to pave the way for Wilson to meet Governor Roosevelt in early July, 1932, for a long explanatory session regarding the domestic allotment.

By early May, Wilson was advising National Chamber of Commerce president Harriman on his public remarks concerning agriculture. Harriman's statements primarily dealt with agricultural planning, and Wilson urged him to speak in terms of the Christgau bill's suggestions for regional planning programs. It may have been well to talk about regional planning developments and the retirement of submarginal lands, but on his recent trip to Washington, Wilson heard only talk about a balanced budget and reduced expenditures, which seemed to exclude any scheme for land retirement through government purchases. Still, he was encouraged in New York by the number of businessmen who believed that a rejuvenated agriculture was essential to general business recovery.[1]

Within the Farm Board, Ezekiel told Chairman Stone that the Wilson plan faced administrative difficulties, but they could be overcome if the board were given sufficiently broad powers. Also

[1] Wilson to Harriman (May 4, 1932); Wilson to Clarke (May 16, 1932), Wilson MSS.

the plan appeared the most promising of all the proposals under discussion for farm relief. The allotment appeared to be workable on a variety of crops, especially wheat and cotton, but severe difficulties might be encountered with hogs and tobacco. Under the plan there would be little danger of inflation, and in Ezekiel's opinion, "At least a start would be made in the direction of rational planning and control of our agricultural production." [2]

In Congress both Marvin Jones and Clifford Hope of the House Agricultural Committee thought that the Farm Board should have no part in the administration of the plan and wanted it under the Department of Agriculture. If Congressman Hope gauged congressional opinion correctly at the moment, to associate the plan closely with the Farm Board would be detrimental to its chances in Congress. But Wilson did not think the Republicans, some farm organizations, and cooperatives would permit the Department of Agriculture to move into this area without the board. Others objected to the suggestion that the Extension Service play a central role in administering the allotment plan. Dr. Alva H. Benton, head of the Department of Marketing and Rural Organizations at the North Dakota agricultural college in Fargo, declared that to involve Extension in the plan would absorb all of its efforts and open the entire Extension program to undeserved criticism if the plan did not succeed. The Wilson plan's reliance on the Extension Service appealed to Tugwell. The use of county agents in conjunction with local farmer committees to administer the plan "was just what had been lacking in all my schemes before," admitted Tugwell. [3]

Although disagreement persisted on specific administrative questions about the plan, Wilson believed that the allotment idea was gaining strength in the corn belt. For "diplomatic reasons" he endorsed a scheme worked out by W. R. Ronald for applying the plan to hogs which would soon be presented to Senator Norbeck. Such a scheme would boost the allotment's stock in the corn belt. "Now in my judgment," wrote Wilson, "what is happening is that

[2] Ezekiel to Stone (May 17, 1932), files of the Economic and Statistical Analysis Division of the Economic Research Service, USDA.

[3] Wilson to Ezekiel (May 18, 1932), files of the Economic and Statistical Analysis Division of the Economic Research Service, USDA; Hope to McCarthy (May 14, 1932); Wilson to McCarthy (May 18, 1932); Benton to Wilson (May 6, 1932), Wilson MSS; Rexford G. Tugwell, Columbia Oral History Collection, Columbia University, New York, N.Y.

this allotment thing has taken hold in the corn belt." He was confident that this spelled the end of the equalization fee and the export debenture and that the allotment would be the "rally point for a new farm relief campaign." In Omaha, Clarke wrote Nebraska Senator Robert B. Howell that Wilson was making "wonderful headway in Washington" with his controlled production plan. He also told Wilson that it would be advisable to see Howell because his voice was always being heard in Washington demanding farm relief. In addition Howell's influence might bring Senator Norris to back the plan, if Wilson had not already made direct contact with Norris. Clarke was confident that as the stock market declined day by day the reaction would be to the allotment's benefit. "The lower it goes the more cooperation we are going to get from industry," he said.[4]

No sooner had Wilson reached Montana in mid-May than he returned to Washington on May 21. En route he visited with Clarke in Omaha and held a long conference with Wallace in Des Moines. To Wallace he explained the general approach in selling the domestic allotment plan and said that cotton and wheat were used as examples most often and wheat much more than cotton because wheat above all commanded Wilson's interest. Wallace said he always had questions about the administration of the plan. Wilson's ideas about associations of farmers in the counties, a referendum, and making the allotments through agricultural committees all appealed to Wallace. In their talk they seemed to agree that they were not formulating a permanent plan for agriculture, but rather a plan to meet the present emergency. A permanent agricultural plan was an entirely different question.[5]

Early in the year on January 9, 1932, representatives of three farm organizations had met in Washington at the behest of Edward O'Neal of the Farm Bureau. They agreed that the Agricultural Marketing Act should be amended by including either the debenture plan, the equalization fee, or "any other method which will make it effective in controlling surpluses . . . and in securing for American farmers cost of production on those portions of their crops sold for consumption in their own nation." Clifford V. Gregory, a spokes-

    [4] Wilson to Englund (May 18, 1932); Clarke to Wilson (May 22, 1932); Clarke to Wilson (May 30, 1932); Clarke to Wilson (May 28, 1932), Wilson MSS.
    [5] Wilson, COHC.

man for the Illinois Agricultural Organization, later claimed that this "other method" left the door open for Professor Wilson's domestic allotment plan. This claim, however, is doubtful because it most likely referred to the demand of John Simpson and the Farmers' Union for cost of production on that portion of the crop which was domestically consumed. It had no reference to production control—a concept that the farm organizations only reluctantly accepted. The Farmers' Union under Simpson's leadership never accepted it.[6]

When Wilson arrived in Washington, the "farm leaders were nosing around trying to get their three headed monster through Congress." Their proposed three-way bill would authorize but not require the Farm Board to use one of the three following plans: (1) the export debenture, (2) the equalization fee, or (3) a diluted version of the allotment plan sponsored by the Farmers' Union that proposed cost of production prices without production control. Supposedly this measure represented a compromise among the three organizations on a common policy, but it was little more than a combination of three individual policies that had been standard for years. Not until June 15 when the Senate recommitted the "three headed monster" to committee was the way cleared for consideration of new legislation. Earl Smith, president of the Illinois Agricultural Organization, accused Wilson of being an outsider in the battle for agricultural legislation. Of Wilson's plan, he said that farmers would be unable to work together on the local level. "It would increase neighborhood jealousies throughout the countryside," he said and called it, the "National Farmers' Quarreling Plan." Smith said that since it was not a farmers' plan they would not cooperate on anything but a McNary-Haugen proposal.[7]

By June 1, a draft of Wilson's domestic allotment bill that had been worked on by Ezekiel and the Senate bill drafting committee was circulating in Washington. The decision to have the bill drafted by a committee in the House came on the eve of the House's consideration of the three-way bill. The move by Texas Democrat

---

[6] Clifford V. Gregory, "The American Farm Bureau Federation and the AAA," *Annals of the American Academy of Political and Social Science*, CLXXIX (May, 1935), 154.

[7] Wilson, COHC; *Congressional Record*, 72d Cong., 1st sess., June 15, 1932, 13000.

Marvin Jones, chairman of the House Agricultural Committee, greatly confused the legislative picture on the congressional farm program according to the *New York Times* for May 31, 1932. The *Times* reported that "heretofore farm relief measures shied away from the idea of subsidizing agriculture," but the new domestic allotment plan made subsidy the foundation of farm aid. In this rather critical article the *Times* said that the plan would guarantee the farmer the domestic price plus the tariff on that quantity of his crop which was domestically consumed. Where the Farmers' Union plan proposed a cost-of-production price as the minimum for farm commodities, the bill being written called for government certificates for the amount of the tariff in addition to the market price to be issued to farmers for the portion of their crop domestically consumed. Sketching the implications of this proposal for the farmers, the article said that under the plan every farm in the United States would be "card-indexed as to its contribution to domestic consumption and the Farm Board could require that it increase or decrease acreages in direct ratio to changes in production and consumption, or withhold its tariff allotment rights." George Peek took the view that the proposed plan was "not sufficiently generous to the farmer, and I am wondering if Mr. Wilson has not permitted himself to become influenced too much by the Eastern industrialists and financiers with whom he has been contacting." [8]

Wilson sent a long summary of his activities on the eastern trip addressed to the "Bozeman Folks" including President Atkinson, Director Linfield, Stockton, and the "boys in the office." In Des Moines he found Wallace strong for the allotment plan and of the opinion that it could be made to apply to hogs. Wallace was very complimentary toward the efforts made by the Montana people in behalf of the relief plan and "thinks that aside from Montana, the Colleges of Agriculture and Extension Service are doing little or nothing to assist farmers in depression or readjustments and expects a decline in the support and income for the agricultural institutions," wrote Wilson. According to Wilson, "Old" Alex Legge welcomed the allotment plan, "swallowing the bait in big chunks." After the interview Legge exclaimed, "Wilson! Go to it. Don't get discouraged. G-o-d D-a-m-n i-t! We are going to get somewhere after all. I am for you but don't tell anybody, because I am afraid it will hurt the

[8] Peek to Davis (May 28, 1932), Peek MSS.

cause." A House subcommittee of the Agricultural Committee presently was working over Wilson's draft of the bill as he had received it from the Senate drafting committee, and Wilson said, "I am staying away at this stage—like extension method of making them feel that they are doing it."

Every morning Wilson said he had breakfast with the Farm Bureau people, but he did not bring up farm legislation because he was waiting for them to come to him. O'Neal told Wilson that he had been around Washington for fourteen years and never saw anyone stir up the agricultural committee like Wilson did with his talk before them on the features of the domestic allotment plan. He admitted, "I am not for your bill, but looks like we would get something." Wilson thought O'Neal would eventually agree to the allotment approach. Earl Smith was another story. He accused Wilson of being backed by the New England power and public utility interests, the life insurance companies, and big business, and said, "There will not be any farm legislation unless organized agriculture is for it." Wilson replied that the Montana Farm Bureau was backing him. To this Smith replied sarcastically, "How many members has the Montana Farm Bureau?" Wilson smiled and said, "Enough to fill the offices." "I let him get a little worked up then I pretended to get sore," said Wilson, "I shook my finger in his face and said that Stockton, Chester Davis and I would not stand for any one to question our motives. We were first in the McNary-Haugen fight in 1924—and for he and Charley Hearst [president of the Iowa State Farm Bureau] to go back and see what a time we had to get them in—Smith then tamed down."

The Grange, Wilson saw as friendly, but "old man" Simpson was the shrewdest and least dependable of them all. Simpson indicated he probably would not support the voluntary domestic allotment plan even if it were worked on a cost-of-production basis. Wilson, however, was not totally despairing at the attitude of the farm organization people. He had learned that the "present farm organization leadership does not stand any too well here. They have lost prestige in their failure to get together on a single plan." What was more important, he thought, it was no great loss to have them opposing the plan, but he pledged "to do all I can to sweeten them up." Inside the Farm Board, he said, Ezekiel was working undercover all the time for the bill.

Still, the domestic allotment was not Wilson's only concern. He planned to have a "dignified member" of Congress introduce the Homestead Repeal bill as soon as possible. After the allotment bill was out of the way, he wanted Christgau to reintroduce the regional readjustment bill and show how it was the logical follow-up legislation for the domestic allotment bill. Finally, he hoped that the present allotment bill would be limited to three years and be very conservative in its approach to attract broader support. Wilson emphasized that it would educate and demonstrate to the farmers what benefits came from production control and suggested that after three years it might be performed on a completely voluntary basis. One unnamed House member, he quoted, laughed at talk about the bill's temporary nature, and said, "If the farmers get a taste of tariff blood you will never get them off unless you reduce the tariff." [9]

Legge wrote Wilson that he should be more explicit on the agricultural commodities to come under the bill's jurisdiction. He thought it should be applied only to those crops on which it was most likely to succeed. Also Legge objected to taking a referendum among the growers of the commodity involved. Why should it not be put into effect as any other piece of legislation and let the benefits accrue to those who decided to participate in the plan? he asked. The most important criticism Legge leveled at the plan was in its administration. Although he realized that the goal was to have the plan administered through already existing agencies, he felt too many were involved:

> Do you realize that the program as set up contemplates involving the Department of Agriculture, the Federal Farm Bureau, the Secretary of the Treasury, the Bureau of Internal Revenue and the Tariff Commission at the Washington end of the line, the State, County and Local Allotment Boards in the territory, plus the Boards of Arbitration and County Agents?

On the same date Legge wrote Chairman Stone of the Farm Board that perhaps the board had better change its "stand pat" policy and back some reasonable program like the Wilson plan instead of being forced to undertake a measure that would be doomed to failure from the outset. The allotment plan avoided dumping surpluses on

[9] Wilson to "Bozeman Folks" (May 29, 1932), Wilson MSS.

the foreign market and also called for production control, which had been unpopular a few years ago but now was "becoming pretty generally accepted." [10]

In a letter to Hyde a couple of days later, Legge said the stumbling block was Simpson's demand for a cost-of-production plan. "Wilson told me over the telephone that was the price that Simpson put on his approval of the project," Legge related, "and of course every body familiar with the situation knows that a cost of production program is impossible." Hyde replied that he had talked with Wilson but had not seen the bill he was sponsoring. He was advised by a member of the House Agricultural Committee that the committee had voted to refuse a report on the Wilson bill by a vote of seven to six. The deciding factor appeared to be that the farm organizations had their own bill which the committee called the "three horned bill." "The failure of the three great farm organizations to support the bill is responsible for the refusal of the Committee to vote it out," Hyde charged.[11] Ardent supporters of the domestic allotment felt it was an outrage that farm relief had to be postponed because of the farm organizations, but with the plan so little known the farm organizations had a distinct advantage.

Senator Norbeck asserted that the failure of the domestic allotment people to win over the farm organizations and more legislative support was because of their unyielding attitude on production control. This crucial point of the Wilson plan was still unacceptable to many. Norbeck noted that Wilson left Washington only when he became convinced it was futile to push for a domestic allotment at this time. While the legislative machinery stymied on the three-way plan, Wilson made plans to go to the Republican National Convention and an agricultural economics meeting to be held in Chicago. At the Republican convention Wilson tried to gain a hearing before the Platform Committee, but his request was pushed aside in the hectic convention atmosphere. From there his thoughts turned to the Democratic convention which was scheduled to meet the

[10] Legge to Wilson (June 1, 1932); Legge to Stone (June 1, 1932), files of the Economic and Statistical Analysis Division of the Economic Research Service, USDA.

[11] Legge to Hyde (June 6, 1932), RG 16, National Archives and Records Service; Hyde to Legge (June 6, 1932), files of the Economic and Statistical Analysis Division of the Economic Research Service, USDA; Ronald to Wilson (June 15, 1932), Wilson MSS.

last of June. Democratic Congressman John N. Norton of Nebraska advised Wilson not to waste time on the party conventions, but to spend time perfecting the bill and making friends with all the anti-Hoover people.[12]

On June 24, Wilson was in Chicago for the meeting of economists sponsored by the Giannini Foundation for Agricultural Economics. In part the meeting was a direct result of the April conference on the domestic allotment. Tugwell came to the conference by special invitation and was given a detailed description of the allotment plan—both its politics and economics in discussions with Wilson and Wallace. After considering it, Tugwell placed a long distance call to Roosevelt. He asked the governor to delay writing the agricultural portion of his acceptance speech to the convention until after he had conferred with his advisers. Tugwell made it clear that the speech should contain some definite commitment to farm relief. Tugwell then told Moley, "Let Wilson see Roosevelt before any other people see him in regards to the agricultural program in the campaign." Shortly after the final campaign cheers of the Democratic convention, Wilson was called to Albany, and there he had a session with Roosevelt on the domestic allotment plan in early July, 1932. Wilson felt especially indebted to Tugwell for opening the doors to this important interview with the governor. The detection of this new farm plan and its growing strength amidst the general confusion on the subject generated by the farm organizations was certainly to Tugwell's credit. "It was an indication of the notable effectiveness of the Brain Trust that Roosevelt almost immediately became aware of it," writes Frank Freidel. Later, Tugwell himself wrote:

> The scheme was called by its proponents "the domestic allotment plan" and its attraction was that it accepted the necessity for limitation of production but depended on elected county committees for the enforcement of generally agreed crop quotas. Keeping the government largely out of disciplinary duties was, I thought, a remarkable contribution. I wanted Franklin to accept the principle at once.[13]

[12] Norbeck to Ronald (June 16, 1932), Norbeck MSS; Wilson, COHC.
[13] Raymond Moley, *After Seven Years* (New York: Harper & Brothers, 1939), p. 41; Moley, *The First New Deal* (New York: Harcourt, Brace & World, 1966), p. 249; Wilson, COHC; Frank Freidel, *Franklin D. Roosevelt: The Triumph* (Boston: Little, Brown and Company, 1956), p. 273; Rexford G. Tugwell, *The Democratic Roosevelt* (Garden City, N.Y.: Doubleday & Company, Inc., 1957), p. 232.

At their face-to-face meeting in Albany, Roosevelt and Wilson first talked of where the Democratic speech on agriculture should be given. The Republicans usually delivered theirs in Des Moines. Wilson thought it would be a mistake for the Democrats to deliver their statement in the corn belt and advised the governor to make his pronouncement in the wheat area. Wilson wanted the speech to be made closer to the areas where agriculture was in most distress and that was, in his opinion, first in the wheat area and second in the cotton region. The corn-hog area was probably "better off" than the other two. Wilson suggested somewhere a little farther west and south, perhaps, where cotton and wheat met—along a line from Omaha to Kansas City. Roosevelt replied that he had been thinking of Topeka and Wilson concurred.

Now Wilson moved to a careful exposition of the problems faced in the wheat areas. He had had much practice in explaining these problems and the plan to remedy the situation beginning with local meetings in Montana two years before. The approach that he found best, and which he proceeded to use on the future President, was "slipping up on the blind side." As he talked of the plan, he put no name tag on it but merely outlined the problems faced by the wheat crop and what steps had to be taken logically to overcome these most obvious difficulties. In the process he avoided direct attack on the McNary-Haugen proposals in order not to offend anyone favoring those plans. Wilson believed that Roosevelt caught the strategy of this approach immediately and said to Moley that this will be the way we will approach the farmer on any plan during the campaign. At this, Wilson said, he thought he remembered Roosevelt throwing his head back with a gleam in his eye, giving a chuckle, and slapping his knee when he caught the tactics of Wilson's conversation.

When Wilson went on to explain some of his ideas about planning in agriculture, withdrawal of submarginal lands, local democratic committees playing a role in decisions on agricultural policy, and the relocation of industry in rural areas, Roosevelt thought a minute and recalled his statements on agriculture while governor of New York and said, "See here, Mr. Wilson. Is this your plan or my plan?" Wilson replied that perhaps only the domestic allotment plan as presented was exclusively his own. Roosevelt was greatly interested in the National Chamber of Commerce president, Harriman, and was impressed with a farm plan that could attract support from business leaders.[14]

Looking back on the meeting between Roosevelt and Wilson, Tugwell said, "What we were looking for was a way of controlling production which would be politically feasible. Wilson thought he had it. That was the contribution achieved by the domestic allotment plan." Wilson explained that the idea for county associations of farmers to work on the allotment committees had occurred to him on his visits to the Canadian wheat provinces where he observed the workings of their local cooperative committees composed of wheat farmers. He endorsed the referendum concept because it would serve to rally popular support to the plan. Although it was charged that farmers would cheat on reporting their individual allotment figures, Wilson felt he had the answer to this charge. The Stillwater County assessor in Montana had once campaigned on a platform to reduce the cost of assessing property for tax purposes. His method was to have each farmer in the county assess the amount of tangible property on his farm and mail the estimate to the assessor's office. When the results were compiled the assessor published them in the local newspaper and farmers scrutinized the reports of their neighbors. This Wilson proposed to do with the acreage allotment for each farmer in the community. Here, in Tugwell's view, was the plan that could place controls on the American farmer in such a way that the regulation would be politically acceptable. Tugwell said he knew the word "control" was anathema to the American people and especially the farmers, but he could see no other way out of the problem short of inflation.[15]

Returning to New York, Wilson met with Tugwell and also Hugh Johnson. General Johnson objected to the committee system in administering the plan because he said that the plan's leadership would not have a united voice. "You've got to put some one in charge to get anything done," he said. After the meeting in Albany, Wilson confessed that he definitely felt "magnetized" by F. D. R.'s personality and there was little doubt whom he would support for President in November. This was all the more reason for Wilson to accept Roosevelt's request that he be available for future consultations on farm policy during the campaign. Tugwell recalled that

[14] Wilson, COHC.
[15] Wilson, COHC; Tugwell, COHC.

Wilson had also won the respect of Roosevelt and that Wilson and his plan immediately captured the governor's interest. Tugwell said:

> Of course, he took the Governor into camp. He always takes everybody into camp. Wilson's the most ingratiating person that ever lived. He waves his arm and talks generally. He looks a little like John Dewey and he has a little bit of the same expansiveness. You have to pick out the gems of sentences in paragraphs of discourse the same as you do with John Dewey. But the gems are there, usually, and he took the Governor into camp.[16]

Back in Washington, Senator Norbeck had introduced a modified version of the domestic allotment plan in bill form to the Senate, which passed without a record vote. The bill found favor in the House where a similar proposal was under consideration sponsored by Congressman Henry T. Rainey of Illinois. In the Senate, however, it was moved that the bill be reconsidered the following day. The next morning, despite Norbeck's efforts to the contrary, the Senate voted to recall the bill from the House, thus killing any chance for agricultural legislation in the session, for Congress adjourned two days later.[17]

After the defeat, Congressman Hope advised the hurried introduction of another allotment bill for publicity purposes. Both he and Norbeck introduced bills into the House and Senate. The Hope-Norbeck bills received no consideration, rendering only the desired publicity. With reference to these legislative maneuverings, Hope wrote that it "all goes to illustrate the fact that it is absolutely impossible to legislate intelligently under present conditions. I think the best thing we can do is to quit and go home as soon as possible and then come back in December and pass the Domestic Allotment bill." These abortive attempts at domestic allotment legislation in the closing days of the session pointed to the direction that national agricultural legislation was to take. Even Peek wrote, "I should not be surprised, however, if this principle [the domestic allotment] would be used in future plans for agricultural legislation."[18]

[16] Wilson, COHC; Tugwell, COHC.

[17] *Congressional Record*, 72d Cong., 1st sess., July 13, 1932, 15194, and July 14, 1932, 15338; *New York Times*, July 15, 1932.

[18] Hope to Wilson (July 15, 1932); Peek to Clarke (July 15, 1932), Wilson MSS.

At the same time Wilson told Hope that the domestic allotment plan was no permanent solution. Any comprehensive approach to the farm problem must involve agricultural planning. On this question he called Hope's attention to the new Christgau bill under preparation. The head of the Bureau of Agricultural Economics, Nils Olsen, saw the Christgau bill as a threat to the functions of the bureau. He wrote that it "takes over pretty fully the activities of this Department and the Land Grant Colleges in supplying leadership and direction in planning readjustments in land utilization." In addition he requested criticisms of the measure from the Office of Farm Management and suggestions "that might be used in connection with a counter proposal." [19]

Despite defeat in Congress, the domestic allotment plan was now a national issue. R. R. Rogers of the Prudential Insurance Company wrote to Wilson expressing optimism: "Undoubtedly the movement gains headway in almost every direction. The thing now is to get it to the farmers themselves." From Mitchell, South Dakota, W. R. Ronald promised to build a bonfire under the bankers in Minneapolis, and another South Dakotan, editor Robert Lusk of Huron, felt he could obtain support from the state's Farm Holiday Association for the allotment plan. "I feel that we would be making a mistake were we to fail to work with this group and direct it to an endorsement of the voluntary allotment plan," he wrote Wilson. Wilson thought that Grimes at Kansas State College would soon come out for the domestic allotment and thus strengthen Hope's position in the state on the issue. Wilson conveyed this confidential information to Hope with the preface: "Kansas is such a pivotal agricultural state and you have taken such a fine aggressive attitude in the matter that I want to go to any limits to help you to assist in getting Kansas lined up satisfactorily." [20]

Harriman at a Minneapolis meeting in July revealed his hand publicly when he announced support of the emergency allotment bill under discussion in Congress. His statement shocked millers and grain men in the city, and they wasted no time in expressing their indignation to him. At a meeting of twenty to twenty-five

[19] Wilson to Hope (July 22, 1932), Wilson MSS; Olsen to C. H. Holmes, Office of Farm Management (July 25, 1932), RG 83, NARS.
[20] Rogers to Wilson (July 19, 1932); Ronald to Wilson (July 19, 1932); Lusk to Wilson (July 22, 1932); Wilson to Hope (July 22, 1932), Wilson MSS.

grain men, including James Bell, president of General Mills, and Charles S. Pillsbury of the Pillsbury Mills, Harriman was given a "very vigorous bawling out." Harriman's only reply was that if "they didn't want him to be President of the National Chamber, the Board of Directors could fire him and like Alex Legge he had an independent income." Wilson made a special effort to inform Tugwell on Harriman's background in response to Roosevelt's interest in the man. He was graduated from the classical course at Wesleyan University in Middletown, Connecticut, and later studied law in the office of Charles Evans Hughes in New York, but never practiced. Instead he invested in cotton textile manufacturing and from this he went into public utilities and formed the New England Water Power Association that provided power to the region's textile mills. "He impresses me," said Wilson, "as being thoroughly democratic in his make-up, is a close friend of Justice Brandeis and other New England liberals." Wilson did not mention that Harriman also had investments in Montana agriculture.[21]

Wilson was also looking ahead to the next session of Congress. On July 16 he had Senator Norbeck introduce two resolutions. One asked for a report at the next session of Congress on the European restrictions on U.S. exports. Wilson knew this document would be embarrassing to advocates of the equalization fee and export debenture. The other called for the economists in the Bureau of Agricultural Economics and in the Farm Board to work on a farm relief plan to be applied to hogs. If the two agencies reported accurately, Wilson thought the reports would show that the voluntary domestic allotment plan would be the only plan which had any chance of helping all three major agricultural sections in the country.

On the local level in the Midwest the farm holiday movement drew public attention. Wilson agreed with his South Dakota friends Robert Lusk and Ronald that "we should show our sympathy with the farmers trying to hold their products off the market for a better price, and then interest them in the permanent solution we are advocating." Ronald thought that "our long-time cause would be furthered by any radical movements of this kind which all make

[21] Wilson to Englund (July 23, 1932); Wilson to Tugwell (July 25, 1932), Wilson MSS.

our plan seem tame." Wilson admitted that he knew very little about the holiday since it had not yet struck Montana, but he was not surprised that such a movement was under way. He was skeptical about the economics and the workability of its proposal, "but this is an outburst of pent-up emotions in farmers' minds which results from the present ridiculous prices." In spite of its impractical approach, he felt, "They will do the cause of permanent farm relief good rather than harm." Wilson thought the farmers' holiday might sweep the country, and he told editor Lusk that he had performed an excellent stroke of business in winning the South Dakota organization to the voluntary allotment plan. "It is just such pieces of strategy as this that will finally put us across," said Wilson. Lusk urged an appeal to the national organization, saying that "Milo Reno seems to be the big shot that should be sold on it." [22]

The domestic allotment plan, however, did not meet with success on all fronts. Dr. Joseph S. Davis of the Food Research Institute of Stanford University wrote an article for the *Northwestern Miller*, July 13, 1932, in which he criticized the plan. Wilson thought Davis was not totally informed on the plan. He also described Davis as a "very conservative man, but I am inclined to think that at the present time he would say that the voluntary allotment plan has more merit to it than any other plan which has yet been suggested." In addition, the Food Research Institute was largely endowed by President Hoover, and Davis was formerly chief economist for the Farm Board. Wilson had no doubt that these associations helped shape Davis's thinking regarding agricultural relief proposals along conservative lines. [23] Turning to his own political position, Wilson told the editor of the *Montana Farmer* that Roosevelt greatly impressed him during a recent interview. He wrote:

> I think I shall have to classify myself this fall as a Roosevelt Republican. Likely the Republicans will criticize him for radicalism and socialism, but I am satisfied that neither of these are justifiable characterizations. I should call him liberal but neither radical nor socialistic in the accepted sense of the term. [24]

[22] Wilson to Ronald (July 27, 1932); Ronald to Wilson (July 30, 1932); Wilson to Lusk (July 27, 1932); Lusk to Wilson (July 30, 1932); Wilson to Lusk (August 3, 1932), Wilson MSS.

[23] Wilson to B. H. Woodworth, Woodworth Elevator Company, Minneapolis, Minnesota (July 27, 1932), Wilson MSS.

[24] Wilson to Lester Cole (July 27, 1932), Wilson MSS.

As early as July 28, 1932, Wilson was sending Moley and Henry Morgenthau, Jr., memoranda for preparation of the governor's agricultural speech. Tugwell hoped that the major Wilson memorandum on agriculture would reach the East before August 4 and wrote Wilson that it was "being awaited with great anticipation." But Wilson's major agricultural memo was not mailed to the brain trust until August 22. It was a twenty-two-page typed document that Wilson had worked on with the advice of Ezekiel, Bushrod Allen, a tax economist in the Bureau of Agricultural Economics, and Wallace in Des Moines. After outlining the need for federally supported agricultural relief, the memo asserted that the purpose of federal relief "should be to provide protection for agriculture adequate to restore agriculture to a parity with industry." The plan should meet two requirements—protection against foreign competition and control of production to avoid excessive surpluses. The only method of effective control of production would be to grant a reward for voluntary compliance with the requirements set by the program. The plan should be financed by a sales tax on the agricultural commodities it included and its administration would be carried out by voluntary local committees. "The need for this relief is so imperative that leading farmers in each county would gladly serve without charge as county and township supervisors. . . ."[25]

The memorandum made little mention of increased credit facilities for the farmer. Wilson fought the inflationary approach to the farm problem in his letters to the governor's advisers. He told Rogers, "I am using the little influence I have by the grapevine route, to keep the Governor from talking a lot of tommy-rot in his speeches about government loans to farmers and a subsidized interest rate." This stand, of course, impressed the insurance and creditor men in the East and showed Wilson's basic economic conservatism as well as his Republican economic orientation quite divorced from the western silverites and inflationary heritage of the agrarian wing of the Democratic party. Wilson thought Tugwell was of much the same viewpoint, but "a little visionary on the farm mortgage interest rate" and more inclined to favor a subsidy to farm mortgages. To correct this trend in the thinking

[25] Wilson to Morgenthau (July 28, 1932); Tugwell to Wilson (August 1, 1932), Wilson MSS; Wilson, COHC; "Essential Elements of a Federal Farm Relief Program," Wilson MSS.

around the governor that was also being promoted by Henry Morgenthau, Jr., and Cornell economist George F. Warren, who advocated the commodity dollar, Wilson urged Rogers to meet with Tugwell and convince him that "we want to raise the price on farm products so that the farmer can pay his interest rate and thereby neither make him dishonest through an attitude of repudiation or an object of government charity through dropping the rate below its economic level." [26]

Peek was of the opinion that while the equalization fee plan would be much simpler in administration, the domestic allotment plan with its state, county, and township committees would have a greater tendency to stimulate organization of the farmers. "If they secured the benefits of such a plan a year or two, any political party that tried to take it away from them later would be out of luck." he said. Looking back over his experience, Peek recalled that there never had been an opportunity to sit down and draft the most ideal farm measure without political considerations. He was irritated that "we had a difference in views among the farmers themselves and among the friends of farmers to say nothing of the antagonism of the opponents." Peek was unaware of Governor Roosevelt's plan for the conduct of his farm campaign. He hoped that he would avoid the contradictory statements that Governor Smith had made regarding the farm problem in 1928. [27]

Meanwhile Ronald started to send articles on the domestic allotment to the *Dakota Farmer*, the *Nebraska Farmer*, the *Michigan Farmer*, the *Farm Journal* in Philadelphia, and the *Prairie Farmer* in Chicago. "Publication of a story on the plan in a few farm papers will automatically gain the interest of the others and make more likely their use of similar articles," he told Wilson. Clearly, both Wilson and Ronald were now bent upon selling the plan to the general farm population. Regarding the agricultural memorandum sent to Moley, Wilson sent a long letter explaining some of the

[26] Wilson, COHC; Wilson to Rogers (August 3, 1932), Wilson MSS; John Morton Blum, *From the Morganthau Diaries: Years of Crisis, 1928–1938* (Boston: Houghton Mifflin Company, 1959), p. 41; Tugwell, COHC, ". . . the Cornell group were not interested in farm relief at all. They had a notion that all you had to do was to manipulate the amount of gold in the dollar. . . . We had trouble with the Cornell group all the way through, in the attempt to work out a farm relief program, because they didn't believe in any."

[27] Peek to Hirth (August 10, 1932), Peek MSS.

rationale behind its statements. He emphasized the "equality for agriculture" ring in the document and said this was designed to attract the attention of the great mass of farmers who had been influenced by the "equality for agriculture" movement in the previous decade. The speech was aimed at the type of farmer who might be influenced to switch his vote from Republican to Democratic. Wilson saw this class of corn-belt and wheat-belt farmer as Republican by heredity, who voted for Hoover four years ago in spite of the "equality for agriculture" campaign against him.

Still Wilson believed the phrase "equality for agriculture" had a magic appeal for the farmer. "It is fixed in his sub-conscious mind and carries both a hope for better times and a resentment against the President and his so-called Eastern Republicans." The recent development on the farm that postdated the "equality for agriculture" movement, Wilson thought, was a general acceptance by the farmers of reduced and adjusted production levels. It was true that they did not believe in it three years ago when the Secretary of Agriculture and the Farm Board "went on their barnstorming and acreage reduction campaign." The demand for reduced production would be a drawing card instead of a liability in this campaign, Wilson reasoned. Finally he urged Moley to notice that the speech bore resemblance to the Democratic attack of four years ago: "It might be helpful to you to read the Smith speech made at Omaha, Nebraska. This explains the reason for the section dealing with Equality for Agriculture."[28]

When Farmers' Union president Simpson invaded South Dakota and attacked the Wilson domestic allotment plan, it brought a stinging reply from Ronald. Ronald wrote Simpson, "I was surprised and amazed by the remarks you made at Yankton." He denied that those supporting the voluntary domestic allotment plan tried to go around the farm organizations. "The support given the plan came first from the Montana State Farm Bureau . . . ," he said, and added, "The first man I tried to see when I went to Washington was John Simpson." Ronald called Simpson's attack on Harriman "unfortunate" and pointed to the fact that Harriman was also being denounced and condemned by enemies of agriculture in the Chamber of Commerce of the United States. "The effect of your

[28] Ronald to Wilson (August 13, 1932); Wilson to Moley (August 22, 1932), Wilson MSS.

remarks was to make Mr. Harriman rather a lone figure in insisting that Congress do something for the farmer," said Ronald. Ronald explained that he had written the *Nation's Business*, the mouthpiece of the United States Chamber of Commerce, asking that they publish one of his articles on the voluntary domestic allotment plan. "The reply from the editor," Ronald related, "was that they do not wish to print anything of the sort." He accused Simpson of unwittingly playing into the hands of those in the United States Chamber of Commerce who still opposed any and all form of farm relief and asked, if some in the East believe it is in their interest to advocate a relief plan for agriculture, "should not we welcome their assistance and cooperation?" This last statement was the keynote of Wilson's entire campaign for the domestic allotment plan.[29]

Regarding the business interests of Montana and showing his continued interest in Wilson's work, President Atkinson of Montana State College wanted Wilson to do some public relations work with the milling and elevator interests of the state, who were disturbed at the prospect of domestic allotment legislation. These business people increasingly contacted the President for a meeting with Wilson, who was rapidly gaining a reputation as the leading authority on the plan in the United States. Atkinson recognized that a meeting of this kind might detract from more important work in the campaign. He wrote, "I am conscious of the fact that the attitude of the people in Montana will not be the major factor in deciding whether or not the Domestic Allotment plan is put into effect," but he felt that a conference with these people might ease some mounting resentment against the college among business interests in the state.[30]

By late August, Wilson was revealing in his correspondence that he had had a personal conference with Roosevelt and that he was a consultant to the governor's research staff in the East. He told Hirth that he had prepared a memorandum for Roosevelt's agricultural speech, but said, "He is a man who does his own thinking and works out his own speeches." Wilson thought that President Hoover laid himself open to attack in his acceptance speech when he said there was no power on earth which could raise prices, and "as I interpreted the paragraph, practically closed the door on

[29] Ronald to Simpson (August 27, 1932), Wilson MSS.
[30] Atkinson to Wilson (August 27, 1932), Wilson MSS.

farm relief." Wilson not only hoped the Democratic candidate would take advantage of these clear-cut and immediate issues to hit the Republican leadership, but also hoped for a pronouncement about the future of agriculture that would "set forth his philosophy with reference to agriculture in the future." As the political campaign progressed, Wilson came to the conclusion that the country was undergoing a vast new political realignment that would continue for years to come. A central issue between the opposing forces would be a nationwide fight to reduce all federal taxes and practically eliminate everything in government except its primary functions of keeping domestic order and providing defense from foreign attack. The fight would be centered on reducing taxes and doing away with bureaucracy. As he viewed the situation in the traditionally Republican Northwest, Wilson prophetically told Ronald, "You will find that we will be classed among the bureaucrats." [31]

Wilson also kept in contact with the Republican campaign. On September 7, he sent Moley a "confidential" letter containing information "from sources which I do not care to divulge" on the Republican agricultural strategy. According to Wilson's sources, neither Secretary Hyde nor any of Hoover's agricultural advisers were consulted about the section dealing with agriculture in his acceptance speech. His advisers were astounded at his reference to the shortcomings of the Farm Board and what many people called "Hoover's closing the door to farm relief." The President's advisers wanted him to say little about agriculture in order to give Roosevelt the chance to make the first speech. They hoped and were confident that the Topeka speech would endorse inflation as the panacea to the farm problem, said Wilson. They also expected the governor to be full of platitudes about the farmer, but to have nothing concrete with reference to surplus problems either in the way of tariff benefits or production control. In the Topeka speech they looked for Roosevelt to outline a national land policy involving the retirement of submarginal lands and reforestation along the lines of his New York program. Most important, they were banking on his proposing a vast inflationary scheme for immediate farm relief.

On the basis of this speech, the Republicans hoped to play on the idea that Roosevelt was a radical inflationist, an eastern W. J. Bryan,

[31] Wilson to Hirth (August 29, 1932); Wilson to Ronald (September 5, 1932), Wilson MSS.

that he had no agricultural philosophy, and no definite plan for meeting the surplus problem. "They are getting ready to ridicule the idea of solving the agricultural problem by planting trees," Wilson added. The people in the Hoover campaign further hoped and expected that Roosevelt would direct most of his attack against the Farm Board and not against the Hoover policies and Republican history for the last twelve years. What they did not want and feared most was the "anti-agricultural attitude of Hoover paraded," according to Wilson. In Wilson's opinion, farmers wanted two things: first, sympathy and, next, some new specific proposals. He felt sure the Republicans would offer neither. The only constructive claim they would make was that the stabilization corporation caused the prices of wheat and cotton to be higher than they would have been otherwise. After considering the developing trend of the campaign and hoping that the "Governor will see fit to develop a sympathetic and forceful speech at Topeka," Wilson concluded that the spring wheat territory would land in the Roosevelt column.[32]

As the days moved closer to the Topeka speech on September 14, the national political campaign took increasing precedence over the campaign for the domestic allotment plan. Wilson told Ezekiel that he had made two trips from Washington to New York and returned by way of Chicago and Des Moines to confer with Wallace and Chester Davis on the memorandum for the governor's speech. At the moment he said, "There is not a great deal of news with reference to progress on the voluntary domestic allotment plan." But Wilson's head had not been entirely turned to the political arena, for he urged Ezekiel to continue talks with Father John Ryan at Catholic University on the domestic allotment plan, and said, "I am particularly anxious that Father Ryan be educated . . . because I want to stir up some Catholics to write him. . . . I think it will help tremendously if we can get Father Ryan and the National Catholic Welfare Council on our side." Later in the month, Father Ryan announced his support of the plan to Wilson. This was an occasion for Wilson to write Ezekiel thanking him for the "wonderful job which you have done in putting this over with Father Ryan. This is going to be very helpful to us."[33]

[32] Wilson to Moley (September 7, 1932), Wilson MSS.
[33] Wilson to Ezekiel (September 9, 1932); Wilson to Ezekiel (September 21, 1932), Wilson MSS.

From Chicago, Davis reported that Earl Smith was disappointed in the farm organizations' three-way bill, but resentful at any plan sponsored by the Chamber of Commerce or insurance men. Smith said he was afraid Wilson was going to "make a fatal mistake" by permitting the domestic allotment plan to appear before the country "labeled as a U.S. Chamber or big business bill." At this Davis said "I tore into him harder than I have had a chance to do before. . . ." Davis pointed to Wilson's early support of the McNary-Haugen fight, his attempts to get the farm groups to support the domestic allotment plan and particularly the effort to get them "to take up the banner and lead the fight." After this, Smith made some concessions, but said Ronald was "a bad man to be contacting the farm groups or Congress." Ronald's tactics were apparently so aggressive that he offended those he was trying to convince. Wilson saw that Smith must be in this group and wrote Davis, "Ronald is a very aggressive chap who gets by very well with some people but unfortunately greatly antagonizes others."[34] Although Ronald might have lacked the finesse that Wilson used in dealing with people and, as Tugwell said, "taking them into camp," he served the cause of the domestic allotment plan well in his tireless efforts, attention to details, and endless footwork that had to be done in the publicity campaign. Wilson, using him as a loyal lieutenant in the field, constantly asked him to answer correspondence and to send his articles on the plan to various people throughout the country.

The opposition to the domestic allotment plan within Montana, which President Atkinson had feared, finally came out against the plan in a letter to Harriman. C. R. McClave, president of the Montana Flour Mills Company, complained about Harriman's support of the voluntary domestic allotment plan at the recent Economic Conference of the National Chamber of Commerce at Colorado Springs. "You asked why millers and grain dealers are so definitely opposed to legislation to make this plan effective?" wrote McClave. "The answer is that it is impracticable, unworkable, exceedingly cumbersome, and if made effective will further complicate the tragic agricultural problems which now confront this country." McClave went on to criticize the unsound economic thinking "by well-

[34] Davis to Wilson (September 10, 1932); Wilson to Davis (September 15, 1932), Wilson MSS.

meaning but inexperienced (and often self-appointed) farm leaders and farm political elements." He concluded that government intervention into the free play of economic forces in the agricultural community was the real cause of the present situation and urged President Harriman to reconsider his position on the proposed domestic allotment plan.[35]

While some in the business community fumed over the question of government intervention into the economy, Roosevelt's campaign train on its western trip arrived in Topeka for his major address on the agricultural question on September 14, 1932. Raymond Moley writes that the forthcoming speech was designed to win the Midwest "without waking up the dogs of the East." It was the product of more than twenty-five people, "but the very heart of the speech was contributed by Wilson."[36] Under the sunny skies of Kansas, Roosevelt spoke to a huge outdoor audience in general terms about the need for land planning in agriculture, attacked the Hoover administration, and called for more initiative from the federal government. Without mentioning any plan by name, he said that he agreed with "reasonable leaders of agriculture" that any approach to the agricultural problem should meet the following specifications:

First: The plan must provide for the producers of staple surplus commodities, such as wheat, cotton, corn in the form of hogs, and tobacco, a tariff benefit over world prices which is equivalent to the benefit given by the tariff to industrial products. This differential benefit must be so applied that the increase in farm income, purchasing the debt-paying power will not stimulate further production.

Second: The plan must finance itself. Agriculture has at no time sought and does not now seek any such access to the public treasury as was provided by the futile and costly attempts at price stabilization by the Federal farm board. It seeks only equality of opportunity with tariff-protected industry.

Third: It must not make use of any mechanism which would cause our European customers to retaliate on the grounds of dumping. It must be based upon making the tariff effective and direct in its operation.

[35] McClave to Harriman (September 13, 1932), Wilson MSS.
[36] Moley, *After Seven Years*, p. 45; Moley, *The First New Deal*, p. 250.

Fourth: It must make use of existing agencies and so far as possible be decentralized in its Administration so that the chief responsibility for its operation will rest with the locality rather than with newly created bureaucratic machinery in Washington.

Fifth: It must operate as nearly as possible on a cooperative basis and its effect must be to enhance and strengthen the cooperative movement. It should, moreover, be constituted so that it can be withdrawn whenever the emergency has passed and normal foreign markets have been reestablished.

Sixth: The plan must be, insofar as possible, voluntary. I like the idea that the plan should not be put into operation unless it has the support of a reasonable majority of the producers of the exportable commodity to which it is to apply. It must be so organized that the benefits will go to the man who participates.[37]

Supporters of the domestic allotment plan applauded the speech. At the offices of the *Mitchell Republican,* Ronald and his staff celebrated when the Associated Press delivered advance copies of the governor's speech. "The language is so familiar," he wrote Wilson, "and the identity of the plan he has in mind was so obvious that we felt warranted in the conviction that after all these years, there is at last a prospect of justice for the farmers." From Omaha Clarke exclaimed in a letter to Wilson, "Oh, boy, what a speech and did he hit the Domestic Allotment plan square in the bull's eye? Congratulations, old boy, on the grand work you did in selling him the plan." State Senator Wilmer from Washington state wrote Wilson, "Of course, you noted Candidate Roosevelt's six points to Kansas farmers? 'Weaseling' was my first reaction but upon closer analysis I am wondering whether Mr. Roosevelt has not been told a lot about Domestic Allotments." Wilson heard the speech over the radio during his work on the Lone Warrior Fairway Farm at Poplar, Montana. He too was pleased with the speech and happy that the governor had not mentioned the domestic allotment plan by name in accordance with the strategy and advice outlined at Albany. Later, Tugwell wrote to Wilson, "I don't need to tell you how pleased I was about the Topeka speech. You—not I—deserve the credit."[38]

[37] *The Public Papers and Addresses of Franklin D. Roosevelt: The Genesis of the New Deal, 1928–1932* (New York: Random House, 1938), I, 704–705.

[38] Ronald to Wilson (September 14, 1932); Clarke to Wilson (September 14, 1932); Wilmer to Wilson (September 16, 1932); Tugwell to Wilson (September 30, 1932), Wilson MSS; Wilson, COHC.

Congressman Hope told Wilson that Governor Roosevelt "did everything but name it in his six point exposition of what he thought was a feasible farm program." Hope felt it was too early to gauge the reaction to the governor's speech in Kansas. Most editorial comment in the state said it was a fine essay on agricultural conditions with some excellent suggestions as to what ought to be done without saying how the desired result was to be brought about. "Of course, the allotment plan has not been discussed generally enough that very many people recognize its similarity to the specifications set up by the Governor," said Hope, but, "his speech would certainly indicate that he is impressed with the plan." Father Ryan, director of the Department of Social Action for the Catholic Church in America, wrote Wilson that he was strongly in favor of the domestic allotment plan, and "it seems to me that if enacted it would comply with all the six specifications set forth by Governor Roosevelt in his Topeka speech." He congratulated Wilson that the governor's proposals referred to the domestic allotment plan "and to no other plan." But the Catholic social reformer seemed well aware that Roosevelt was playing politics somewhat deceptively when he did not identify the plan in the speech. "But I hope that either Governor Roosevelt or the Democratic National Committee will find ways to make this identification public," Ryan wrote Wilson, "and to set forth as clearly as possible the 'Domestic Allotment Plan' as the specific means by which the Democratic Party intends to obtain better prices for the staple agricultural products." [39]

After hearing the broad implications of the Topeka speech, Wilson felt confident in hoping for a general reform in agriculture. It would, of course, be broader than the voluntary domestic allotment plan and should contain the ideas involved in land policy, agricultural planning, decentralization of industry, cooperative marketing, taxation, and financial reform. Roosevelt's speech was constructed in such a way that for the "enemy" to attack the proposed six points or the domestic allotment plan, they would first have "to penetrate this very plausible front line trench involving a

---

[39] Hope to Wilson (September 17, 1932), Wilson MSS; Ryan to Wilson (September 17, 1932), files of the Economic and Statistical Analysis Division of the Economic Research Service, USDA.

reconstruction program and a new agricultural industrial balance. This would tend to take the edge off of such a direct frontal attack on the Voluntary Domestic Allotment Plan," said Wilson.[40]

Still, Wilson was irritated with attacks on the domestic allotment plan, especially from the grain trade and the millers. He wrote McCarthy in Duluth, "I am disappointed the grain men and millers will probably take such a hostile, antagonistic attitude. Class or group antagonisms are very distasteful. . . ." When the September 7, 1932, issue of the *Northwestern Miller* published an attack on the domestic allotment and on Harriman's support of it, Wilson expressed his disappointment, saying, "In my judgment most of the arguments that have thus far been faced against the plan are the bunk." But in a letter to Chester Davis he saw another side of the question: "I am tickled to death to have this attack come from the *Northwestern Miller*." Wilson thought it would boomerang in favor of the plan for it dispelled the charge that the domestic allotment plan was a United States Chamber of Commerce and big-business bill. Congressman Hope also noted that the *Modern Miller* for August 20, 1932, had paid the plan the "compliment of a critical attack."[41]

With general comment on the Topeka speech suggesting that the six points laid out ideal goals, but ones impossible to fulfill, Wilson thought the time for a national campaign on the meaning and significance of the domestic allotment plan had come. He looked forward to another meeting in Chicago the last of September of the executive committee for the domestic allotment plan to consider raising funds to conduct a national educational campaign. He recognized that people criticized the Topeka speech because of its vagueness, but this was the price that had to be paid for not mentioning the plan directly. If the governor had referred to it by name, the opposition would "call it unconstitutional, un-democratic, socialistic, and all the bad names that are in the catalog. As it stands at the present time they cannot do this," said Wilson. "The opposition will have to attack the six points and so far I have not read any editorial criticism of the six points," Wilson wrote to Bishop O'Hara

[40] Wilson to Englund (September 15, 1932), Wilson MSS.

[41] Wilson to McCarthy (September 14, 1932); Wilson to Davis (September 15, 1932); Hope to Wilson (September 17, 1932), Wilson MSS.

in Helena asking him to join the educational effort in "fighting for a larger share of national income to go into agriculture." [42]

Before leaving for Chicago on September 21, Wilson met with Roosevelt in Butte as the candidate's campaign train moved to the West Coast. Roosevelt was in a confident mood and very satisfied with what he had said at Topeka. Although the domestic allotment plan had run a good course, the farm organizations now presented a serious hurdle. Wilson was unsure about the strategy to be used with representatives of the farm organizations in Chicago. He suggested that perhaps a direct, aggressive approach to them might serve the purpose, but he was also aware of the obstacles that Ronald had encountered using this method. When Wilson returned from Chicago, he was beginning to believe that the farm organizations had no choice other than to turn to the domestic allotment plan. He wrote Senator Hampton P. Fulmer of South Carolina, who had helped introduce a portion of the domestic allotment bill the previous summer, "It is my judgment that they were at first inclined to stand off at a little distance, but they are reading the writing on the wall and are now beginning to anticipate the election of Governor Roosevelt." With this fact becoming more apparent, Wilson thought that "you will see them shifting over toward the voluntary domestic allotment as fast as they can gracefully change positions." Also in Chicago it had been decided not to establish a national committee to carry on propaganda and education for the domestic allotment plan. "We have come to the conclusion now that such a committee is not necessary especially if the farm organizations will take up the program. I think the strategy is to wait and see before anything further is done." [43]

The Topeka speech was not the only major address on which the Roosevelt brain trust asked Wilson to express his opinion. His knowledge of the midwestern farmers' political mind was utilized for the Sioux City, Iowa, tariff speech September 29, 1932. At Butte he had been given two memoranda on two separate tariff speeches. One proposed a program for a "horizontal cut in the existing tariff." The other called for "modification of tariffs by

[42] Wilson to Ronald (September 15, 1932); Wilson to O'Hara (September 21, 1932), Wilson MSS.

[43] Wilson to Clarke (September 20, 1932); Wilson to Black (October 7, 1932); Wilson to Fulmer (October 6, 1932), Wilson MSS.

negotiation." After a night's reflection on the speeches, Wilson sent his advice to the Roosevelt campaign special at its Santa Barbara, California, stop. From an economist's point of view he praised the horizontal cut in the tariff, but "from the standpoint of political strategy and from the standpoint of agriculture, I am absolutely of the opinion that it would be very unwise for the Governor to make the speech proposing the horizontal cut," he said. Instead he advised, "It would be a master stroke of political strategy for him to make the 'tariff by negotiation' speech."

To support his reasoning, Wilson said that the address at Sioux City would be mostly to farmers who had in the past been Republicans and who must be convinced that it is safe to shift to the Democratic party under Roosevelt's leadership. "I am a son of one of these Iowa farmers," said Wilson, "and I think I know their psychology thoroughly." For two generations their minds have been inculcated with the high tariff ideas, and "anything which has the sound of reduction of the tariff causes cold shivers to go down the Iowa farmer's back," he wrote. Wilson thought Hoover would reinforce this prejudice in his agricultural speech in Des Moines by telling farmers that the tariff was giving the American farmer great protection, "and were it not for these tariff walls the American farmer would be much worse off than he is now and would be subject to the dumping of cattle from Argentina, wheat from Canada, etc." Wilson had it on good authority that the Republicans were counting on the Democrats to support across-the-board reduced tariffs, "which would be repulsive to their [the farmers'] accustomed habits of thought."

Therefore, Wilson felt Roosevelt could deliver a master stroke of strategy by proposing "tariff by negotiation." He could stress the point that the United States would reduce its tariffs only "on a trading basis" if other nations reduced theirs in return. "I think this proposal will please all of our middle-western Republican farmers who will see the 'horse-trade' philosophy in it and this deeply ingrained high tariff complex in their subconscious minds will not be offended," concluded Wilson. Wilson, however, was afraid that Hoover might also come out for "tariff by negotiation." That morning he had received from one of his contacts in the Department of Agriculture a letter that led him to believe that Secretary Hyde was suggesting a high tariff speech but at the same time inserting a reciprocity proposal. When Moley showed Wilson's letter to Roosevelt, he seemed deeply impressed. "Roosevelt read this letter two or three times. Then he looked up and said: 'You'd better get Tom Walsh and Key Pittman [both high tariff Democrats] to work with you on the speech.'"[44]

Although Roosevelt followed the suggested course of action in his Sioux City speech, Wilson was afraid of any further pronouncements by the governor on tariff policy. He knew the Republicans were eager to seize on any statement in order to play on the "fear complex" that the Democrats were going to have free trade and ship cattle from the Argentine and permit agricultural goods to be dumped on the domestic market. "It is for this reason I think the Governor should not say any more about the tariff than he said at Sioux City but press hard on the constructive side of his program," Wilson wrote Tugwell.[45]

In his arguments for the domestic allotment plan, Wilson often described himself as a tariff isolationist. He took this position to denote the disappearance of world markets and the necessity for protecting the domestic market and regulating production to its demands through the domestic allotment plan. "I lean toward the tariff isolation policy," he wrote James S. Milloy of the *Minneapolis Tribune*, "and, of course, it is for this reason that I believe the Domestic Allotment Plan is worthy of trial, both on the grounds of its making the tariff effective on the portion of the product domestically consumed and its production control features." When Black learned that Wilson was arguing for reduced production and the domestic allotment on the grounds that it would make for "national self-sufficiency," he objected. "My interpretation," said Black, who was in no way a tariff isolationist, "of the Allotment Plan is that it offers a way of controlling production upward as well as downward, as may be in the best interest of the farmers of the country and the rest of the nation."[46]

Wilson replied that there was no disagreement between himself and Black, except that in selling the domestic allotment plan to

[44] Wilson to Moley (September 21, 1932), Wilson MSS; Moley, *After Seven Years*, p. 49.

[45] Wilson to Tugwell (October 8, 1932), Wilson MSS.

[46] Wilson to Milloy (September 15, 1932); Black to Wilson (October 20, 1932), Wilson MSS.

tariff-minded Republicans, he found it good tactics to talk of the country's self-sufficiency. Usually he explained that the plan gave the government the machinery to reduce production, if necessary. He always sketched the two roads that could be followed in the nation's economic relationship to the rest of the world. The first plotted a course marked by reduced tariffs, canceled war debts, co-operation with Europe, and international markets. The second was aligned with the present Hoover and Republican party policy that stood for higher tariffs, which meant eventual isolation. Since the latter was closest to what the future probably held, given the present international situation, it was understandable that production must be reduced to a domestic level. "I think I find that this rather loose thought of retirement to a domestic basis has rather wide popular acceptance," said Wilson, with his eye to the political barometer. Regardless of one's economic ideals, "We have to hook the domestic allotment plan on somewhere and I have been trying to hook it into that general strata which is [*sic*] in the subconscious mind of so many people but I always say that we will adjust our production to what we can consume domestically and export to advantage," said Wilson. When it came to selling an idea to the public in an effective fashion, the Montana professor did not appear to be above some degree of intellectual opportunism.[47]

Wilson's internationalist beliefs appear in a statement he gave to southern editor Clarence Poe of the *Progressive Farmer and Southern Ruralist* at Raleigh, North Carolina, who inquired about his high tariff position. He wrote of his devotion to an international economic community, but said the world of the present was unlikely to develop along these lines and until it did the United States had to be prepared to live in the imperfect world of national economic barriers. His full statement was as follows:

> Now I challenge anyone to be anymore of an internationalist in theory than I am. I accept all of the economic arguments against tariff and in favor of the principle of comparative advantage throughout the world, but as a realist I am inclined to believe that like many of the other good and true ideas in the world, the world, nevertheless at present, is not going to accept such doctrines. I hope it will and I shall do everything that I can personally towards reduction of tariff, towards cancellation of war debts,

[47] Wilson to Black (October 20, 1932), Wilson MSS.

towards international cooperation through the League of Nations or any of those kinds of policies which tend to reestablish the world on a community basis. Again as a realist, I am afraid that the world, at least in the next few years, is not going to move in that direction.

He concluded that an analysis of foreign price-supporting measures in a recent mimeographed report of the Bureau of Agricultural Economics confirmed his opinion.[48]

The traditional Republican agricultural speech at Des Moines brought nothing radically new into the campaign. Asked from the Roosevelt campaign headquarters what he thought of its impact, Wilson replied that he felt that the net result would be to Governor Roosevelt's benefit. To others he said, "My personal opinion is that as far as wheat farmers in the Northwest are concerned he [Hoover] would have been better off if the speech had not been made." Wilson still felt the governor stood squarely behind the voluntary domestic allotment plan: "He doesn't know entirely what it is all about but he has so committed himself that I do not see how he can backwater." Later in October as the election came closer and with the farm organizations still on the fence, Wilson understood that the plan's eventual adoption would depend on Roosevelt's decisions. "If he will stand four square on his six points that is one thing—personally I am skeptical if he will do it," wrote Wilson, as the thought of the governor turning the matter over to the farm organizations crossed his mind. He feared that after their hasseling the plan would be caught in a paralyzing compromise or be forced out entirely.[49]

National Farm Bureau President O'Neal, Wilson believed, was the most diplomatic of the farm leaders. Shortly after the Topeka speech, O'Neal announced his intention "to smoke Governor Roosevelt out" on his specific proposals. "After it became apparent from the Governor's western trip that the whole agricultural section of the United States was going to landslide towards the Governor," O'Neal changed his tune and said that he thought it was up to the farm organizations to cooperate with Roosevelt, if elected President.

[48] Wilson to Poe (October 26, 1932), Wilson MSS.

[49] Wilson to Black (October 7, 1932); Wilson to Guy Bush, president, National Swine Growers Association (October 8, 1932); Wilson to Ronald (October 24, 1932), Wilson MSS.

Wilson also feared a headlong break toward the domestic allotment by the farm organizations in the December session of Congress. They would be on hand, ready to offer a multitude of suggestions and "will have a thousand and one ideas and we will get a kind of monstrosity out of the whole thing." He preferred their clear-cut opposition to a sudden attempt to jump on the winning bandwagon and remake it to suit their tangled ideas.[50]

Wilson wrote Tugwell that he was uneasy about the suggestions of the influential farm organization paper, the *Prairie Farmer*, which was now talking of the domestic allotment plan in such terms as, "It needs to be perfected still further and particularly it needs to be made more simple." Wilson said that he was much afraid "that the specific meaning of this in the minds of many of the farm organization leaders is that the allotment feature should be cut out altogether." Regarding these power groups in agricultural politics, Wilson felt that the strategy in guiding the domestic allotment plan had to be aimed at one central goal: "to prevent the plan from being dehorned and the production control taken out of it."[51]

To preserve the production control feature and avert paralyzing modifications, Wilson wanted to be in Washington in the weeks after the election and during the congressional session in December. Although he disliked being away from Montana, Wilson told Black, "I am tremendously afraid that our child will get very badly disfigured if there is not someone on guard a good deal of the time." Also Wilson was concerned that either he or Harriman should have a conference with Roosevelt shortly after the election. He told Harriman that it was important that he convey a philosophy to the new President about economic planning and "how the voluntary domestic allotment plan fits as a segment in this philosophy." Again Wilson reiterated that if Roosevelt stood pat on the six points of Topeka, "we stand a good chance to get the right kind of a bill."

On the brighter side of the Hoover agricultural position, Wilson felt convinced that the President could support the principles of the Christgau bill. He claimed that Tolley and Black were responsible for Hoover's promise in the Des Moines speech to make the Department of Agriculture over into a planning institution. This idea was also being pushed in the Roosevelt circles through Tugwell.

[50] Wilson to Black (October 7, 1932), Wilson MSS.
[51] Wilson to Tugwell (October 8, 1932), Wilson MSS.

Wilson predicted that if he could work closely with the Roosevelt people in briefing the new administration, "We might be able to make an advance all along the line, that is, get the Allotment Bill, the Christgau Bill, and a good aggressive land policy bill." Even some of the leaders in the grain and milling trade were softening their attitude and saying that although their philosophy was laissez faire, they would rather deal with the supporters of the domestic allotment than radicals.[52]

Soon it became apparent to Wilson that finances and duties at the college would preclude any possibility of his working permanently in Washington for the domestic allotment plan. He recognized the generosity of President Atkinson in allowing him to be away from his post at the college for long intervals, "but there is a limit to the amount of time one can be away from his post and still draw a salary from the institution."[53] In addition, the college was also under criticism from influential sources in Montana concerning Wilson's activities in behalf of a national farm relief plan. To strengthen his position in any future investigation of his activities, Wilson requested Stockton to write a letter "on your typewriter" to President Atkinson with the date April 5, 1932. He suggested that the letter on Farm Bureau stationery include the following material:

> Our organization has always been friendly towards the principles of agricultural education, research and extension work. We believe that these are fundamental to a healthy and prosperous agriculture. We also believe that our State College of Agriculture, with its affiliated institutions, are created by the people to assist farmers not only with their long-time problems but with such emergencies as arise. The greatest kind of an emergency has arisen in Montana agriculture and we are, therefore, calling upon the institution to render such services as it can with this emergency. The emergency to which I refer is the disparity between the prices of things which farmers have to sell and the price at which they have to buy and the low prices, particularly with reference to wheat.

[52] Wilson to Black (October 7, 1932); Wilson to Harriman (October 21, 1932), Wilson MSS.
[53] Wilson to Ronald (October 24, 1932), Wilson MSS.

Wilson said the economic threat to Montana agriculture could be compared to insect and weather disasters for which the assistance of the college had often been solicited:

If the state were infested with swarms of grasshoppers or some insect or land parasite or, as far as that is concerned, any problem in agricultural production, I am sure you would put the entire resources of the institution behind the problem. Now we are confronted with an economic problem, and while I realize that institutions in the past have been somewhat cautious in facing economic problems, I think the present emergency demands action and I hope that the Montana State College will see fit through its Department of Agricultural Economics to meet this emergency by doing everything within its power towards the development of constructive economic action and legislation designed to raise agricultural prices so that they will have fair purchasing and debt paying power and to restore some sense of equality for agriculture. The Montana Farm Bureau Federation feels that you have a very capable man in the Department of Agricultural Economics and we trust that the institution will meet this problem in a fearless but nevertheless constructive and scientific manner. In so doing, you may subject yourself to some narrow criticism but I want at this time to pledge the support of the Montana Farm Bureau Federation to such activities as you may put forth in the problem outlined above.

He admitted that the request for college assistance in working for a farm relief program perhaps broke precedent:

Again, I cannot too greatly impress upon you the seriousness of the present emergency and the services which I am requesting. We may request you to break many established precedents as far as the administrative policy of the institution is concerned. However, this may be on behalf of distressed Montana producers. I want to request this emergency service from your Agricultural Economics Department.[54]

The immediate emergency in Montana was reflected in the widespread rejection of Extension services in the counties by voters who objected to its continuing burden on the tax rolls. From Wilson's point of view this was another reason in favor of the domestic

[54] Wilson to Stockton (October 22, 1932), Wilson MSS.

allotment plan, because he thought that "the Extension Service has got to go a little wider now than just education." He envisioned a place for Extension in administering a new farm plan: "I think if they could be connected up with some actual concrete proposal for agricultural relief and reconstruction it would tend to help them to hold their ground." But Wilson was not at all optimistic about the present situation in Montana. The decline of wheat prices that followed Hoover's agricultural speech cast a deep gloom over Montana. "I can feel it everywhere I go," Wilson wrote. He also detected a "fear complex" among people in the middle class who were concerned about what the future would bring.[55] Here as in other parts of the country Wilson felt the "fear of fear itself" stalking through the depressed wheatlands as the nation prepared to elect its Depression President.

[55] Wilson to E. J. Bell (October 28, 1932), Wilson MSS.

CHAPTER NINE

Concluding the Domestic Allotment Campaign

A month from now it will be useless to duck the fact that once launched, it compels national planning.—Russell Lord

Election night, November 8, 1932, brought the expected presidential victory to Governor Roosevelt and the Democratic party. On the agricultural front a winter of uncertainty lay ahead. Roosevelt was determined that the farm organization leaders should commonly agree on a new agricultural program and should accept responsibility for it.[1] Wilson had strong doubts that any such agreement could be reached. In vain he hoped for an agricultural relief measure from either the December or February session of Congress. Both sessions finished in political acrimony and endless debate on the domestic allotment plan. Repeatedly, congressmen with little insight into the bill proposed amendments that distorted it. For this reason Wilson was relieved when the two sessions of Congress concluded without passing a farm relief act. He looked to strong leadership from the executive branch of government after the inauguration.

The "Hundred Days" fulfilled his hopes for executive action. On May 12 the Agricultural Adjustment Act, which had been introduced in March to Congress, was signed by the President. In sending the bill to Congress, Roosevelt commented, "I tell you frankly that it is a new and untrod path, but I can tell you with equal frankness that an unprecedented condition calls for the trial of new means."[2] The act was designed to achieve agricultural

[1] Rexford G. Tugwell, *The Democratic Roosevelt* (Garden City, N.Y.: Doubleday & Company, Inc., 1957), p. 232.

[2] As quoted in Arthur Schlesinger, Jr., *The Age of Roosevelt: The Coming of the New Deal* (Boston: Houghton Mifflin Company, 1959), p. 39.

adjustment; most important, it granted the executive discretionary power to achieve this end through various methods. One of these methods was the domestic allotment plan for basic agricultural commodities.

As the domestic allotment supporters collected their trophies from the battlefield of pre-election politics, new dangers loomed ahead for the farm plan. From South Dakota, W. R. Ronald told Roosevelt that little would come of the governor's declared purpose to work with the farm organizations in developing new farm legislation. He recalled the impossibility of bringing their leaders together on a common program in the past, and pointed out the failure of Wilson's "Herculean effort" to swing the leaders of the Farm Bureau behind the domestic allotment. Ronald declared, "It will in the end devolve upon your leadership to show the way." The legislation, in Ronald's opinion, would have to be worked out by the administration in conjunction with skilled economists, and then presented to Congress. There would be no virtue in waiting for either the farm organizations or Congress to formulate legislation. Ronald also rejected the suggestions that the broad masses of the farmers be educated to the principles of the domestic allotment immediately in order to convince their leaders. This would take years of educational effort when all that was needed for an immediate program was a group of experts to formulate the bill.[3]

Wilson was also aware that in spite of his efforts no great progress had been made with the farm organizations. Farm leaders, especially, suspected the allotment plan's demand for production control and claimed it would be impossible to enforce. Among farmers, Wilson believed, there was growing sentiment for an across-the-board price fixing plan that would license all grain dealers and require them to pay a fixed price for the domestic portion and another price for the exported portion of the crop. Hopefully, Wilson believed, this ground swell of radical economic thinking could be used to persuade the millers and the grain men that the domestic allotment plan was the most conservative of all proposals and deserved their support. Still, Wilson had faith that the national farm organizations, especially the Farm Bureau, would lend support to the domestic allotment.

[3] Franklin D. Roosevelt Library, President's Personal File 74, W. R. Ronald to Roosevelt (November 2, 1932); Ronald to John J. Cadigan, president of New World Life Insurance Company, Seattle, Washington (November 9, 1932), Wilson MSS.

He requested a new series of letters from Stockton to various Farm Bureau state presidents on the plan and the general agricultural situation. In the letters, he said, attention should be specifically called to the six points of Roosevelt's Topeka speech and also that the voluntary domestic allotment plan was the only plan that could possibly meet these specifications.[4]

Presently Wilson faced dissension in the ranks of the domestic allotment supporters. Ronald's overzealousness had carried him to a position on the plan that Wilson could not support. Reacting to the criticism that the plan would produce too much centralization of bureaucracy in Washington, Ronald put forth a suggestion that called for state administration of the allotments to farmers. Under his scheme the Secretary of Agriculture would announce the amount of each commodity under the plan that had been allotted to each state in proportion to its production in the last ten years. After a significant proportion of farmers agreed to limit their production in return for benefit payments, the funds would be distributed to the state treasurers by the federal government, permitting the states to administer the benefit payments to the farmers. This money would be given to the states in a manner similar to the federal aid-to-roads program. Although Wilson saw a political advantage to this approach, he could only foresee general confusion if the states administered the plan. In his view the present voluntary domestic allotment plan with its state and county committees was sufficiently decentralized, but admittedly "they would be under the direction of a Federal agent." To avoid the petty politics involved in state governments, he felt it was necessary to establish a direct link between the local farmer in the country and the federal government.[5]

Although Wilson was skeptical about many of Ronald's well-meaning efforts, Ronald seemed to have only the greatest admiration for the Montana professor. In early November, he informed Wilson that he would like to see him as Secretary of Agriculture and intended to suggest his name to Governor Roosevelt. Because he felt that Wilson was not politically minded, Ronald thought he would

[4] Wilson to Bowden (November 5, 1932); Wilson to Ronald (November 7, 1932); Wilson to Stockton (November 9, 1932), Wilson MSS.

[5] "With States the Units of Nation-wide Cooperation by Producers," pamphlet by Ronald, files of the Economic and Statistical Analysis Division of the Economic Research Service, USDA; Wilson to Black (October 7, 1932); Wilson to Tugwell (November 28, 1932), Wilson MSS.

render unprecedented service to the cause of agriculture. Wilson apparently squelched this suggestion, for Ronald admitted later in November that he had "laid off it entirely by your request," although it was coming from other quarters. Returning to his favorite complaint—the farm organizations—Ronald said he did not believe Wilson should be upset at the "political gesturing in the direction of the farm organizations." He thought Roosevelt could be trusted to handle them effectively. In his opinion the farm leaders would be on the defensive if they asked the governor to yield on the specifications laid out at Topeka. Again he congratulated Wilson on showing such foresight in his contribution to the Topeka speech: "You certainly were thinking a long way ahead when you induced him [Roosevelt] to handle it in this way at Topeka." [6]

Wilson had more immediate concerns to occupy his mind than speculation about the appointment of the Secretary of Agriculture. As the political fortunes of the domestic allotment plan rose, it came under increasing attack from influential sources. Dr. Joseph Davis of the Food Research Institute at Stanford criticized the plan because of its expensive administrative machinery. He suggested that the expense of the plan be borne entirely by the beneficiaries in the counties. In this manner he felt that many of the smaller wheat growers would elect not to participate in the plan and a great amount of unnecessary administrative effort could be avoided, because curbing the production of the smaller wheat growers would play no major part in the plan's overall goals. Wilson's assistant at the college, C. C. Conser, replied to Davis pointing out that the main objection to his suggestion would be political. There would be no initial political support for the plan "if this large and politically powerful group of small wheat growers should find themselves outside the benefits of the proposed legislation." Wilson, however, later congratulated Davis on his article and said he appreciated the helpful suggestions it contained, adding, "It has stimulated constructive thinking rather than partisanship." [7]

[6] Ronald to Wilson (November 3, 1932); Ronald to Wilson (November 28, 1932), Wilson MSS.

[7] Davis to Wilson (November 8, 1932); Conser to Davis (November 10, 1932); Wilson to Davis (December 23, 1932), Wilson MSS; J. S. Davis, "The Voluntary Domestic Allotment Plan for Wheat," *Wheat Studies of the Food Research Institute*, IX (November, 1932), 23–62.

Wilson knew that the plan faced rough sledding with the farm organizations. He felt the pivotal group would be the Farm Bureau Federation and especially the attitude of the Illinois Agricultural Association under the leadership of Earl Smith. Wilson still was unconvinced that they would ever completely embrace a production-control scheme. Except for the Farmers' Union and John Simpson, whose opposition was assured, Wilson believed the position of the farm organizations would in the end depend on the pressure brought to bear on them by the President. No broad support for the plan could be expected from the general public in Wilson's opinion, because "unfortunately the public at large doesn't understand the plan and are very easily mixed up on it." He was also convinced that great numbers of people did not accept the production-control features of the plan.[8]

A voice from the opposition, Frederick J. Lingham, president-elect of the National Millers Association, congratulated Wilson on the excellent political work that had been done in Washington on behalf of the domestic allotment plan. He did not know exactly to whom he should address his congratulations, but he said, "I really mean just what I say, though I am on the other side of the question, I certainly can appreciate the good work being done, from a political standpoint." At the end of November, when Wilson began totaling his expenses since the previous April on the domestic allotment campaign, he became increasingly aware of how expensive the "good work" had been to him personally. He was certain that total expenses for travel, telegrams, and phone calls amounted to at least eight hundred dollars and told Ronald that he could not go much further in this direction.[9]

Although the personal expense to Wilson for the campaign had been high, broad support for the plan was beginning to be evidenced in many quarters. From Oregon state it was confidently predicted that the Eastern Oregon Wheat League would endorse the plan and that Oregon congressmen would follow its lead. From Minneapolis, C. H. Hornburg, vice-president of the Deere & Webber Farm

[8] Wilson to Ronald (November 25, 1932), Wilson MSS.

[9] Lingham to Wilson (November 29, 1932); Wilson to Ronald (November 30, 1932), Wilson MSS; Elmer Starch suggests that Wilson's expenses were closer to $3,000. He bases this assertion on his personal observation of Wilson's uncompensated travel and hotel bills, Starch to author (May, 1967).

Implement Company, telegraphed Wilson that unless farm relief legislation could be achieved in the next session of Congress, "the northwest will go broke." He requested information on the allotment plan, about which he and President C. C. Webber were only slightly informed, in order that they might be helpful in pushing future legislation. Later in the month Hornburg wrote Wilson, "Mr. Webber and I have done some hard work in promoting farm relief (the allotment plan) and it has been conducive to results." He reported that businessmen formerly opposed to the plan were now in a receptive mood, and "others are ready to fight for it to help bring agriculture out of its present condition." In Omaha, Louis Clarke said that the *Omaha World-Herald* devoted its lead editorial to the domestic allotment plan the day after the election. He said he had a difficult time in selling the idea to the paper, "but from now on I think we shall have their hundred per cent cooperation." Another businessman in Minneapolis wrote Wilson that he was interested in the prosperity of the Northwest and the domestic allotment plan because of his ownership of stocks in wholesale grocery houses operating in all of the northwestern states.[10]

When curious wheat farmers inquired about Wilson's role in promoting the domestic allotment plan, Wilson usually declined to designate himself as the main spokesman in Montana's drive to obtain a national farm relief program. He explained that he had undertaken this effort only after the vice-president of the Montana Farm Bureau Federation had written the college president for aid in achieving a national program to relieve the low agricultural prices in the state. Wilson wanted a great deal of credit to go to President Atkinson if the domestic allotment plan received approval by Congress. Wilson wrote praising the college president's decision to honor the state Farm Bureau's request for assistance:

> The president of our College thought that this was a fair request and made arrangements for me to give considerable of my time to this problem. As a consequence I have been working on it almost incessantly since the middle of April. Therefore, if any-

[10] E. R. Jackman, extension agronomist, Corvallis, Oregon, to Wilson (November 18, 1932); Hornburg to Wilson (November 10, 1932); Hornburg to Wilson (November 28, 1932); Clarke to Wilson (November 10, 1932); W. K. Nash of the Nash Company to Wilson (November 30, 1932), Wilson MSS; *Omaha World-Herald*, November 9, 1932.

thing is to come from it the President of our college, Mr. Alfred Atkinson, is entitled to very great credit. It would have been very easy for him to have said that such a request was out of the ordinary and to have stated that it would interfere too greatly with my regular work.[11]

The agricultural Committee of the National Chamber of Commerce was also moving in favor of immediate farm relief legislation. A meeting of the committee and representatives from agriculture, including Henry Wallace, George Peek, Earl Smith, and M. L. Wilson, was scheduled for November 21 in Chicago. The *Mitchell Evening Republican* reported that the meeting represented "big business joining hands with the farmer in seeking a solution to restore rural buying power and reform of the national economic system." Ronald wrote that the committee of industrialists, financiers, and manufacturers met with farm representatives and agreed that farm prices were "intolerable." He reported that General Robert E. Wood, president of Sears, Roebuck and Company and chairman of the meeting, said, "We believe that prosperity would come to all of us if the farmer could get some of it." One of the main resolutions adopted by the gathering proclaimed, "Agriculture has found it particularly difficult to adapt itself to this post-war situation because it has been unable to use effectively such methods of control as the tariff and the corporate form of organization." The attitude of these businessmen showed Ronald there undoubtedly would be overwhelming sentiment in the months to come for comprehensive agricultural relief legislation. It was up to Roosevelt to see that this legislation took the form of the voluntary domestic allotment plan. In articles on farm relief, Ronald kept emphasizing that whether the public was aware of it or not "the Wilson voluntary acreage allotment plan" was the chief item in the new President's farm relief program.[12] Although Wilson had expended most of his energies on the domestic allotment approach to farm relief, his attention still focused on how the land should be utilized in the future. He told Clarke that as soon as the domestic allotment plan or some other price-raising plan passed Congress, all of his work would then be thrown into a struggle for government purchase

[11] Wilson to E. E. Baker, farmer from Harwood, North Dakota (November 26, 1932), Wilson MSS.

[12] *Mitchell Evening Republican*, November 21 and 22, 1932.

and retirement of submarginal lands. He reiterated his old theme that had been with him when he began the domestic allotment campaign: "I am more and more convinced that the allotment plan is a very good service palliative but the thing goes fundamentally deeper than the allotment plan can reach and we must have a plan for land purchase and retirement." Wilson was convinced that Roosevelt would support long-range land-reform policies.[13]

On November 29, Moley called Wilson to Warm Springs, Georgia, to discuss political strategy on future farm legislation. Unable to reach Warm Springs in time to meet with the President-elect, Wilson proceeded directly to Washington. At this point and after watching the controversies in Congress over the details of the previous farm relief and domestic allotment bills, Wilson was convinced that the "next bill should be made much more general and much of the administrative features left to the administrative agents." This suggestion, of course, was to be realized in the Agricultural Adjustment Act in May with its grant of broad discretionary powers to the executive. Wilson was also aware that the political position of the domestic allotment plan was not as strong as it should be because of the lack of a general public educational and propaganda campaign in the previous summer. As a result, it was open to modifications from diverse and influential sources. The essential ideas of the allotment plan were by no means safe from attack in the coming months. Victory was near, but the entire plan could easily be lost. Wilson drew the following analogy to the plan's fate in the next two months:

> Steering the allotment plan now is about like taking a delicate birch bark canoe down a torrential mountain stream with boulders, water falls and all kinds of destructive obstacles. Whether or not it can be taken through these rapids which I am afraid will flow pretty fast for the next 60 days is a very great problem.[14]

Russell Lord, free-lance journalist and author, caught some of the spirit of the early New Dealers as they prepared to converge on Washington. In Wilson, Lord saw an optimism that was determined to correct the calamities of the present situation through planned

[13] Wilson to Clarke (November 25, 1932), Wilson MSS.

[14] Wilson to Ronald (November 30, 1932); Wilson to Bowden (November 25, 1932), Wilson MSS.

and creative human action. His fresh approach to problems wiped away the skepticism of the previous years that had fed upon the idea that nothing could be changed in a world that stood impervious to change. Lord told Wilson, "You've started something tremendous." He probably echoed the sentiments of many disillusioned intellectuals and writers of the twenties, as they viewed the revolution taking place in Washington, when he said, "Simply to get in at the edge of it has brought me to life again." Lord explained that he had been "going flat, writing and writing and writing neutral things, and often neutral things I didn't give a damn about." He thanked Wilson that by his example and fortitude in the domestic allotment campaign he had given "a withering skeptic something to be for, for a change." [15]

Lord detected something more far reaching in Wilson's efforts than the immediate achievement of a farm relief program. There was something simple and at the same time profound about the manner in which Wilson had "eased this thing through just the right channels from vague body of thought to a new national philosophy. . . ." What was more remarkable, Wilson had kept himself out of the limelight through the entire operation. Lord concluded that "a month from now it will be useless to duck the fact that once launched, it compels national planning." On December 15, Walter Lippmann termed the domestic allotment approach to the farm problem, with its controlled production features and individual contracts between the government and farmers who agreed to reduce production in return for benefit payments, "the most daring economic experiment ever seriously proposed in the United States." [16]

In Washington, Wilson conferred with Wallace, Congressman Marvin Jones, Henry Morgenthau, Jr., Professor William I. Myers of Cornell, Rex Tugwell, Mordecai Ezekiel, and Frederick P. Lee, an attorney who was asked to draft an acceptable congressional allotment bill. The next weeks set a fast pace for Wilson in the highly charged political atmosphere of Washington in December, 1932. Events in the city occurred so rapidly that Wilson had little time for

[15] Lord to Wilson (December 15, 1932), Wilson MSS.
[16] Lord to Wilson (December 19, 1932), Wilson MSS; Walter Lippmann, *Interpretations, 1933–1935*, ed. Allan Nevins (New York: The Macmillan Co., 1936), pp. 74–75.

lengthy communications with his backers in Montana and the Dakotas. Consequently, through most of the month Ronald operated without complete information on the turn of events in Washington. On December 5, Ronald wrote that there would be no need to compromise with the farm organizations when the businessmen and economists as well as the President would support controlled production. Of course, it was understood that there could be no control of production "except by the allotment plan." Ronald believed his advice was confirmed when National Farm Bureau President Ed O'Neal declared publicly in favor of the domestic allotment plan. From his post in South Dakota, Ronald accused Congress of drifting on farm relief and flouting the will of the President-elect by not following a course of legislative action that led directly to the passage of the domestic allotment.[17]

In part to keep Ronald on the right line of attack, Wilson, upon arriving home in Bozeman on December 21, wrote him a long letter relating the events in Washington during the past weeks. He wrote that at the initial meeting in December the broad strategy on the farm relief measure was developed. House Speaker John Nance Garner was bent upon passing a relief bill at this session of Congress and had instructed Marvin Jones to prepare a bill "ready to jam through." The bill that Jones presented to the meeting was carelessly drawn, according to Wilson, and did not call for production control until the second year of its operation. Wilson said that Tugwell, Wallace, and he were disappointed in many provisions of the Jones bill. Representatives of the governor's position at the meeting agreed to authorize lawyer Lee to recast the bill. They impressed upon Jones that production control must begin immediately. In addition, those who represented the Roosevelt point of view "told Jones that it would be suicidal to press the matter without bringing in the farm organizations." Wilson, Wallace, and Tugwell informed Jones that farm organization people would take offense "at the thing being jammed along ahead of them." This would be especially evident when they had already set a date of December 12 for a general meeting of farm organization representatives and cooperatives to agree on a unified program. Afterward, Jones saw the wisdom of postponing the effort in order to work with

[17] Ronald to Wilson (December 5, 1932), Wilson MSS; *Mitchell Evening Republican*, December 5 and 21, 1932.

the farm organizations. He spoke with Garner and secured approval to hold up the drive for the farm bill to enable the farm organizations to catch up.

Wilson explained that O'Neal's statement backing production control came only after Roosevelt informed the Farm Bureau leader that "nothing would go with him except production control." When Wilson spoke to the Farm Bureau convention in Washington, he felt that his talk along these lines was generally well received. Representatives of the leading packing houses, Swift, Armour, Wilson, and Cudahy, were also on hand in Washington for a meeting with Wallace and Wilson. Although the meeting was "perfectly friendly" and a plan was developed to form a pork corporation to distribute unsold pork to the poor, "it was quite clear to me," said Wilson, "that the packers had agreed upon positive hostility and nothing whatsoever could be done which would change the picture."

Wilson journeyed to Chicago for a meeting of a subcommittee of the Chamber of Commerce's Agricultural Committee in General Woods' office on December 10. There, a new scheme for agricultural relief was put forth by some of the packing, milling, and Wall Street interests. It proposed renting 30 per cent of the wheat, corn, and cotton acreage at a cost of 350 million dollars to be borne by the federal Treasury. Wilson said he asked Fred Sargeant of Northwestern Railroad how he could justify this direct appropriation from the Treasury. Sargeant replied that the plan would ultimately make money for the government because it would stimulate business and thereby increase the taxes that could be paid. In Sargeant's opinion the domestic allotment plan was not quick enough. "We must have positive action immediately," he said. Then, Wilson, wincing under the type of remark that businessmen had often made to him as a college professor, said, "He took a sort of a dig at me and at the allotment plan as being too theoretical."

After the Chicago meeting, Wilson traveled with a group of farm organization people back to Washington for their meeting on December 12. At the Harrington Hotel in Washington, where the conference was to be held, Wilson suffered an attack of flu and was confined to his room for four days. But, he said, "I really got no rest because someone was in my room most of the time" conferring on the events of the conference. His place at the meetings was taken by Tugwell, who kept him informed of its progress. "There were a number of very great surprises," Wilson wrote. O'Neal, of course, endorsed the allotment plan while John Simpson condemned it and L. J. Taber of the Grange remained neutral. C. E. Huff of the Farmers National Grain Corporation said no plan could work on wheat unless it controlled production. Also, Earl Smith took the position that any effective plan for the corn belt must control the supply of hogs. The Grange contended that farmers would not sign contracts and "they would not stand for any plan involving contracts." At the meeting Morgenthau forewarned the farm representatives that a new farm plan must contain two essential provisions for the governor's approval: "First, it must be in the Department of Agriculture and second, it must involve production control and follow the general philosophy set forth in his Topeka speech."

A day and a night's general discussion followed these initial decla- rations. On the second day Lee began to work with Tugwell, Ezekiel, and others on the drafting committee. They started with the Jones bill. Much to Wilson's surprise Earl Smith declared that the bill should call for immediate production control. Others suggested that the provisions for an individual contract should be eliminated the first year for faster administration, but retain the restricted produc- tion requirement for the following year. Later, Wilson wrote Clarke that a "milestone was turned on December 12th and 14th when the national farm organizations and the co-ops . . . voted unani- mously to get behind the principles of the Voluntary Domestic Allotment Plan." Late in the afternoon of the second day the farm organization draft was completed. "Up until this time," Wilson observed, "old man Simpson had been pegging away just as hard as he could, but I believe considerably to his surprise nobody paid any attention to him."

From Wilson's viewpoint, the bill seemed adequate. Although it did not call for contracts the first year, it would be administered the second year along the same lines of the original domestic allot- ment proposal. On one point it differed significantly. It used the ratio price in determining the rate of payments to farmers instead of the standard attempt to make the tariff effective. This would, as Wilson pointed out, please men like Harriman who talked of "a fair price" and also the Democrats who had a natural distaste for the word "tariff." Most important the bill left the details of administration to the Secretary of Agriculture. Now the difficulty lay in guiding the bill through the Senate and House committees without being defrocked of its important elements. But Wilson had little hope of passing it in the short session of Congress. The important accomplishment stood in bringing the farm organizations into the fight on the side of production control. Now it was their fight.

Wilson closed his letter to Ronald with the hope that the South Dakota newspaperman would support Wallace for Secretary of Agriculture, saying, "It is absolutely necessary that he be Secretary of Agriculture to put this over." Of course, Wilson foresaw that a man who was sympathetic to the principles of the domestic allotment plan had to be installed as Secretary because of the wide-ranging discretionary powers that were likely to be granted him under a new farm bill.[18]

The day after Christmas, Wilson left Bozeman again for Washington and a meeting of the American Farm Economic Association in Cincinnati on December 28 to 30. At the conference of economists, Premier John Bracken of Manitoba was present with his economic advisers. Talks with the Premier explored the possibilities of a general international wheat agreement. "It was agreed if the domestic allotment plan were enacted here efforts would be made to develop such international action later." Ezekiel called this the "first preliminary International Wheat Conference." Bracken, as Ezekiel recalled, was amazed that "these problems of state craft in the United States were being handled by beardless youths."[19]

In Washington, Wilson testified before the House Agricultural Committee on behalf of the bill formulated at the December meeting. During his brief stay in Washington from January 1 to 6, Wilson talked extensively with Tugwell and Wallace. In his diary Tugwell noted that Wilson and Wallace were "pretty determined general inflationists." Wilson would have been the first to deny this charge, and perhaps Tugwell was merely expressing his preconceived ideas

[18] Wilson to Ronald (December 22, 1932); Wilson to Clarke (January 15, 1933), Wilson MSS.

[19] Ezekiel to Tugwell (October 20, 1939), files of the Economic and Statistical Analysis Division of the Economic Research Service, USDA; *North Dakotan*, January, 1933 (The Greater North Dakota Association, Fargo, North Dakota).

about western farm leaders' positions on inflation. In a general comment about both Wilson and Wallace, Tugwell wrote comparing the two men: "Wilson's mind, though it is one of those poetic, intuitive ones, is far more elusive. He is much more difficult to get close to. . . . To know Wallace and Wilson well makes a good deal of sacrifice worth while." [20]

By January 10, Wilson was back in Montana. Until he was asked to come to Washington in March to testify before congressional committees by Secretary Wallace on behalf of the administration's farm bill, Wilson remained in the West away from the events in Washington. In late January he wrote a friend in Washington, "I feel lost in the wilderness and will be mighty glad to have a word from you in regard to your size up of the situation in Washington." What little he did hear from Washington perturbed him. He thought it had been a mistake for the Senate committee to "hold hearings or mess around with the matter," and could not understand why Roosevelt had encouraged this. The only way Wilson could explain the "present drift" was that the President-elect wanted the situation to "develop into a sort of hopeless muddle" which he could step into and exert positive leadership after March 4. Privately he believed that the bill, as now modified by the House, was dangerous. He did not care to say this publicly because it would be interpreted as criticism of Chairman Jones. From another viewpoint he saw it as a "step in an evolutionary process" that would be completed after the inaugural when an administration bill would be "rammed through by the party whip." [21]

Wilson believed that members of Congress did "not get the production control idea at all." Only the weight of Roosevelt placed squarely behind the concept could save it from its enemies in Congress. Wilson also believed that the benefits of production control could be explained more easily if the bill were argued on a tariff basis rather than on parity. "Theoretically parity seems much better to me," Wilson said, "but I am sure the country has been educated

[20] Franklin D. Roosevelt Library, Record Group 31, Tugwell Diary, pp. 46, 48.

[21] Wilson to C. R. Noyes (January 23, 1933); Wilson to Robert Lusk (January 20, 1933); Wilson to L. H. Godard, Bloomington, Illinois (January 27, 1933), Wilson MSS.

so much to the phrase 'making the tariff effective' that they would have had much less opposition if they would have argued it on a tariff basis rather than otherwise." But Wilson understood that the Democrats preferred to talk about "parity" instead of "making the tariff effective." [22]

Since the farm organizations had changed their positions to support the domestic allotment plan, Wilson believed that the Voluntary Domestic Allotment Committee should dissolve. "We never had any money and it is absolutely impossible to raise any," he said. Toward the last of January, Wilson told Chester Davis that he had no inside information on who was to be the new Secretary of Agriculture. But Wilson emphasized that he had been repeatedly saying, "If Governor Roosevelt did not know enough to select H. A. Wallace under the present circumstances it was just good-bye as far as the administration was concerned." A month later Wilson was informed that Wallace had received the nod from the new administration for Secretary of Agriculture. Confidently Wilson wrote to Bishop O'Hara in Great Falls that Wallace would push for a new domestic allotment bill that would be an effective compromise between the different elements in Congress and also be economically sound. The proponents of farm relief legislation, of course, differed greatly in their views. Tugwell said their positions could be divided into four viewpoints: (1) those who called for price-fixing by legislation or regulation; (2) those who advocated disposal of surpluses abroad; (3) those who would place the responsibility for increasing prices on the processors and rely on cooperative marketing agreements; and (4) those who asked the farmer to reduce acreage and supply output in order to raise agricultural incomes. Around these four positions debate swirled on the administration's farm bill during March and April, 1933. Tugwell might have added a fifth group who called for general inflationary moves to raise agricultural prices and reduce farm indebtedness. [23]

Of course, Wilson supported the controlled acreage position, but in doing so he also acknowledged that it was a static view of the

---

[22] Wilson to J. S. Davis (January 28, 1933), Wilson MSS.

[23] Wilson to Clarke (January 15, 1933); Wilson to Chester Davis (January 20, 1933); Wilson to O'Hara (February 27, 1933), Wilson MSS; Tugwell, *The Democratic Roosevelt*, p. 275.

growth possibilities for the American economy in the future. He referred to many economists such as Harold Laski, who saw

> a kind of disintegration of the world capitalistic order and because of our inability to make social adjustments in the matter of distribution of wealth, collective organization, etc. to the machine age, we may be moving into a rather static condition which the German philosopher Spengler has called, "The New Dark Ages."

Wilson felt this view was perhaps too pessimistic, but certainly American agriculture was traveling this road if export opportunities did not improve. For this condition he felt that the domestic allotment plan was the most logical adjustment, and he prided himself with the satisfaction that he had been instrumental in presenting it to the nation. Wilson admitted that his ideas about the international scene were limited and that in talking of this subject he always felt "more or less gripped in the provincialism of the Northwest." He told John D. Black that isolationism was to have a strong political appeal in the future: "I honestly believe that the hard times have intensified in the minds of our people isolation ideas rather than diminished them—all of which makes me rather pessimistic." [24]

While the domestic allotment plan had now drawn the support of the Farm Bureau, it lost the backing of the influential Henry I. Harriman. Harriman had switched his position to support government land purchasing, which members of the business community, including Sydney Anderson, vice-president of General Mills, now advocated. Ronald saw the whole attempt as a sham relief program designed to divide the support on a united farm program. Ronald believed that tremendous pressure had been brought to bear on Harriman and in order to satisfy critics, "He is doing this at least as a gesture. I cannot believe that after all he has done on the other plan, he could at heart desert it." But Ronald was confident that these maneuverings would not sidetrack the domestic allotment plan because Roosevelt was determined to carry through the promises of the Topeka speech. [25]

Wilson also agreed that Harriman must have come under tremendous pressure from his antiallotment friends in the Chamber of

[24] Wilson to Chester Davis (February 21, 1933); Wilson to Black (February 4, 1933), Wilson MSS.
[25] Ronald to Wilson (February 25, 1933), Wilson MSS.

Commerce. The land-leasing plan did not upset Wilson, but he was disappointed that President Hoover condemned the allotment plan and came to the support of the land-leasing scheme just three days before he left office. In one of his few caustic remarks about Hoover, Wilson wrote:

> While I have felt all the time that President Hoover was not particularly farm minded and that he had made a lot of mistakes in his farm policy, I nevertheless had a good deal of sympathy for him but I must admit he did a rather cheap thing when he mixed in the farm relief matter the week before he went out of office. I would have taken his suggestion about land leasing and that kind of thing much more sympathetically if he had put them forth last year.

Although a government land-leasing program spread over two or three years appeared to be economically sound, Wilson thought it would take as much machinery and involve as much difficulty as the allotment plan.[26]

While Wilson was in Washington during March, he found that the Democratic Senate leadership had formulated a complete line of strategy on the farm bill. Wallace told him that the matter was being taken care of within the high councils of the administration and that there was little that could be done from the outside. Russell Lord also felt the hum of activity in Washington and felt as if a firm hand had now taken over the reigns of government. "Like all of us, I have been in a constant spin of activity," he wrote Wilson, "but Lord! for the first time in ten or fifteen years I feel as if I were alive all over, and that this cockeyed world is taking us somewhere." In Montana the discontent was not as vocal as Wilson had anticipated. No one seemed to understand the administration's farm bill. He could only say that "farmers have faith that Roosevelt will do something for them but they do not quite know what it will be."[27]

In these closing days of the domestic allotment campaign, W. L. Stockton began to differ with Wilson on the feasibility of putting the domestic allotment plan into effect immediately. He was afraid

[26] Wilson to C. C. Webber (March 6, 1933), Wilson MSS.
[27] Wilson to Noyes (April 6, 1933); Lord to Wilson (March 19, 1933), Wilson MSS.

that national legislation on the plan was proceeding too fast for the country, which would be unprepared for it. "Now don't try to put it into effect till it is sold—till the farmers are made to want it," he wrote Wilson. If the plan were instituted "in a half baked condition," he said it would suffer a setback that would destroy any possibility for similar farm relief for many years to come. Wilson replied that he understood Stockton's point of view, but asked him to consider the great pressure for immediate action which would force the Secretary of Agriculture to take very drastic measures within the next few months.[28]

Senator Norbeck was hesitant about supporting a farm bill that left so many critical decisions to the Secretary of Agriculture, but realized that the administration had to have somewhat of a free hand in meeting the present situation. Gerald Nye of North Dakota asserted that he would support the farm bill because it offered the only prospect at the present time for achieving relief. Nebraska's Senator George Norris agreed with President Roosevelt when he said, "To some extent it is an experiment, but personally I believe we have reached the point where we are justified in attempting something of this kind." Senator Burton K. Wheeler believed that an inflated currency would be the most direct route to an improved agricultural situation, but conceded that he would stand for the bill. If the administration did not soon turn to remonetizing silver or even issuing paper currency, Wheeler feared that this farm bill would not dent the agricultural depression and the "democratic party will make itself look ridiculous." However much he disagreed with the administration, Wheeler attacked representatives of the grain trade and millers who opposed the administration's farm bill because it interfered with natural economic laws. To Frederick Lingham of the Millers National Federation he said, "Trouble is that you have not been leaving it to the natural laws, because of the fact that you have been passing legislation, class legislation in favor of the group here in the East." Another northwestern representative believed that the present farm bill was itself inspired by Wall Street. Congressman William Lemke of North Dakota told a sympathizer in South Dakota, "We have before us an idiotic farm

[28] Stockton to Wilson (April 7, 1933); Wilson to Stockton (April 7, 1933), Wilson MSS.

relief bill which, at best, is but a toe hold fathered by such incompetents as the New York coupon clippers and a newspaper Secretary of Agriculture." [29]

After much legislative debate, the farm bill reached the President's desk on May 12, 1933. It was now a three-part measure. Title I dealt with Agricultural Adjustment aimed to give farmers "equality of purchasing power." A wide range of power was extended to the Secretary of Agriculture to achieve this end, and prominent among them was the power to employ the domestic allotment plan for producers of certain staple commodities—tobacco, cotton, wheat, and hogs. Title II, the Emergency Farm Mortgage Act, and Title III dealt with monetary issues and included the inflationary Thomas Amendment that authorized the President to issue greenbacks, remonetize silver, or to alter the gold content of the dollar, if he deemed it necessary. [30]

The domestic allotment was first to be applied to wheat. The man chosen to direct the program as head of the Wheat Section in the AAA was M. L. Wilson. Roosevelt had proposed Wilson as Assistant Secretary of Agriculture, but Tugwell advised against it because he wanted Secretary Wallace to have a stronger administrator for an assistant. Tugwell believed Wilson could better serve closer to the mechanics of the domestic allotment plan. In his view this plan eventually would lead to a national land-planning project that Wilson could direct. In relation to this, Wallace wrote Wilson in February, 1933, "Don't take under secretary of agriculture. We want you for something more important—Lord of the Land." Wilson's appointment committed the AAA to production control and eventually gave him a voice in land-planning ideas that

[29] *Mitchell Evening Republican*, March 17, 1933; Senate Committee on Agriculture and Forestry, *Agricultural Emergency Act to Increase Farm Purchasing Power*, March 17, 24, 25, 27, 28, 1933, 73d Cong., 1st sess., p. 178; Wheeler to Stockton (March 25, 1933), Wilson MSS; Lemke to Arthur W. Watwood of Aberdeen, South Dakota (March 25, 1933), William Lemke Papers, University of North Dakota, Grand Forks, North Dakota; Edward C. Blackorby, *Prairie Rebel: The Public Life of William Lemke* (Lincoln: University of Nebraska Press, 1963), pp. 194–195.

[30] Schlesinger, *The Coming of the New Deal*, pp. 44–45; *Documents of American History*, ed. Henry Steele Commager (New York: Appleton-Century-Crofts, Inc., 1958), pp. 422–426.

emerged as land-withdrawal programs under the Soil Conservation and Domestic Allotment Act of 1936.[31]

Generally, newspaper reaction to the farm bill in the Northwest was cautious and at the same time optimistic. In the administration of the new bill the *North Dakotan* in Fargo believed that the interests of the Northwest and the spring wheat country would be ably represented by M. L. Wilson in his position as head of the Wheat Section in the AAA. The Watertown, South Dakota, *Public Opinion* referred to Roosevelt's comment that the bill outlined an "untrod path" and said, "the untrod path cannot lead us into greater despair than we have already known." Another South Dakota paper, the *Huronite*, said that South Dakotans could be proud of the part they had played in securing the enactment of the domestic allotment plan. It paid tribute to Wilson, but asserted that "it was in South Dakota that Mr. Wilson first secured real support for his program of farm relief." The paper congratulated South Dakotans George A. Starring of Huron, W. R. Ronald, and Senator Norbeck on the farm victory.[32]

Although not overly enthusiastic about the Democrats or Secretary Wallace, the *Fargo Forum* believed the bill pursued a wise course in attempting to adjust supply to demand. From the heart of the North Dakota wheat country the *Minot Daily News* was eager to try the new experiment and said, "This method, after the terrific failures of the laissez-faire policy, is certainly worth trying." The conservative *Western Progressive* in Helena, Montana, felt that government efforts for farm relief should only be directed at the encouragement and development of cooperatives. This was the path to permanent recovery of agriculture. From the plains area of Montana's wheat country, the *Havre Daily News* dealt extensively with the allotment plan and hoped it would be applied in time to

[31] Franklin D. Roosevelt Library, Record Group 31, Tugwell Diary, p. 98; Wallace to Wilson, February 22, 1933, files of the Economic and Statistical Analysis Division of the Economic Research Service, USDA; Edwin G. Nourse, Joseph S. Davis, John D. Black, *Three Years of the Agricultural Adjustment Administration* (Washington, D.C.: The Brookings Institution, 1937), n. 5, pp. 83–84; Robert J. Morgan, *Governing Soil Conservation: Thirty Years of the New Decentralization* (Baltimore: Johns Hopkins University Press, 1965), pp. 41–44.

[32] *North Dakotan*, May, 1933; *Public Opinion*, May 12, 1933 (Watertown, South Dakota); *Huronite*, May 13, 1933 (Huron, South Dakota).

support the 1933 crop. The paper boasted of Wilson's position as head of the Wheat Section and said, "Out here in Montana where he is so well-known, there is pleasure and pride over his selection." The editorial was confident that Wilson would protect the interests of the high protein spring wheat sections in the administration of the new plan and concluded, "He has been one of our trusted leaders in this state and if anyone can accomplish the task we feel that M. L. can." [33]

M. L. Wilson stands as a central figure in the search for a national agricultural program. From the Honyocker country in Montana to the hub of federal administration in Washington was a long road. In 1934 he served as director of Subsistence Homesteads in the Department of the Interior, and from 1934 to 1940 was successively Assistant Secretary of Agriculture and Under Secretary; from 1940 to 1953 he held the post of director of Extension Service in the department. As head of the Wheat Section in the AAA, Wilson was in a position to institute the domestic allotment approach for controlled production on the principal crop of his agricultural region. Although not a politician, he was close to the politics of wheat during the twenties, observed the Farm Board experiment, and was involved in the search for a new agricultural program preceding the 1932 election. His familiarity not only with the politics of wheat, but also with agricultural politics in general had served him well as he undertook a broad campaign to sell the domestic allotment plan for relief of the wheat crop and other commodities to influential circles in the American economic, social, and political power structure. Wilson's success in making the political break-through with the New Deal administration placed him and his plan in a key position to shape the early emergency measures of Roosevelt's farm program.

While the domestic allotment plan had received its political sanction, many regarded it as only the first step in a general revision of American agricultural policy. As a westerner Wilson's primary interest was in land policy and land use. The domestic allotment approach to farm relief had only been a second choice as a road to general agricultural reform. The first choice, of course, was a land

[33] *Fargo Forum*, June 27, 1933 (Fargo, North Dakota); *Minot Daily News*, May 13, 1933 (Minot, North Dakota); *Western Progressive*, June 23, 1933 (Helena, Montana); *Havre Daily News*, May 16, 1933 (Havre, Montana).

reform measure that called for economical use of land in relation to the market demands for its production. When it became apparent that the benefits of land legislation could not reach the local communities to meet quickly the crisis that had been intensifying since 1930, emphasis shifted from land reform to the more immediate benefits of the domestic allotment plan. But still the plan was regarded as a step in the direction of eventual land reform. As Russell Lord and Walter Lippmann observed, the domestic allotment plan would eventually compel agricultural planning.

In the attempt to convert what had once been an idea in academic circles of agricultural economics into an administrative reality, Professor Wilson departed from the impartial and uninvolved role of the academic man in American society by taking a stand in favor of a definite national policy. He and others in the distressed wheat areas responded to the special needs of their agricultural region. Wilson's effort to devise farm legislation and offer expert advice stood within the precedents established in the twenties when officials from the Bureau of Agricultural Economics and economists from the larger universities offered aid to farm legislative drives. Others point out that this tradition had its roots in early twentieth-century progressivism:

> These people took progressivism's positive attitude toward government action for economic purposes, translated it into specific programs for the farmer, and reinterpreted old ideas about his importance, placing a new emphasis upon farm purchasing power and its relation to national prosperity. These intellectual and political activities laid the groundwork for changes in government practices during the 1930's.[34]

In short, Wilson's role in the thirties was not necessarily a new one and contained elements of continuity with what had preceded it in the persisting progressivism of the twenties.[35]

[34] Richard S. Kirkendall, "The Great Depression: Another Watershed in American History?" *Change and Continuity in Twentieth-Century America,* eds. John Braeman, Robert H. Bremner, Everett Walters (Columbus: Ohio State University Press, 1964), p. 155.

[35] John M. Gaus and Leon O. Wolcott, *Public Administration and the United States Department of Agriculture* (Chicago: Public Administration Service, 1940), pp. 64–65, referring to the AAA state, "Here again there was no sharp break with movements and ideas that had been developing throughout

The campaign for the domestic allotment plan raises several questions. One of the most obvious questions is why, in the light of the disastrous conditions of northern plains agriculture, there were not more leaders in the colleges and the communities of the northern Great Plains states pushing vigorously for national relief legislation and devising programs of significant reform. Of the land-grant colleges in the northern Plains, Montana State College appeared to be the only institution which recognized that the problems of the wheat crop extended beyond the questions of efficient production and marketing. At Montana State College, Wilson was given a wide latitude of freedom, which few other state college professors enjoyed, to seek agricultural reform legislation from the federal government. This enabled him to span, in part, the gap between the worlds of academic economics and the world of politics, personalities, and interest groups. From the community of academia, Wilson brought and sold a plan to help agriculture's crumbling economic life; his freedom of action enabled him to gain access to Roosevelt's brain trust, where he received the general commitment of the incoming administration to the principles of the domestic allotment plan.

For years the fortunes of the wheat crop on the northern Plains had a direct bearing on the political temper of the region. Many solutions had been put forth to remedy the crop's declining market, but they had either lacked a political sanction or had been economically unworkable. With the advent of the New Deal and the sophistication of the domestic allotment plan by Wilson, both of these impediments had been swept away. The lessons of a preceding decade of wheat politics were now used to nurture the growth of a national agricultural program.

---

the postwar period. . . . Individual officials had been called upon freely by Congressmen for assistance in the drafting of legislation, despite the opposition to various farm-relief measures by the Secretaries and Presidents of the time"; Arthur S. Link, "What Happened to the Progressive Movement in the 1920's?" *American Historical Review*, LXIV (July, 1959), 844–845.

Bibliography

MANUSCRIPT MATERIAL

Chester C. Davis Papers. Western Historical Manuscripts Collection. University of Missouri, Columbia, Missouri.

Mordecai Ezekiel. Columbia Oral History Collection. Columbia University, New York, New York.

Herbert Hoover Papers. Herbert Hoover Library. West Branch, Iowa.

William Lemke Papers. University of North Dakota, Grand Forks, North Dakota.

Samuel McKelvie Papers. Nebraska State Historical Society. Lincoln, Nebraska.

Peter Norbeck Papers. University of South Dakota, Vermillion, South Dakota.

George W. Norris Papers. Library of Congress.

North Dakota–Montana Wheat Growers Association Papers. University of North Dakota, Grand Forks, North Dakota.

George N. Peek Papers. Western Historical Manuscripts Collection. University of Missouri, Columbia, Missouri.

Franklin D. Roosevelt Papers. Franklin D. Roosevelt Library. Hyde Park, New York.

O. C. Stine. Columbia Oral History Collection. Columbia University, New York, New York.

H. C. Taylor Papers, Collection Various. Columbia University, New York, New York.

Howard R. Tolley. Columbia Oral History Collection. Columbia University, New York, New York.

Howard R. Tolley Speeches. University of California, Documents Division, Giannini Foundation Library. Berkeley, California.

Rexford G. Tugwell Diary, 1933. Franklin D. Roosevelt Library.

M. L. Wilson. Columbia Oral History Collection. Columbia University, New York, New York.

M. L. Wilson Papers. Montana State University Library, Bozeman, Montana.

Files of the Economic and Statistical Analysis Division of the Economic Research Service. United States Department of Agriculture, Washington, D.C.

Record Groups 16 and 83 of the National Archives and Records Service. Washington, D.C.

Annual County Extension Agent Reports, 1932 and 1933, for Nebraska, South Dakota, North Dakota, and Montana, located at the respective state colleges in Lincoln, Brookings, Fargo, and Bozeman.

NEWSPAPERS AND FARM PERIODICALS

Dakota Farmer, Aberdeen, South Dakota.

Fargo Forum, Fargo, North Dakota.

Farm Journal, Philadelphia, Pennsylvania.

Farm, Stock, and Home, St. Paul, Minnesota.

Havre Daily News, Havre, Montana.

Huronite, Huron, South Dakota.

Minot Daily News, Minot, North Dakota.

Mitchell Evening Republican, Mitchell, South Dakota.

Montana Record-Herald, Helena, Montana.

Nebraska Farmer, Lincoln, Nebraska.

New York Times, New York, New York.

North Dakotan, The Greater North Dakota Association, Fargo, North Dakota.

Omaha World-Herald, Omaha, Nebraska.

Public Opinion, Watertown, South Dakota.

Wallace's Farmer, Des Moines, Iowa.

Washington Post, Washington, D.C.

Western Progressive, Helena, Montana.

GOVERNMENT PUBLICATIONS

U.S. *Congressional Record*, 71st Cong., 2d sess.

U.S. *Congressional Record*, 72d Cong., 1st sess.

United States Department of Agriculture Year Book of Agriculture, 1919, 1920, 1921, 1923. Washington, D.C.: Government Printing Office.

U.S. Senate Committee on Agriculture and Forestry, *Farm Relief Proposals*, April, 1932, 72d Cong., 1st sess.

U.S. Senate Committee on Agriculture and Forestry, *Agricultural Emergency Act to Increase Farm Purchasing Power*, March 17, 24, 25, 27, 28, 1933, 73d Cong., 1st sess.

U.S. Senate Subcommittee of the Committee on Manufactures, *Senate Hearings*, 72d Cong., 1st sess. S. 6215.

UNPUBLISHED DISSERTATIONS

Kirkendall, Richard S., "The New Deal Professors and the Politics of Agriculture." Ph.D. dissertation, University of Wisconsin, 1958.

Stone, James A., "Agrarian Ideology and the Farm Problem in Nebraska State Politics with Special Reference to Northeast Nebraska, 1920–1933." Ph.D. dissertation, University of Nebraska, 1960.

BOOKS

Bellush, Bernard. *Franklin D. Roosevelt As Governor of New York*. New York: Columbia University Press, 1955.

Black, John D. *Agricultural Reform in the United States*. New York: McGraw-Hill Book Company, 1929.

Blackorby, Edward C. *Prairie Rebel: The Public Life of William Lemke*. Lincoln: University of Nebraska Press, 1963.

Blum, John Morton. *From the Morgenthau Diaries: Years of Crisis, 1928–1938*. Boston: Houghton Mifflin Company, 1959.

Braeman, John, Robert H. Bremner, and Everett Walters, eds. *Change and Continuity in Twentieth-Century America*. Columbus: Ohio State University Press, 1964.

Brinton, J. W. *Wheat and Politics*. Minneapolis: Rand Tower, 1931.

Burlingame, Merrill G., and K. Ross Toole, eds. *History of Montana*. Volume I. New York: Lewis Publishing Company, 1957.

Capper, Arthur. *The Agricultural Bloc*. New York: Harcourt, Brace and Co., 1922.

Casselman, Paul Hubert. *The Cooperative Movement and Some of Its Problems*. New York: Philosophical Library, 1952.

Commons, John R. *The Distribution of Wealth*. New York: Macmillan and Company, 1893.

Cowling, Ellis. *Co-operatives in America: Their Past, Present, and Future*. New York: Coward-McCann, Inc., 1938.

Dorfman, Joseph. *The Economic Mind in American Civilization, 1865–1918.* Volume III. New York: The Viking Press, 1949.

Drache, Hiram M. *The Day of the Bonanza: A History of Bonanza Farming in the Red River Valley of the North.* Fargo: North Dakota Institute for Regional Studies, 1964.

Finklestein, Louis, ed. *American Spiritual Autobiographies.* New York: Harper & Brothers, 1948.

Fite, Gilbert C. *Farm to Factory: A History of the Consumers Cooperative Association.* Columbia: University of Missouri Press, 1965.

———. *George N. Peek and the Fight for Farm Parity.* Norman: University of Oklahoma Press, 1954.

———. *Peter Norbeck: Prairie Statesman.* University of Missouri Studies. Volume XXII. Columbia: University of Missouri Press, 1948.

Freidel, Frank. *Franklin D. Roosevelt: The Triumph.* Boston: Little, Brown and Company, 1956.

Gaus, John M., and Leon O. Wolcott. *Public Administration and the United States Department of Agriculture.* Chicago: Public Administration Service, 1940.

Genung, A. B. *The Agricultural Depression Following World War I and Its Political Consequences.* Ithaca, N.Y.: Northeast Farm Foundation, 1954.

Hargreaves, Mary Wilma M. *Dry Farming in the Northern Great Plains, 1900–1925.* Cambridge: Harvard University Press, 1957.

Hicks, John D. *The Populist Revolt.* Minneapolis: University of Minnesota Press, 1931.

———. *Rehearsal for Disaster: The Boom and Collapse of 1919–1920.* Gainesville: University of Florida Press, 1961.

Hoover, Herbert. *The Memoirs of Herbert Hoover, the Cabinet, and the Presidency, 1920–1933.* Volume II. New York: The Macmillan Company, 1952.

Howard, Joseph Kinsey. *Montana: High, Wide, and Handsome.* New Haven: Yale University Press, 1959.

Kirkendall, Richard S. *Social Scientists and Farm Politics in the Age of Roosevelt.* Columbia: University of Missouri Press, 1966.

Lippmann, Walter. *Interpretations, 1933–1935.* Allan Nevins, ed. New York: The Macmillan Co., 1936.

Lord, Russell. *The Agrarian Revival: A Study of Agricultural Extension.* New York: American Association for Adult Education, George Grady Press, 1939.

———. *The Wallaces of Iowa.* Boston: Houghton Mifflin Company, 1947.

Lubell, Samuel. *The Future of American Politics.* New York: Harper & Brothers, 1952.

Malenbaum, Wilfred. *The World Wheat Economy, 1885–1939.* Cambridge: Harvard University Press, 1953.

McCune, Wesley. *The Farm Bloc.* New York: Doubleday, Doran and Co., 1943.

Moley, Raymond. *After Seven Years.* New York: Harper & Brothers, 1939.

———. *The First New Deal.* New York: Harcourt, Brace & World, 1966.

Morgan, Robert J. *Governing Soil Conservation: Thirty Years of the New Decentralization.* Baltimore: Johns Hopkins University Press, 1965.

Morlan, Robert L. *Political Prairie Fire: The Nonpartisan League, 1915–1922.* Minneapolis: University of Minnesota Press, 1955.

Nourse, Edwin G., Joseph S. Davis, and John D. Black. *Three Years of the Agricultural Adjustment Administration.* Washington, D.C.: The Brookings Institution, 1937.

Olson, James C. *History of Nebraska.* Lincoln: University of Nebraska Press, 1955.

Rasmussen, Wayne D., ed. *Readings in the History of American Agriculture.* Urbana: University of Illinois Press, 1960.

Raymer, Robert George. *Montana: The Land and the People.* Volume II. Chicago: The Lewis Publishing Company, 1930.

Robinson, Elwyn B. *History of North Dakota.* Lincoln: University of Nebraska Press, 1966.

Rölvaag, O. E. *Giants in the Earth.* New York: Harper and Brothers, 1927.

Saloutos, Theodore, and John D. Hicks. *Agricultural Discontent in the Middle West, 1900–1939.* Madison: University of Wisconsin Press, 1951.

Schell, Herbert S. *History of South Dakota.* Lincoln: University of Nebraska Press, 1961.

Schlesinger, Arthur M., Jr. *The Age of Roosevelt: The Coming of the New Deal.* Boston: Houghton Mifflin Company, 1959.

———. *The Age of Roosevelt: The Crisis of the Old Order, 1919–1933.* Boston: Houghton Mifflin Company, 1957.

Shideler, James H. *Farm Crisis, 1919–1923.* Berkeley: University of California Press, 1957.

Shover, John L. *Cornbelt Rebellion: The Farmers' Holiday Association.* Urbana: University of Illinois Press, 1965.

Soule, George. *Ideas of the Great Economists.* New York: The Viking Press, 1952.

Spillman, W. S. *Balancing the Farm Output: A Statement of the Present Deplorable Conditions of Farming, Its Causes, and Suggested Remedies.* New York: Orange Judd Publishing Co., 1927.

Taylor, Henry C., and Anne Dewess Taylor. *The Story of Agricultural Economics in the United States, 1840–1932.* Ames, Iowa: Iowa State College Press, 1952.

Toole, K. Ross. *Montana: An Uncommon Land.* Norman: University of Oklahoma Press, 1959.

Tugwell, Rexford G. *The Democratic Roosevelt.* Garden City, N.Y.: Doubleday & Company, Inc., 1957.

Wallace, H. C. *Our Debt and Duty to the Farmer.* New York: The Century Co., 1925.

Zucker, Norman L. *George W. Norris: Gentle Knight of American Democracy.* Urbana: University of Illinois Press, 1966.

ARTICLES

Anderson, Clifford B. "The Metamorphosis of American Agrarian Idealism in the 1920's and 1930's." *Agricultural History,* XXXV (October, 1961), 182–188.

Black, John D. "The McNary-Haugen Movement." *American Economic Review,* XVIII (September, 1928), 405–427.

———. "The Progress of Farm Relief." *American Economic Review,* XVIII (June, 1928), 252–271.

Chambers, Clarke A. "The Cooperative League of the United States of America, 1916–1961: A Study of Social Theory and Social Action." *Agricultural History,* XXXVI (April, 1962), 59–81.

Christensen, Alice M. "Agricultural Pressure and Governmental Response in the United States, 1919–1929." *Agricultural History,* II (January, 1937), 33–42.

Colman, Gould P. "Government and Agriculture in New York State." *Agricultural History*, XXXIX (January, 1965), 41–50.

Dalrymple, Dana G. "The American Tractor Comes to Soviet Agriculture: The Transfer of a Technology." *Technology and Culture*, V (Spring, 1964), 191–214.

Davis, J. S. "The Voluntary Domestic Allotment Plan for Wheat." *Wheat Studies of the Food Research Institute*, IX (November, 1932), 23–62.

Fite, Gilbert C. "The Agricultural Issue in the Presidential Campaign of 1928." *Mississippi Valley Historical Review*, XXXVII (March, 1951), 563–584.

————. "John A. Simpson: The Southwest's Militant Farm Leader." *Mississippi Valley Historical Review*, XXXV (March, 1949), 563–584.

————. "Peter Norbeck and the Defeat of the Non Partisan League in South Dakota." *Mississippi Valley Historical Review*, XXXIII (September, 1946), 217–237.

Garrett, Garet. "That Pain in Our Northwest." *Saturday Evening Post*, CXCVI (April 12, 1924), 46–48.

Gleason, J. P. "The Attitude of the Business Community Toward Agriculture During the McNary-Haugen Period." *Agricultural History*, XXXII (April, 1958), 127–138.

Gregory, Clifford V. "The American Farm Bureau Federation and the AAA." *Annals of the American Academy of Political and Social Science*, CLXXIX (May, 1935), 152–157.

Huffman, Roy E. "Montana's Contribution to New Deal Farm Policy." *Agricultural History*, XXXIII (October, 1959), 164–167.

Johnson, William R. "National Farm Organizations and the Reshaping of Agricultural Policy in 1932." *Agricultural History*, XXXVII (January, 1963), 35–42.

Jorgenson, Lloyd P. "Agricultural Expansion into the Semiarid Lands of the West North Central States During the First World War." *Agricultural History*, XXIII (January, 1949), 30–40.

Kirkendall, Richard S. "A Professor in Farm Politics." *Mid-America*, XLI (October, 1959), 210–217.

————. "Four Economists in the Political Process." *Journal of Farm Economics*, XLI (May, 1959), 194–210.

Kirkendall, Richard S. "Franklin D. Roosevelt and the Service Intellectual." *Mississippi Valley Historical Review*, XLIX (December, 1962), 456–471.

———. "Howard Tolley and Agricultural Planning in the 1930's." *Agricultural History*, XXXIX (January, 1965), 25–33.

Larsen, Grace H., and Henry E. Erdmen. "Aaron Sapiro: Genius of Farm Co-operative Promotion." *Mississippi Valley Historical Review*, XLIX (September, 1962), 242–268.

Link, Arthur S. "What Happened to the Progressive Movement in the 1920's?" *American Historical Review*, LXIV (July, 1959), 833–851.

Norbeck, Peter. "The Voluntary Allotment." *Farm Journal*, LVI (October, 1932), 5–6.

Saloutos, Theodore. "Spring Wheat Farmer in a Maturing Economy." *Journal of Economic History*, VI (November, 1946), 173–190.

———. "The Expansion and Decline of the Nonpartisan League in the Western Middle West, 1917–1921." *Agricultural History*, XX (October, 1946), 235–252.

———. "William A. Hirth: Middle Western Agrarian." *Mississippi Valley Historical Review*, XXXVIII (September, 1951), 215–232.

Shideler, James H. "Herbert Hoover and the Federal Farm Board Project, 1921–1925." *Mississippi Valley Historical Review*, XLII (March, 1956), 710–729.

———. "The Development of the Parity Price Formula for Agriculture, 1919–1923." *Agricultural History*, XXVII (July, 1953), 77–84.

Slichter, Gertrude Almy. "Franklin D. Roosevelt and the Farm Problem, 1929–1932." *Mississippi Valley Historical Review*, XLIII (September, 1956), 238–258.

Starch, E. A. "Farm Organization as Affected by Mechanization." *Bulletin No. 278* (May, 1933), Montana State College of Agriculture Experiment Station, Bozeman, Montana, pp. 1–102.

Strong, Helen M. "Export Wheat Producing Regions." *Economic Geography*, VIII (April, 1932), 160–164.

Tontz, Robert L. "Origins of the Base Period Concept of Parity." *Agricultural History*, XXXII (January, 1958), 3–13.

Tugwell, Rexford G. "Reflections on Farm Relief." *Political Science Quarterly*, XLIII (December, 1928), 481–497.

Wilson, M. L. "Experimental Method in Economic Research." *Journal of Farm Economics*, XI (October, 1929), 578–583.

———. "The Fairway Farms Project." *The Journal of Land and Public Utility Economics*, II (April, 1926), 156–171.

———. "Research Studies in the Economics of Large Scale Farming in Montana." *Agricultural Engineering*, X (January, 1929), 3–12.

Winters, Donald L. "The Persistence of Progressivism: Henry Cantwell Wallace and the Movement for Agricultural Economics." *Agricultural History*, XLI (April, 1967), 109–125.

MISCELLANEOUS

Wilson, M. L. "Land Utilization." Economics Series Lecture no. 25, April 16, 1932. Chicago: University of Chicago Press, 1932.

Conference on Economic Policy for American Agriculture. Edward A. Duddy, ed. Chicago: University of Chicago Press, 1932.

Documents of American History. Henry Steele Commager, ed. New York: Appleton-Century-Crofts, Inc., 1958.

North Dakota Industrial Program. Bismarck: State Printers, 1920.

Proceedings of the Forty-Fourth Annual Convention of the Association of Land-Grant Colleges and Universities. Washington, D.C., November 17–19, 1930. Charles A. McCue, ed. Burlington, Vt.: Free Press Printing Co., 1931.

The Public Papers and Addresses of Franklin D. Roosevelt: The Genesis of the New Deal, 1928–1932. Volume I. New York: Random House, 1938.

E. A. Starch to author (May, 1967).

Jules Alexander Karlin to author (October 2, 1967).

INTERVIEWS

Interview with M. L. Wilson, November, 1965. Chevy Chase, Maryland.

Index

Legge, Alexander, 48, 64, 66, 74, 75, 76, 82, 83, 87–88, 90, 146, 148, 149, 155
Lemke, William, 194–195
Lindley, Troy, 115
Linfield, F. B., 56, 80, 81, 146
Lingham, Frederick J., 181, 194
Lippmann, Walter, 185, 198
Lord, Russell, 184–185, 193, 198
Lowden, Frank, 41–42, 137
Lusk, Robert, 123, 131, 132, 154, 155, 156
Lusk, Willard C., 123, 131

McCarthy, Walter R., 65, 66, 68, 75, 117, 122, 133, 167
McClave, C. R., 163–164
McCormick, W. S., 22, 89, 112
McGraw Hill Book Company, 66
McKelvie, Sam, 63–65, 89, 90
McNary, Charles, 137
McNary-Haugen proposals, 4, 41, 71, 82, 83, 116, 124, 132, 139, 145; bills, 24, 26, 27, 29, 32–33, 34, 35, 44, 71, 135; and Black, 44, 45; campaigns of 1920's helped to prepare business for agricultural reform legislation of 1930's, 28; and Davis, 29, 30, 38, 42, 119, 147; Jardine's purge of Department of Agriculture of McNary-Haugenites, 27; and Peek, 12–13, 28–29, 42, 135; and Stockton, 29, 120–121, 134, 147; and wheat-cotton alliance, 30–31; and Wilson, 2, 7, 29, 38, 68, 78, 128, 147, 151, 163
Mechanized farming, 39–40
Meyer, Eugene, 21
Meyer-Mondell mission, 21–22, 23
Michigan Farmer, 158
Millers National Federation, 194
Millet, Daniel, 74
Milloy, James S., 170
Minneapolis Grain Exchange, 71
Minneapolis Tribune, 109, 170
Minot Daily News, 196
Missouri Farmer, 116, 129

Missouri State Farm Bureau, 115
Mitchell Republican, 122, 132, 165, 183
Modern Miller, 167
Moley, Raymond, 42, 150, 151, 157, 158, 159, 161, 164, 170, 184
Mondell, Frank, 21
Montana: "capitalistic family farm," 50–51; Communists, 97–98; drought, 93, 95–96; election of 1928, 41–43; attitude toward Farm Board, 76; "next year country," 17, 25; United Farmers League, 102; low-cost production of wheat, 49–52; effect on politics of wheat problems, 1920's, 17–18; wheat problems, 1930's, 82
Montana Equalization Fee Committee, 4
Montana Farm Bureau Federation, 94, 103, 120, 147, 174–175, 182
Montana Farmer, 69, 83, 156
Montana Farmers' Union, 68, 130
Montana Flour Mills Company, 163
Montana Record-Herald, 21
Montana State College, 2, 3, 54, 56, 121, 174–176, 182–183, 199
Montana State Farm Bureau, 4, 29, 68, 82, 88, 103, 112, 114, 128
Montana Wheat Growers Association, 22
Morgenthau, Henry, Jr., 157, 158, 185, 188
Moser, C. O., 123
Murphy, Frank E., 109
Myers, William I., 185

National Advisory Council on Radio Education, 122
National Agricultural Conference, 1922, 12, 15
National Catholic Welfare Council, 162
National Chamber of Commerce. *See* Chamber of Commerce of the United States
National Cooperative Council, 122